Million
Dollar
Consulting

Million Dollar Consulting

The Professional's Guide to Growing a Practice

Fifth Edition

Alan Weiss

New York   Chicago   San Francisco   Athens   London
Madrid   Mexico City   Milan   New Delhi
Singapore   Sydney   Toronto

1 2 3 4 5 6 7 8 9 0   DOC/DOC   1 2 1 0 9 8 7 6

ISBN   978-1-259-58861-7
MHID   1-259-58861-0

e-ISBN   978-1-259-58862-4
e-MHID   1-259-58862-9

Product or brand names used in this book may be trade names or trademarks. Where we believe that there may be proprietary claims to such trade names or trademarks, the name has been used with an initial cap or it has been capitalized in the style used by the name claimant. Regardless of capitalization used, all such names have been used in an editorial manner without any intent to convey endorsement of or other affiliation with the nameclaimant. Neither the author nor the publisher intends to express any judgment as to the validity or legal status of any such proprietary claims.

This publication is designed to provide accurate and authoritative information in regard to the subject matter covered. It is sold with the understanding that neither the author nor the publisher is engaged in rendering legal, accounting, securities trading, or other professional services. If legal advice or other expert assistance is required, the services of a competent professional person should be sought.

—From a Declaration of Principles Jointly Adopted by a Committee of the American Bar Association and a Committee of Publishers and Associations

McGraw-Hill Education books are available at special quantity discounts to use as premiums and sales promotions or for use in corporate training programs. To contact a representative, please visit the Contact Us pages at www.mhprofessional.com.

For all of you who, since 1992, have read my books, attended my events, participated in my experiences, and been coached or mentored in my communities.
I always learn more than anyone else. Thank you.

CONTENTS

ACKNOWLEDGMENTS   ix

INTRODUCTION   xi

CHAPTER 1
What Is a Consultant, Anyway? Is It Someone Who Comes
to Study a Problem and Remains to Become a Part of It?   1

CHAPTER 2
Build It and They Will Come:
But Only if You Let Them Know That You've Built It!   15

INTERLUDE I
The Yin and Yang of Clients and Prospects   31

CHAPTER 3
The Relationship Business: Learning How to Sell Yourself   41

CHAPTER 4
How to Maximize Fees: Money Left on the Table
Isn't There in the Morning   57

CHAPTER 5
Proposals: Never Negotiation, Always Summation   71

INTERLUDE II
The Concept of Value   83

CHAPTER 6
The Estimable Consultant: How to Build
Your Practice by Building Your Esteem   93

CHAPTER 7
The Cyberspace Consultant:
Houston, Let's Not Have a Problem   109

CHAPTER 8
Delivering the Goods: Taking the Express Lane   127

CHAPTER 9
Thought Leadership: It's Fine to Stand Out in
a Crowd So Long as You Look Good Standing There   143

CHAPTER 10
The Ethical Consultant: How to Do Well by Doing Right   159

CHAPTER 11
The Global Community: The World Is Next Door   171

CHAPTER 12
Designing Your Own Future:
Taking Control of Your Fate   177

CHAPTER 13
Creating a Company: But What Kind?   183

CHAPTER 14
Leverage: More Output for Less Input   199

CHAPTER 15
Creating and Sustaining Your Endeavor:
Cathedrals Last for Hundreds of Years   211

APPENDIX   227

INDEX   269

ACKNOWLEDGMENTS

Bᴇᴛꜱʏ Bʀᴏᴡɴ was the senior editor at McGraw-Hill in 1991 when my agent, Jeff Herman, presented the idea for this book to her. Just before production was to start she said to me in her office, "We need a final title—your current one doesn't work."

"Betsy," I said, "it's simply a book about how to make a million dollars consulting."

"There it is," she said, and my life was changed.

My continuing gratitude to Betsy, Jeff, and the wonderful people at McGraw-Hill over these past 25 years.

INTRODUCTION

In 1990 I wrote a proposal for what would have been my fourth book, entitled *Confessions of a Consultant*. The premise was to alert corporate executives about what was going wrong unbeknownst to them, and what combination of internal and external resources was needed to become more effective. After all, I was an organization development consultant, working with Fortune 1000 firms.

That book idea was rejected by 15 publishers. Then one day my agent called on my brand-new car phone, hardwired to the dashboard, and said, "I'm at McGraw-Hill." I was ecstatic—he was at one of the premier publishers on the planet. "They like the book idea?" I shouted.

"No, they hate it."

"Jeff," I said, "do you know what this call is costing me?"

"They want to know," he said calmly, "if you can write a book about how you can make seven figures a year as a solo consultant."

"I can do that in six minutes," I said.

"I'm going to tell them six months," he replied, "I'll get back to you later. I'll call you at your office—this connection is awful!"

And there you have the beginning of what is today a global franchise that changed my life to one of helping entrepreneurs and experts to build their businesses, improve their self-worth, and live the lives to which they aspire. You are reading the fifth edition of the book and, more important to me, its twenty-fifth anniversary edition. I've written 60 books that appear in 12 languages, more books on consulting than anyone, ever, and this book remains my bestseller by a wide margin.

Some of you are rereading it, and some of you are joining me for the first time. I've rewritten almost all of it from scratch, meaning I haven't used past files to abridge and modify but wrote it entirely "from my head onto the screen" with no notes. You will find prior material presented differently and new material never presented before.

This profession has provided me—and many I've coached—with a fabulous life. You can accommodate new technologies, globalization, shifts in mores, changing demographics, and new discoveries. You can do all of that *if* you create and sustain a high level of self-worth. We are not "selling" services, not "taking" money. We are offering value and generating equitable compensation as a result of a huge return on investment for the buyer.

I've found that the most fundamental success factor is one's mindset. As you read on, I'm hoping that I can influence your mindset to appreciate your own value and act in a manner commensurate with it. After that, it's up to you.

Alan Weiss
East Greenwich,
Rhode Island
June 2016

Million Dollar Consulting

WHAT IS A CONSULTANT, ANYWAY?

IS IT SOMEONE WHO COMES TO STUDY A PROBLEM AND REMAINS TO BECOME A PART OF IT?

I'm sitting on a cliff overlooking the Pacific in Laguna Beach, California, where I'm holding a meeting for global consultants in my community. The hotel manager, who's stopped by to meet me, asks, "When did you realize you would be a consultant?"

The answer is the day I was hired to be one.

No one I know has studied to become a consultant. Don't confuse MBA students with nascent consultants. They are simply students with advanced degrees in finance. (I have three graduate degrees, and not one has ever helped me in my marketing or delivery in this profession.) They may well enter Deloitte or McKinsey, but they do so as worker ants who are expected to carry tasks many times their own weight. They are expendable, paid X, and billed out at X times three to cover costs and produce profit.

Come to think of it, worker ants have a more creative life.

WE ARE ALL CONSULTANTS (OR ARE WE?)

The dictionary will tell you, tersely, that a consultant is someone who provides advice *professionally* (italics mine). That means, as I interpret it, for money. Thus, some of us are "amateur" consultants and some "professional." I guess the former are sort of quasi-consultants in the manner that the Federal Reserve is a quasi-governmental entity or a Mercury is a quasi-Ford.

But advice is cheap. When we consider consultants in this book, we're talking about *expertise*. Consultants are experts, not mere advice givers. You may give me advice about skiing, which you engage in sporadically, and it may be enough to sustain me in an upright position for a few minutes at a time. But the ski instructor, who is paid for expertise, can show me how to traverse, slalom, recover from being off balance, and take a fall correctly. That expertise is better than your casual advice.

So while we are surrounded by advice (especially if we have a significant other in our lives and *especially* if we have children old enough to talk), we're not surrounded by expertise. We, and organizations, have to find it and either maintain it (employees) or situationally secure it (brief engagements by experts).

This book is about solo consultants and boutique firm owners. Although prior versions of this book and my other works are often read by consultants working for large organizations, the focus here is on the solo practitioner.[1] With that in mind, here is the definition of a consultant for our purposes:

> **Consultant:** *An expert in one or more identified areas who partners with a client to improve the client's condition.*

Once you walk away from a successful engagement, the client's "state" should be better than it was when you got there, ideally in conjunction with previously determined and agreed-upon objectives (more about that later).

---

[1]Some readers of the four prior editions consistently complained that I don't address large firms or building large firms. There's a reason for that—*it's not the intent of this book or my work!*

Please consider the relationships shown in Figure 1-1. I said that a consultant "partners with" a client. That is the upper right in Figure 1-1, collaborator. There are two dynamics in consulting interactions. One is the importance of the issue involved (vertical axis), and the other is the transfer of skills to the client for continued and sustainable success (horizontal axis).

If you work on an important issue with zero transfer of skills, you're simply an *independent expert* (upper left). You ski, but you can't teach me to ski. Think of an expert witness in a trial who testifies about proper heart stent implants but can neither perform the procedure nor teach it.

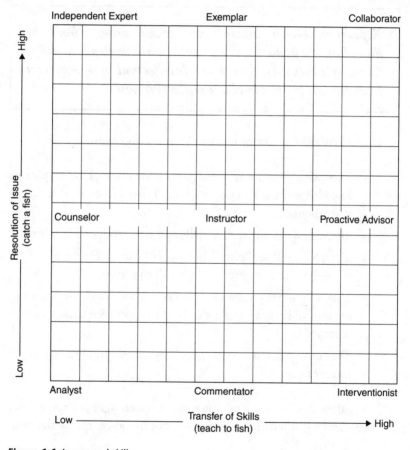

Figure 1-1 Issues and skills

If you transfer significant skills but not for an important issue (lower right) then you're an *interventionist*. By that I mean that you help people learn how to respond to complaints from customers, or change a tire in the body shop, or underwrite risk in an insurance policy. You've done these things yourself and can teach them. But you teach them generically, not because there is an urgent issue at the moment.

The upper right, *collaborator*, represents the real value in consulting, where you are both transferring skills *and* doing so as a vital issue is resolved. That's where the highest value and concomitant highest fees reside.

> *Expertise: **Great consultants teach others how to do what they do and do not create codependencies. Counterintuitively, the more intellectual property you transfer, the more the client will value you.***

Here are the traits of professional experts who consult:

- They have content knowledge (how to make glass) or process knowledge (how to make decisions) that can be transferred to their clients.
- They can speak conversationally and easily about their value.
- The never "sell" or "pitch," but rather focus on contributing and offering value to improve the client's condition.[2]
- They continually expand their expertise through the development of additional intellectual property, experiences, and experimentation.
- They charge based on value, never by a time unit, head count, or boxes of materials.

I realize this last trait is somewhat threatening, even today after I've been writing about this for 25 years, but if you charge by the hour

---

[2]If you're looking for help with an "elevator pitch," find a book from the 1950s. If someone pitched me on an elevator, I'd stop it at the next floor and toss the pitcher out.

you're an amateur, and by definition in this book, not a professional. We'll cover the basis of fees in Chapter 4, though I suspect some of you immediately turned to that chapter, in which case, welcome back to the beginning!

When expertise becomes so obvious and apparent that the consultant is sought out by clients, a powerful brand has been created, based on the allure of one's expertise. When that happens, credibility, terms, fees, and other factors are no longer any kind of obstacle or barrier.

THE MILLION DOLLAR METAPHOR

In the introduction I talked about the origins of *Million Dollar Consulting*. Sometimes it's better to be lucky than good.

However, as catchy as that title and notion may be,[3] I understood from the outset that it's a metaphor. It represents the fuel you require for the lifestyle you desire. That may be $450,000, or $1.4 million, or $6 million. Wealth is discretionary time; money is simply the means to obtain wealth. (Hence, some people pursue money so rabidly that they decrease their wealth.)

More important, however, is the issue of the labor involved to get there. Years ago, my accountant said to me as I was beginning to become really successful, "Alan, reducing debt is as important as making money." He demonstrated the cost of carrying debt, the power of being debt free, and so forth. As a result of his advice, except for my mortgage (which has certain advantages to maintain) and a couple of car leases, I'm completely debt free.

The analogy is that while building revenues is important, *reducing labor intensity is just as important*. The reason is that too many people are racing around generating money while eroding their wealth. They are making money but losing time.

---

[3]Someone published a subsequent book called *Six Figure Consulting*. I believe they're going in the wrong direction. What's next, *How to Lose Money in Consulting*?

Expertise: You can always make another dollar, but you can never make another minute.

Thus, the secret to Million Dollar Consulting as a metaphor is that you have to continually work smarter, not harder. The progression often looks like this (read from bottom to top):

- Retainer
- Project oversight
- Project implementation
- Work at client request
- Subcontractor

At the bottom, *subcontractor*, you're working on someone else's product and at that person's command and discretion, very much like being someone's employee. And many of us have to start that way to earn money—nothing embarrassing about that unless you're still doing it years later. Above that, *we work at the client's request*, often as a result of a request for proposal (RFP), with the client's specifications to be met.

In *project implementation*, you are collaborating with a client and internal people to design and executive an initiative. In *project oversight*, you have designed what others are implementing and you are simply providing guidance. Finally, as a trusted advisor, you are on *retainer* with the client paying for access to your "smarts" and not any kind of deliverable or presence on site.

The bottom of the list is highly tactical, the top highly strategic. The key is to minimize labor while maximizing fees. Trusted advisors do that the best.

As you can see in Figure 1-2, the maximization of increasing fees *while decreasing labor* is dependent on a strong brand. As your career progresses, your brand should build, and the ultimate brand is your name. If someone says, "Get me an excellent strategy consultant," and your name could be pulled from that hat, that's nice. But it's better when someone says, "Get me Janet Murphy, she's the best strategy consultant around." In the latter case, fees don't matter, *nor does the labor*, because people are seeking results, not the maximum use of your time. (We'll talk more about branding later in the book.)

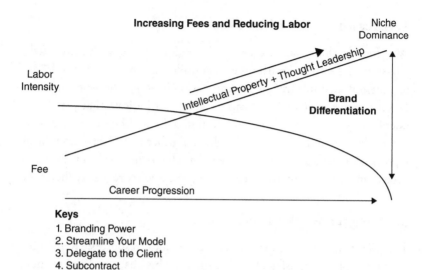

Figure 1-2 Million Dollar power

Case Study

Hewlett-Packard was my client for 10 years. At one point my buyer called and said, "Alan we need this project done, we know you're the best one to do it—will you take it on? We need your conclusions within 30 days, it's mission critical."

I said, "Sure, my fee will be $75,000, payable now, and you'll have my recommendations within 30 days."

She asked when I could get to Mountain View, California. I live in Rhode Island. "I'm not coming out," I said.

"You're going to do this in a month and never be here?"

"I can do this by phone, e-mail, and Skype, and I know you report to someone in Hong Kong whom you never actually see in person, right? Now let me get to work."

And I did.

Whether you are new to the profession or veteran, it's always a good time to examine whether you are reducing your labor and not merely increasing your revenue. There are three important aspects to doing this:

1. Streamline Your Business

We often do things because we've *always* done them. We've invented a "six-step sales strategy" without ever considering whether the results can be accomplished in three steps. Alliteration is no justification for labor! Never promise a client "ten focus groups." Just indicate that you'll conduct focus groups, because you might find out what the true patterns are after only five, so don't "owe" the client another five.[4] I gave up writing reports 25 years ago when I realized that clients neither read them nor need them, but consultants keep offering them to try to justify their fees.

2. Delegate Work to the Client

The client has significant infrastructure and resources. Remember the power of the transfer of skills earlier in this chapter? Engage client resources and obtain buyer permission to use them to do whatever they can do in your stead. Most consultants never even consider this *because their fees are tied to the time they spend on-site.*

3. Subcontract

It's cheaper to find people who can conduct interviews, focus groups, observation, surveys, and so on than to do it yourself. Classroom trainers and facilitators are a dime a dozen. Why? Because they can't market themselves, can't "make rain," and are dependent on the work of others to gain income. Using them reduces your labor despite the relatively small cost of employing them. (Don't recommend this book to them.)

WHERE DO YOU BEGIN?

You require three things to be successful in this business:

- *Passion.* You must love what you do.
- *Competency.* You must be good at what you do.
- *Need.* You must identify or create client need.

[4]And with value-based fees, discussed later, the amount of time you spend never influences your fee.

If you have passion and competency but no need, you have a message no one wants to hear. If you have passion and need but not competency, you'll always be an "also-ran." If you have need and competency but no passion, you're simply your own employee with a grinding nine-to-five job.

Essentially, the great careers in consulting are built around what you love to do and are great at doing. It is not a process of continual addition, but actually one of culling.

Case Study

When you see Michelangelo's David *in the Accademia Gallery in Florence, your breath is taken away, no matter how prepared you think you are to view it. The detail and colossal nature are overwhelming.*

In what may be an apocryphal story, it is said that Michelangelo carved David from a single piece of discarded marble he bought from someone else. When asked how he managed to carve the masterpiece from the single block of marble, he replied, "I merely carved away everything that didn't look like David."

Carve away everything that you aren't great at and don't love, and you'll create the artwork of your career.

To begin, state your value proposition. This is a brief statement of how the buyer is improved after you leave, hence, it is *always* a business outcome or result, never an input or deliverable. Here are some examples of poor value propositions:

- We provide training in leadership skills.
- We help telemarketers use their time better.
- We assist in the creation of clear communications.

The following are excellent value propositions:

- We reduce sales closing time and acquisition costs.
- We turn customer complaints into additional sales.
- We reduce undesired attrition.

Note that these three propositions are all demonstrably related to bottom-line business improvement. Your value proposition is simply the point of your arrow, enabling you to penetrate lack of interest and resistance. When the other person says "How do you do that?" that's the opening you need to begin the sales conversation. (And if the buyer says "I don't believe you can do that," it's great, because a question or objection is a sign of interest. It's apathy that will kill you.)

Once you have your value proposition, you're ready to find your ideal buyer. First, write your one-sentence value proposition as a business outcome here:

_____

_____

_____

Your ideal buyer is that economic buyer who can spend money for your value proposition, and who would probably find it at least attractive and possibly critical.

In Figure 1-3 you can see a three-dimensionality to the usual bell curve. Toward the left we have people who are apathetic or only pretend to be interested. In the middle are aspirational people, fence-sitters, perhaps. But then come serial developers and "hang tens" (a term from surfing that means those who take the biggest risks for the greatest ride). Note that the depths of these populations are key. In other words, you're better off with a mailing list or audience of relatively few people on the far right than you are with tens of thousands on the far left or even middle.

Buying lists for a few pennies per name from people overseas may seem like a bargain, but it is not, for two reasons: The first reason is that cold-calling doesn't work. But the second is that such lists are never useful in terms of your ideal buyers.

An ideal buyer for someone in the closely held business market might be the business owner. For someone in the Fortune 1000 market, it may be anyone with profit and loss (P&L) responsibility. More narrowly, if your value proposition is something like "We increase the average size of sales and improve cross–product line selling," then your ideal buyer is probably the sales vice president.

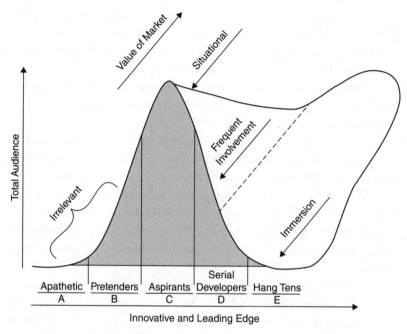

Figure 1-3 Finding the ideal buyer

Consider your value proposition from above, and write here who your ideal buyer probably is by title or position:

_____

> **Expertise: You have limited time and money. Don't waste either pursuing the wrong buyer or nonbuyers.**

Note that human resources is practically never a buyer, but is only the gatekeeper "protecting" real buyers. We'll discuss circumventing them later in the book.

Your value statement reflects your passion—how you want to contribute to others. Now let's look at what you're great at.

IMMODESTLY GREAT

Let's be clear: We do not grow and prosper by correcting weaknesses; we grow and prosper by building on strengths. Most "self-help" books assume you are somehow "damaged" (i.e., not as good as the author) and provide remedial work. I do not. I want to remind you that we all succeed best by applying our existing strengths to challenges and opportunities, and surmounting problems in the same manner.[5]

To accomplish this, determine your "sweet spot," which is what you are great at doing consistently (as compared to your value proposition, which is your passion for helping others).

In Figure 1-4, I've created an example of my sweet spot, which is boutique consulting. I am great at helping solo practitioners and small firm owners improve their results and dramatically grow their businesses.

The "spokes" around the sweet spot are factors or components of it. You can see the four I've chosen, but there could be more or less. If we considered value-based fees, that might be a separate component, but I'd include it here under acquiring business. There is no "right answer," only the ability for you to map out what you're great at.

If your sweet spot is "formulating strategy" (note that these don't have to be business outcomes, they are things you do well), your components might include:

- Establishing values
- Identifying a driving strategic force
- Anticipating competitive strategies
- Translating into accountabilities

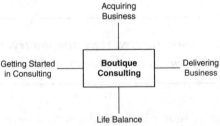

Figure 1-4 The "sweet spot"

[5]Dr. Martin Seligman, at the University of Pennsylvania, has done the best work on positive psychology of anyone I know. See his book *Learned Optimism* (Simon & Schuster, 2011), for example.

Take a moment to sketch out your sweet spot and four to six components. The components are *not* delivery mechanisms (e.g., coaching) but should be aspects of your sweet spot:

Sweet Spot: _____

Component:_____

Component:_____

Component:_____

Component:_____

The final consideration here is a vital one: What intellectual property (IP) will support those components?

If you return to my sweet spot, you'll find that I've written books, created workshops, recorded audio, filmed subscription series, and created speeches about all of those components. If you consider people who are "thought leaders," such as Marshall Goldsmith, Seth Godin, Marcus Buckingham, or Steven Covey, we've all done this.

The sweet spot and components give you the direction for creating IP that will establish your competency in others' eyes, and we've established that this is one of the three areas (with passion and market need) that are critical to your success and effective branding.

> ***Expertise: IP doesn't exist, and isn't created, in a vacuum. It should be created within your competency and passion to support your name and brand.***

The recognition of your value proposition (your passion around your contribution), your ideal buyer (the person who will invest in your passion because there is perceived need that exists or you create), and your sweet spot (the thing you're great at doing and want to do and that gives you great satisfaction), is the heart of your success in growing a solo practice and/or a boutique firm. Too many people leap into consulting as though they can simply "help" others without thinking about their own value, target audience, or future gratification.

The research and my experience are overwhelming in showing that people are most motivated by gratification in the work they do and recognition of the use of their talents to achieve results. (And, as we well know, motivation is intrinsic and must come from within. We can't "motivate" other people.)

So why would we give clients that advice, but not follow it ourselves? If we're to be successful helping others, then we have to first help ourselves.

> *The oxygen mask rule: You put your own mask on first before attempting to help others. The same principle applies in consulting and in any career: You have to help yourself before you can truly help others.*

Now that we have a basis for who we are and what we do, let's examine some aggressive approaches to launching, sustaining, and dramatically growing a practice.

BUILD IT AND THEY WILL COME

BUT ONLY IF YOU LET THEM KNOW THAT YOU'VE BUILT IT!

Marketing is the art and science of creating need. You can reach out to people to do this, *but it's far more effective to attract them to you.* When you knock on a door, you have to justify why you want entry. When people knock on your door, they're happy to pay the price of admission.

CREATING MARKET GRAVITY

Consultants (and others in professional services) often make the mistake of thinking that they have to reach out to others, or that they are too new to the business to expect others to come to them.

Both of these beliefs are fallacious.

The "build it and they will come" apothegm from the movie *Field of Dreams* is also fallacious, in that they can't come if they don't know what you've built. Ergo, the effective strategy is "Build it and tell them you've built it, and they will come."

I call this approach *market gravity*. The idea is to create a gravitational pull that compels your ideal buyers to seek you out. When buyers approach you because they've heard of you and are interested in your value (gravity), they seldom look into credibility or inquire about fees.

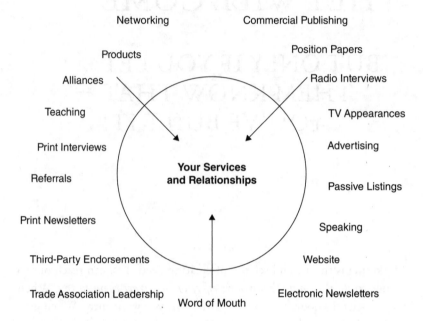

Figure 2-1 Creating market gravity

Their basic question is, "I have this issue, how would you go about help-ing me?"

As you can see in Figure 2-1, there is a plethora of opportunity to generate and sustain market gravity. In no special order, starting at 12 o'clock:

- *Pro bono work.* Find a highly visible charity and offer your services (e.g., if you're an expert in recruiting talent, offer to attract volunteers). Make sure you meet the board members and major donors, who may well be buyers or recommenders (referral sources).

- *Commercial publishing.* Write articles for newsletters, newspa-pers, magazines, and so forth. For your ideal clients, find out what they read or what publications are produced by associa-tions to which they belong. Of course, the most profound com-mercial publishing is a book from a major publisher.

- *Radio and TV interviews.* Start with local talk radio shows and cable television and work your way up to network affiliates and syndicated shows. Write to the producer (not host or talent) and *suggest the benefits for the show's audience.*

- *Advertising.* While not usually very productive for our profession, it can be useful in the arts, charity work, and other fund-raising organizations where "movers and shakers" contribute.

- *Passive listings.* Make sure your business is to be found on Google, in local phone books, and on professional association lists, as appropriate.

- *Speaking.* Pursue trade association executive directors to speak at upcoming conferences.[1] If there is a visitors or convention bureau in your city, meet the executive director and offer to be a resource when a group requests a local speaker or needs a replacement for an out-of-town speaker who can't make it.

- *Web presence.* Your website isn't a sales tool, but it is a credibility statement for those who have met you or heard about you and want some background. Be sure your physical address is on your site (some people want to send you checks!), as well as video testimonials and typical client results or case studies.

- *Word of mouth.* Pursue viral marketing by equipping your clients and colleagues with an understanding of the full panoply of value you can provide, as well as the types of projects you engage in.

- *Trade association leadership.* If you take on a key role in a professional association, you'll find that you'll be quoted, interviewed, and consulted on best practices and trends in business.

- *Third-party endorsements.* Encourage evangelism. Find ways to bring your clients and prospects together, in reality and/or virtually.

- *Hard copy, print newsletters.* These sometimes stand out in the crowd because they are not simply additional electronic communications arriving daily.

---

[1]An excellent resource is National Trade and Professional Associations of the United States: https://www.associationexecs.com/national-trade-and-professional-associations-directory.

- *Print interviews.* Make yourself available to be cited in your field of expertise. You can to this through outlets such as Expert-Click.com.

- *Teaching.* Noted consultant Edgar Schein, wrote, "If you want to really understand something, try to teach it." Explore whether a local college would accept you as a visiting lecturer or adjunct professor on occasion.

- *Alliances.* Sometimes someone with noncompeting but complementary skills comes along, where 1 + 1 = 120. A small business strategy expert teamed with a financial advisor would be an example, marrying both business and family needs.

- *Products.* Products can add to your brand and provide passive income, including subscriptions, videos, manuals, and so forth.

- *Networking.* This is particularly effective when not done at obvious places (trade association meetings) but at places where the proper people gather (fund-raisers, for example). The key is just to begin the relationship and secure a meeting, not to try to make a pitch over cocktails.

- *Referrals.* This is the most profound and highest-quality aspect of market gravity, since a peer is endorsing you to another peer, with all the credibility that attends such a recommendation.

Of all of these (and other) gravity factors, referrals, networking, and speaking have the best potential for short-term business and fairly rapid cash.

> *Expertise: Some market gravity is passive (listings) and some is active (referrals). The key is to constantly review your market gravity for the most effective components and exploit them.*

Keep these numbers in mind:

- If you see two economic buyers a week on average, that's 100 a year.

- If half become seriously interested, you have 50 quality leads.

- If half of those agree to see a proposal, that's 25 proposals.

- If half of your proposals are accepted (and you'll see later that it should be 80 percent), then you have 12 pieces of business.

- If your average sale is $50,000, you have a $600,000 year. If it's $100,000, you have a $1.2 million year.

Do you see why I say, "Keep these numbers in mind"? That's what you need the gravity to produce.

THE ACCELERANT CURVE

I've developed the Million Dollar Consulting® Accelerant Curve (Figure 2-2) to help you understand the outcomes of your gravitational pull. It's no use to attract buyers unless they result in conversion to a customer or client. (Mark Smith provided the elementary idea for this during one of my Million Dollar Club meetings.)

Basically, the vertical axis is barrier (or lack of barrier) to entry (to find you, get to know you, appreciate your value). The horizontal access is increasing value and fee and *declining* labor. (I know that sounds counterintuitive, but bear with me.) Therefore, as you go to the right, your offerings increase in value and intimacy and decline in labor, but there are greater barriers to entry (price, commitment, time). On the left, people can get to know you readily (a free download, podcast, inexpensive booklet) and "ride" the accelerant curve toward more complex relationships.

There are "bounce factors" on the curve that propel people farther, faster. Someone reading this book may decide to attend my Million Dollar Consulting® College, all the way on the right in my "vault."

Otherwise, without bounce factors, the power of your brand and the building of trust will move people down the curve. On the extreme right is your vault, which means offerings unique to you. (At position 12 you may be offering high value that someone else offers, such as strategy work, but your vault might be a "six-hour strategy" that no one else can offer.)

Parachute business is business from buyers entering on the right side of the curve from the outset, not needing to come down the curve.

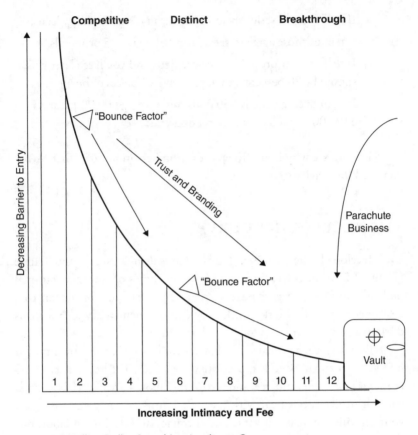

Figure 2-2 Million Dollar Consulting Accelerant Curve

This is caused by strong word of mouth (remember Figure 2-1), referrals, speaking, and so on. Your credibility and value are perceived as so strong that a "toe in the water" (pilot or test) is not deemed at all necessary or even advisable.

Take a moment to decide, ideally, at present or in the future, three value offerings you would create on the left, middle, and right of the curve, and two offerings that would be in your vault. The left side of the chart is generally representative of competitive offerings, the middle of distinct offerings, and the right of breakthrough offerings, culminating in the vault's unique offerings.

What makes sense for you to highlight or create at this point?

Left

1. _____
2. _____
3. _____

Middle

1. _____
2. _____
3. _____

Right

1. _____
2. _____
3. _____

Vault

1. _____
2. _____

Unless you actively and consciously prepare the points and offerings on the curve, they will not occur. You may find yourself heavily loaded on the left, with no higher-level offerings to which to drive clients, thereby sacrificing revenue. Or you might find yourself tilted on the right, with significant offerings but without the "feeder" mechanism on the left to attract people to them.

> *Expertise: The accelerant curve does not arise by default. It must be consciously planned and examined for adjustment as you become more successful.*

Note that similar offerings may occupy different places on the curve. For example, "coaching" may be on the left for remote phone support; in the middle for periodic meetings and feedback; and on the right for close shadowing, evaluating meetings, and critiquing presentations. It's all coaching, but with significantly different value to the clients in different situations.

Case Study

I was working with Allergan many years ago, coaching various managers. I was asked to coach the CEO because people raved about my help. I cited a fee five times the fee I had been charging.

"How can that be?" someone asked. "Every coach we've brought in here over the years at your level doesn't even charge what you're charging us now for middle management."

"First," I said, "the impact of the improvement of the CEO's performance will be 20 times that of all your middle management put together. Second, why don't you tell the CEO that you refuse to pay more for his coaching than you pay for a middle manager?"

They signed the contract on my terms that afternoon.

I explained that trust in you (the trusting relationship) plus your brand power create movement—acceleration—down the curve. Let's take a look at the process of building, nurturing, sustaining, and gaining equity from your brand.

BRILLIANT BRANDING

Cognitively, a brand is a representation of uniform value. People don't go into a McDonald's to browse. They have made a prior buying decision based on the brand, knowing that they will find a consistent experience (even globally, with minor cultural variations). A Mercedes represents a certain kind of status, as does a Brioni suit or a Bulgari watch.

However, viscerally and emotionally, a brand is what people think of you when you're not around. It is an abstract simulacrum, which is why executives looking for strategy help instinctively once said, "Get me McKinsey" and, contemporarily, people in need of urban transport say, "Let's Uber."

Brand creation begins with the three components we discussed earlier: passion, competency, and market need. I said that confluence creates your brand. In Figure 2-3 you can see a detailed breakdown. The three components create your business positioning (e.g., "strategy for modern times"), and then your brand(s) (e.g., "Six-Hour Strategy" or "The Strategic Sprint"),[2] which is then inserted into your market gravity. Customers are attracted, their needs are fulfilled, and this creates still more market need.

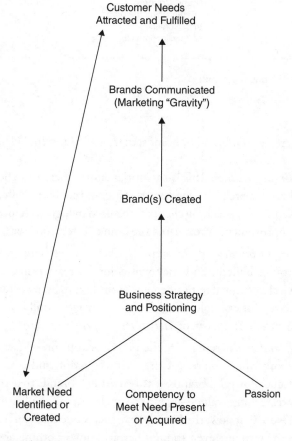

Figure 2-3 Brand sequence

[2]Keep in mind that the *ultimate* brand is your name.

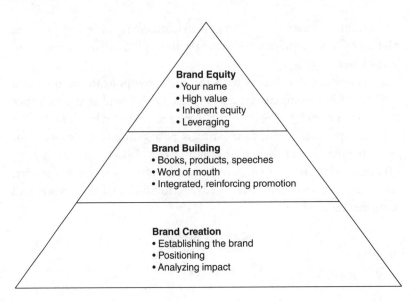

Figure 2-4 The brand pyramid

To create your brand or brands, there are three steps (Figure 2-4):

1. *Brand creation.* This is the initial effort where you choose your brand, match it to your positioning, and analyze its effectiveness. One of my coaching clients specialized in high-tech medical firm improvement. We created the brand "Lifeblood" for her.

2. *Brand building* is the step of "Once you've built it, tell them you've built it, and they will come." Create print, electronic, viral, continual reinforcement of the brand. Don't create a newsletter, for example, titled *Strategic Strengths*. Call it *Janet Boyd's Strategic Strengths*, or *The Strategic Sprint Strengths*.

3. *Brand equity* represents the power of your brand (what people think when you're not there) in attraction and is worth huge value. Powerful brands at this writing—brands that themselves create huge value—include Google, Apple, Coke, and Nike. (Note that powerful brands have such value that you'll find "Ferrari" watches, even though Ferrari knows nothing about timepieces. It leases its name and brand to watchmakers who can profit more simply using the name.)

> *Expertise: It's never too early or too late to create, refine, and/or abandon brands. Monitor their effectiveness constantly.*

To illustrate the importance of your brand's success at the effective juncture of the three critical marketing elements, consider the relationship shown in Figure 2-5.

Two of the three factors are obviously insufficient. The key payoff is worth repeating: A brand enables market gravity to more readily attract people to you, and when people knock on *your* door, credibility is assumed and fees are whatever you say they are.

A brand, whether a phrase, a combination of words, or your name, is a way of informing people that "you've built it" (your value) and they can come.

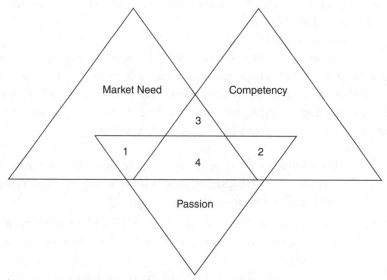

1. Brand is a clever concept, but substance can't be delivered.
2. Brand is ideally suited to you, but market is unreceptive.
3. Brand is potentially effective, but isn't supported.
4. Brand is magic.

Figure 2-5 The three critical elements of an effective brand

Advisory: A note before we proceed. If you are building a solo practice, which will generate cash for you every year but which obviously won't be sold since it consists only of you, work toward your name as the brand. But if you're building a boutique firm in which you reinvest every year so that you can sell it one day, make the business the brand so the brand equity is of value to the purchaser and the brand value is not dependent on your continued presence.

UNIFIED FIELD THEORY

The brilliant mathematician and polymath Stephen Hawking has been laboring for a long time to find a unified field theory for the universe. That is, a set of rules and laws that explain *all* the various known facts about the cosmos in concert, without contradiction and with self-reinforcement. This pursuit eluded Einstein.

It has also eluded Hawking.

However, I can show you a unified field theory for consulting success based on the early chapters of this book. I present this so that you can avoid the errors (or at least correct them) that so many others of us have made in not understanding how the marketing of consulting services "fits together" to form a cogent explanation of our universe:

1. The starting point is your value proposition (see "Where Do You Begin?" in Chapter 1), in which you state your passion for helping clients improve their condition.

2. The next step is your sweet spot (Figure 1-5), where you identify what you are great at doing and the few, key components surrounding it.

3. Carve away everything else and create your *David*, the artwork of your career, based on those two factors.

4. Find your ideal buyers (Figure 1-4) for that value and competency. Remember that quality is more important than quantity.

5. Use market gravity (Figure 2-1) to attract those buyers to you, through mechanisms appropriate for them and at which you excel.

6. Place them on your Accelerant Curve (Figure 2-2) with the intent of moving them through brand, trust, and "bounce factors" toward your vault with the benefits to you of high fee, low labor intensity, and high perceived intimacy.

I'm not setting myself up with Einstein and Hawking. In fact, I'm trying to prove the opposite—that consulting success isn't rocket science. There are no unknown mysteries of the cosmos here. So why don't people abide by the simplicity of excellent consulting and accelerate their careers?

Expertise: The steps are easy, but we keep getting distracted by squirrels.

My white German shepherd, Bentley, will run across the yard in pursuit of a squirrel, then stop to scratch, then watch a leave blown by the wind, then relieve himself, then take off after a different squirrel—all within 60 seconds. He'll sometimes chase and catch a Frisbee, then wander over and watch some dogs in another yard, with the Frisbee still in his mouth.

Dogs, as we all know, are easily distracted. But so, it seems, are consultants. (The great comedian Steven Wright once observed, "I'd like to be able to daydream, but I keep getting distracted."

Case Study

Jeannie called me to ask how to handle a potential small start-up project. The husband and wife owners were at $2 million in sales, had 12 people on staff, and feared they were focusing too much on delivery and not enough on marketing.

> *"What should I charge?" she asked, "and how much time do you think I'd need? They only have $12,000 they can spend, and not all at once."*
>
> *"Jeannie," I asked, "why are you considering this when your average project is a $75,000 to $125,000 strategy project for a Fortune 1000 company?"*
>
> *"It's easy money," she said, "and they're only an hour from my house."*
>
> *"You don't need the money, it's not in your area of expertise, and you're going to be swamped with questions. Walk away. If you don't walk away, don't call me, because I'm not helping with crazy projects."*

I receive calls like this about once a month. One of my coaching clients, who normally works with leadership skills in huge multinational companies, has an almost fatal penchant for taking on small law firms experiencing personnel problems with their high performers. The first two times, he was fired once and had to walk out once. The third time I refused to talk to him about it, but I bet he's still at it. He makes over a million dollars a year, but he adds to that income useless grief from totally inappropriate clients.

We all have a tendency to keep yelling "Squirrel! Squirrel!" and running full tilt in another direction. We see "money on the table" and think we should sweep it up. Yet this isn't at all consistent with the unified field theory, and in fact it undermines our progress toward profit.

The reasons that we chase squirrels instead of finding treasure are:

- We think "easy money" is always "safe money," but it rarely is. The smaller the project, the more demanding the client. The more cash is tight, the more insistence on a huge ROI on your modest fee.
- We think the project is easy. It rarely is. These buyers are looking for a "magic bullet," which takes one of two impossible forms:
  1. You are supposed to solve an intractable problem quickly and completely.

2. You are supposed to demonstrate that the client's prior approaches and work are not at fault, *even though they demonstrably are.*

- We fear we may never acquire another piece of business. I'll talk much more about self-esteem later in the book, but let's establish here that many consultants have a bad case of the "imposter syndrome" and fear they will get "caught" someday in the near future. So if you've been "faking it," you need to make as much as you can before someone determines that you're not really "making it."

- We see others do something that seems appropriate for us. ("If he can do it, I can do it!") Yet this flies in the face of what you're truly passionate about and great at. There are people making good money miniaturizing computer chips or creating pomegranate ice cream, but that doesn't mean that you can make money at it the way they are.

Thus, I'm not merely advocating a sequential, coherent approach to value, clients, and offerings as an academic nicety, I'm admonishing you to utilize the discipline to keep you on the right track. The "squirrel" you see is seldom relevant to your day, is almost impossible to catch, and in the long run actually tastes awful. (Someone once claimed that fox hunting was the unspeakable in pursuit of the inedible.)

For those of you who are newcomers to the profession, this chapter contains a great way to become immediately focused and raise your chances of immediate success hugely. For those of you who are veterans, you have the opportunity here to significantly realign your efforts, creating far more fulfillment and success.

You have to be happy and well to treat others well, because this is the ultimate relationship business.

THE YIN AND YANG OF CLIENTS AND PROSPECTS

We tend to use *client* generically. When I ask people who their ideal buyer is, they tell me "General Electric," or "utilities," or defense contractors. These aren't buyers, they are buildings.

An economic buyer is a person who has the ability to write a check (have a check issued) for your value without the approval of anyone else. When a prospective buyer says to you, "I think we can go forward once I run this by my boss," you're not talking to an economic buyer, just a feasibility person. Almost everyone in human resources or training and development is a feasibility person—they have no budgets of their own, they are merely middlemen[1] and gatekeepers.

Thus, your ideal buyer may be someone in a large company with P&L responsibility, or the executive director of a nonprofit, or the owner of a small business. Those are people whose needs can be discovered, created, and addressed.

There is also a profound difference between your existing buyers ("clients") and potential buyers ("prospects"). The former know you and love you, and the latter usually have little or no idea of who you are. And even if they do, and your brand and repute impress them, they still have no emotional bond with you. This is a critical distinction, *because logic helps people to think, but emotion urges them to act.*

---

[1]While I try to remain sensitive to gender in all that I do, *middleperson* sounds to me like *middle earth* and some kind of hobbit.

TWO DIFFERENT CAMPS

We often make the mistake of transference: believing that our interactions with clients carry over to our interactions with prospects.

They do not.

Figure I1-1 shows that we have three dynamics between ourselves and buyers. We may have a product (tangible purchase, such as a computer or book), a service (intangible purchase, such as insurance or advice), and a relationship (feeling of trust, such as reliance, confidentiality, safety, and ego needs). Apple produces great products, provides excellent service (via the Genius Bar), and generates a relationship of being hip and having the cachet of the best technology in the field. No one needs a Bentley for transportation, but one does need it for ego, to proclaim one's place in the world, and for a guarantee of the best in safety and engineering.

A strong product relationship (breakthrough in the chart) is insufficient in tough times. *It's the breakthrough relationship that creates the benefit of the doubt.* Thus, most U.S. airlines never receive the benefit of the doubt because they are mistrusted and have not established strong relationships with customers.[2] In tough economic times, people readily abandon normal alternatives and brands unless there is a strong relationship creating adherence to their offerings. When your Bentley has a flat, you shrug and

	Competitive	Distinct	Breakthrough
Product			
Service			
Relationship			

Figure I1-1 Client dynamics

[2]Frequent flyer status and air clubs have become commodities. In the old days carriers such as Pan Am made these amenities by invitation only. Then, it was a privilege. Today, it's considered a right.

call Bentley's roadside assistance, knowing it will be fixed with minimum inconvenience. When an American airline cancels a flight, the passengers believe it's a conspiracy because of a light load. The cable company, insurance companies, banks, and others often spend great amounts on their products and services while allowing their relationships to go to hell.

With your existing economic buyers, you should always be striving for the breakthrough relationship. This is characterized by:

- You and the buyer immediately disclosing information that has a material bearing on the success of the project (e.g., learning that a key person is being courted by a rival, or that the board is considering a divestiture).

- The buyer asking your opinion on key decisions and following your advice.

- The rejection and overcoming of complaints about the project (and, often, you) from those threatened by it.

- Mutual flexibility in deviating from a prescribed course to take advantage of opportunity and/or make better use of time and expertise.

Now the question becomes: How do we transfer this great relationship dynamic to *prospective buyers*?

CREATING CROSSOVER

How do we share the love? How do we create the same levels of trusting relationship that exist with longtime clients in brand-new prospects? Osmosis doesn't work, but, fortunately, some techniques do.

- *Create evangelists.* Encourage clients (buyers and nonbuyers alike) to spread the word. Find and befriend those people who have most supported your projects, initiated new ones, and been credited with success. Keep a special list of such people.

- *Provide opportunity.* Invite evangelists to events you host. Ask them to coauthor publications. Cite them in your books. Invite them to participate in a speech you're making. Create access to them for your prospects.

- *Use testimonials, references, and case studies shamelessly.* Video testimonials are extremely impressive and can be recorded on a phone camera. They needn't be professionally done. Obtain permission to use names with case studies, and have a list of "platinum references" that you don't use often (so as not to annoy those on the list) but do use with discretion for very high potential prospects. These testimonials should be on your website, in your blog, in your newsletter, in your e-mail signature file, in your conversation, in your speeches, and so forth. *People are much more readily and speedily impressed by their peers' commentary than by your own.* You need to be the choreographer who brings the dancers into harmony.

Case Study

I was in my first few weeks of working for a consulting firm in Princeton, New Jersey. As part of my orientation, I was sent to one of the firm's clients, Florida Power & Light, to take part in its training and graduation ceremony.

At the event, several company employees spoke to the group of assembled senior managers about the consulting firm's great approaches, results gained on the job while still in a training mode, and dramatic plans for expansion of the effort. Several managers present asked the consulting team members that night if they could discuss their own departments' participation in the near future.

"It's like being paid to be paid further," said one of the consulting team leaders.

THE RAPID TRANSFORMATION

When you are meeting with a true economic buyer for the first time, here's how to accelerate the positive, trusting relationship that existing buyers already have with you:

- *Create a peer-to-peer dynamic.* Don't appear as a supplicant of the buyer, and don't be obsequious.

- *Always keep in mind that you are there to offer value,* not to "take" anything. You are not "selling" in the sense of seeking money, but "offering" in the sense of an equal transaction, dramatic improvement, and equitable compensation.

- *Gauge the other person's sense of speed.* I'm not talking about personality profiles, which are notoriously ineffective (we are far too complex to be branded a "green" or "low Z" or "NINNY"). If the buyer wants to go fast ("What can you do for me?"), go fast. If the buyer wants to move slowly ("Tell me about yourself"), move slowly.

- *Guide the conversation.* Remember the boat rides for children in the amusement parks? The boats seemed steerable, but they were actually guided by the current and kept oriented by the nearby walls. They would always arrive at the intended destination. Your conversation should be the same with the buyers, allowing for twists and turns, but always directed by your "current and walls" toward your destination of trust, conceptual agreement, and a proposal.

- *Show confidence.* You must exhibit the confidence in yourself and conviction needed to convince the other party that you're strong and competent. You can't be afraid to make statements such as:

"I know I can help you."

"You and I are meeting at precisely the right time."

"I have better means of approaching this than what you've tried in the past."

"Let me suggest how we can best work together."

- *Push back when appropriate.* You can't seem to be "chasing money" or too readily agreeing. There is a reason the buyer is taking the time to talk to you, and it's because he or she has a need (or at least a "want") that is unmet, and there is a suspicion that you may have the answer. However, the buyer's doubts will seldom be met by your blanket agreement (or else the issue would long ago have been resolved). Thus, logically, what's required is someone suggesting that the buyer's alternative is not the best, his or her evaluation not valid, his or her suppositions not based on empirical evidence.

These are the conversational ways in which you begin to bring the buyer into your frame of reality and normative behavior. You begin to create the trust that those you've already worked with find to be absolutely an asset and important, yet despite their accolades, testimonials, and endorsements, you still have to convince the person in front of you!

THE CLIENT AS PROSPECT

It's important to regard your existing buyer, in most cases, as a prospect as well. The credibility challenge here is not in convincing the buyer you can be of help—presumably, you've already demonstrated that—but in convincing the buyer *that you can be of help in additional areas and dimensions.*

Case Study

I'm in the National Speakers Association Hall of Fame, which is an honor accorded to fewer than one percent of all professional speakers. I'm well known and, considering my fees, well regarded. I am also, obviously, a very successful consultant, which is why you're reading this book.[3]

I had been working for the CEO of a major life insurance company for about six months when he approached me and asked me to find him a good speaker! He told me he was on the program committee of the American Council of Life Insurance, and it needed a keynoter for its annual conference of 250 insurance CEOs and COOs.

"Mike," I said, "I'm your guy!"

"Alan," he replied, "this is serious. I need someone who does this for a living."

The problem, of course, was that Mike knew me solely as an organizational development consultant and really had no reason to explore my background beyond that. I actually had to resell him on my merits. The result was obtaining that keynote and a lot of new business.

---

[3]But don't let that stop you from also reading my *Million Dollar Speaking* (McGraw-Hill, 2011).

As I've mentioned, I tell people in my coaching community that they need to see two buyers a week on average. It's just an average, but it's required if you wish to pursue great results and wealth. That means that if you're speaking to a dozen buyers at an event, you've covered six weeks.

Now tell me this: Who is more likely to proceed to next steps in high ratios—new buyers or existing buyers? That's a no-brainer.

So what I'm telling you here is that if you see your existing buyers also as prospective buyers, and if you include them to the maximum degree in your two-buyers-a-week drill, you will significantly improve the percentage of new business that results. It's all in the numbers.

Yet we often miss this clear, noncomplex, direct route to improving our businesses *because we don't see existing buyers as prospective buyers, only as "past" buyers.* This is both ludicrous and dangerous. If Mike hadn't approached me, I never would have had that new business. But if I had made my capabilities more apparent at the outset, I would have guaranteed his coming to me for the assignment. I shouldn't have depended on him to know I had this skill, and you shouldn't depend on luck or the fates or your charm.

Include all of your buyers in your "prospects" category and treat them accordingly, knowing that you don't have to re-create the trust and belief that you would with a true prospect because that's a line you don't have to cross again with them.

THE BUYER LIFE CYCLE

No matter what markets you favor or buyers you find ideal, two sales are made when you successfully conclude an agreement. The first occurs when the proposal is signed and you receive your check to begin. The second occurs when you derive referral and repeat business from that buyer.

Too often, consultants ignore or forget the second sale, thereby denying themselves half of the business potential.

All client relationships come to an end. I worked with Merck for 12 years and Hewlett-Packard for 10. I thought that was extraordinary. But I'm still working to this day with companies and people I first met through those early corporate relationships. These are the scenarios for which you must be prepared, especially considering that your current buyers are also your current prospects:

1. The buyer leaves through retirement, a new job offer, promotion, disability, and so forth. You should have been meeting the buyer's peers, subordinates, and relevant others during your tenure. Only if the replacement comes from outside the organization would you be at a disadvantage.

2. Follow your buyers to new positions within the same organization or in new ones. I've worked with some buyers through four organization changes and several career alterations. Why wouldn't your "smarts" transcend organizational boundaries?

3. Assiduously create referral business. Ask for referrals, inside and outside the organization, at least every two months. Ask by name if possible ("I'd love to be introduced to Jane Jones") or by title ("Can I meet your counterpart for Asia?").[4]

4. Elicit contemporary testimonials, case studies, and war stories as your tenure progresses. Video is especially important, as I've noted earlier.

5. If your buyer is replaced by someone from outside the organization, offer to "debrief" and bring the new person up to speed on the project and its trajectory.

6. Never cease marketing to new prospects. In any one year, a ratio of about 80 percent repeat business and 20 percent new business is quite good. It represents great continuity but also the infusion of "new blood."

7. Create and nurture your "evangelist" group. These may not all be buyers, but they are people who sing your praises in public, helping your "brand." Remember: A brand represents what people think about you when you aren't present. It eliminates the necessity of you being present to be considered.

Figure I1-2 shows a simple schematic for tracking many of the people you should be in touch with and developing as prospective sources

---

[4]For a detailed examination of the methodology of successful referral business, see my book *Million Dollar Referrals* (McGraw-Hill, 2012).

Figure I1-2 "Touch points" with a client

of business. You can see how "existing" and "new" business tend to blur because organizations are diverse and can accommodate your talents in many ways.

In summary, your clients and your prospects can be entirely different or may be largely the same. Just as a prospect can become a client, a client is also a prospect. Once you can accept that blend, you'll find yourself in a far more powerful position to build and sustain your business.

THE RELATIONSHIP BUSINESS

LEARNING HOW TO SELL YOURSELF

Realtors, insurance people, car salespeople—they are all oriented toward high interpersonal relations. After all, they meet people looking to make individual purchases, and their future is largely based on referrals from happy customers.

Yet they are just selling a product or service. You're selling you.

The coauthor of my first book in 1988, The Innovation Formula, *said to me, "You know, you can't really sell anything except yourself, but you're damn good at it."*

—Mike Robert

THE VITAL CREATION OF TRUST

Trust is the firm belief in the reliability, truth, credibility, and conviction of someone else. It is the keystone component in building relationships, gaining conceptual agreement (which we'll discuss later in the chapter), and gaining the benefit of the doubt. This is essential for a new consultant, a veteran consultant, and, for that matter, anyone who is trying to influence anyone else at any time.

We don't automatically grant or gain trust. We may not be skeptical or cynical, but there's no sound reason to trust a stranger, and even less so if the stranger asks for money! We'd be naive to simply put our faith in random people, and we'd be fantasizing if we expected others to do so with us. (This is why telemarketing is harder than face-to-face marketing, because the former omits body language and gesture, key components in relationships and interpreting communications. Telemarketers try to compensate by using your first name immediately and asking a "soft" question: "Hello, Alan, and how are you this wonderful day?")

The reason for trust is to gain honesty from buyers and thereby learn what you require to be of help to them with their needs and to create a proposal that will effectively address those needs. If I don't trust you, I'm not going to share things of any import with you. If you don't trust me, you're not going to believe a word I say. I heard it said once of a rather unscrupulous manager, "He lies when he says Hello."

The sequence in the process of acquiring business looks like this:

Project Launch
Proposal Accepted
Conceptual Agreement
Need Identification
Issues Discussion
Trusting Relationship
Determination of True Buyer
Initial Meeting
Leads

You need sufficient trust with a nonbuyer to be directed to the true buyer, but you need significant trust with the true buyer to initiate a discussion of issues.

You may have to "push back" against what you're told. If a buyer says, "Motivation issues are easily solved by paying more money," you need to say, "If you give an unhappy employee more money, you simply create a wealthier unhappy employee." You need the buyer to say, "Tell me more," and not, "I simply don't agree." If the buyer trusts you, then additional advice will be sought.

The heart of a proposal is the conceptual agreement on objectives (outcomes), metrics (measures of success), and value (ROI on the investment). No one is going to share those details with someone he or she doesn't trust.

Expertise: Behind every corporate objective are personal objectives. To find them, you must have a trusting relationship.

Proposals are most effective when they satisfy personal objectives of the buyer in additional to business issues. For example, a desire for more collaboration among departments might mean that the buyer is weary of wasting time playing referee among disputing parties. How would you find that out? Only if the buyer offers it as a result of trusting in your judgment and advice.

As you can see in Figure 3-1, trust can begin with referrals, identification of expertise, affiliation needs, and respect. However, true, sustaining trust is built on an emotional connection. *Think of it as the honest belief that the other person has your best interests in mind.* He is not trying to sell the most expensive option, and he is not trying to gain at your expense. He is trying to help you achieve your goals and will only succeed if you succeed. That is the emotional connection.

What are the indicators of trust? How do you know it's possible to move on and engage in substantive conversations? This is vital, since too many consultants simply sit down and go into a pitch, or through a checklist, or—shiver—start showing PowerPoint slides.

The indicators of trust are:

- The buyer does not allow interruptions by phone, e-mail, or people entering the meeting room.
- The buyer looks you in the eye.
- Humor is used, and the mood is not somber.
- You're asked questions seeking your advice. ("Have you seen firms like ours that don't have a chief marketing officer?")
- You're told things you didn't ask about. ("This is confidential, but we'll be eliminating the human resources department.")

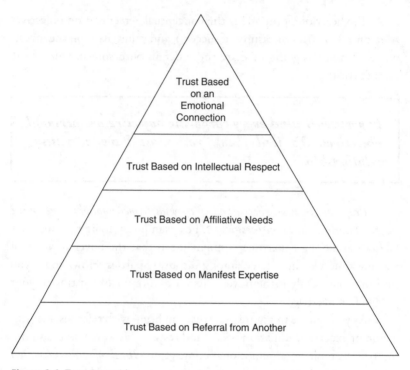

Figure 3-1 Trust Pyramid

- You are not delegated to lower-level people.
- You are asked to stay longer than the meeting time frame.

Indicators of distrust, in addition to the converse of the above, are:

- You are asked for references.
- You are asked to explain in detail how you would work in the current environment.
- You are asked about "deliverables" and tasks.
- You are asked what your "rates" are.
- You are asked about your education.[1]

---

[1]This may seem innocuous, but in 30 years I've been asked exactly once, by the CEO of Merck, what school I attended.

As you can see, you can calibrate trust building as the conversation progresses. This is essential, since you can no more proceed with the sales acquisition process without trust than you can build a house without a foundation.

There is one more condition to examine while we're on the subject of trust. The only worse condition than not having trust is having had it and lost it. It is more difficult to regain lost trust than it is to establish it in the first place. Just ask Lance Armstrong, the disgraced cycling champion, or Brian Williams, the once-suspended news anchor.

The lesson here is that you must walk the talk and talk the walk. Always be on time. Never gossip. Don't cut corners. Never exaggerate what you can accomplish. Use evidence and observed behavior, not supposition or third-party claims.

Case Study

I was telling a division president that he had to replace his most trusted subordinate because the subordinate was undermining people, providing no leadership, and micromanaging (he directed in what order people should attend activities at a company picnic, for example). I was apologizing for the news to a man who held a PhD in chemistry and would go on to become CEO of a global pharmaceutical firm.

"Alan, don't worry," he said, "I have to take your word because we're both scientists using evidence and the scientific method."

That was a huge sign of trust—though I was tempted to turn my head to see what scientist had walked into the room behind my back!

LANGUAGE

Every business is a communications business, and all communications rely on language to be effective and accurate. That may seem obvious, but most people pay scant attention to this vital tool in relationship building. Here is the immutable sequence in our profession:

- Language controls discussions
- Discussions control relationships
- Relationships control business

Is that clear enough? You can't omit the first step and set of skills and expect to be successful in this profession.

Here are the attributes of powerful language that will create dynamic relationships and large projects:

Peer Level

You can't be a supplicant or appear obsequious. You should appear as a peer of the buyer. That means your examples should be relevant to his or her level and situation, and your frames of reference should be appropriate for the industry. For example, in a bank you needn't be a financial expert, but you should know what a loan defalcation is. In manufacturing environments, you should know what "supply chain management" refers to. Your language should, therefore, change given the:

- Hierarchy (front line, mid-management, executive)
- Strategic vs. tactical
- Profit vs. nonprofit
- Manufacturing vs. services
- Closely held vs. corporate giant
- Domestic vs. multinational

It's simple to change your language, examples, and metaphors to match the context of your business dealings so long as you don't fall into the trap of "pitches" and "scripts."

Directionally Oriented

Remember those boats in the amusement park that you thought you were steering but actually stayed in the channel, always moving in the direction of the ride's completion? You should create the same channel for your conversation's completion.

There's an old line, "No wind is a good wind if you lose sight of your destination." Enter into discussions with language prepared to move toward your destination: a proposal submitted, meeting the real buyer, gathering information, exploring budget—whatever your immediate goal may be. Don't allow the conversation to drift out of your channel. You should own the ride. But there is too much irrelevant language, such as "How do you like this job?" or "What are your worst nightmares?" or "What are your priorities?" These are banal questions that don't lead toward your destination.

A fanatic is someone who loses sight of his goal and consequently redoubles his efforts.

—Philosopher George Santayana

Illustrative Speech

A picture may be worth a thousand words, but a metaphor is worth a thousand pictures. Think of illustrative speech as the use of language to accelerate your progress toward your intended objectives.

Here are the most common techniques:

- *Metaphor:* A metaphor is a word or phrase representing an action not immediately applicable to create memorability. I often use "the oxygen mask principle" to demonstrate that we need to take care of ourselves before attempting to help others (just as flight attendants tell you during every airplane takeoff announcement).

- *Simile:* This is the comparison of one issue with another unrelated one, often using "like" or "such as": His search was as desperate as a blind man trying to find a black cat in a dark room.

- *Metonymy:* A word or phrase used to represent something else to which it is closely linked but not an actual part. We see memos that say "from the desk of" (really from the writer) or "the White House has said . . ." (really from the press secretary).

- *Synecdoche:* One aspect of something is used to represent the entirety. We use "9/11" to indicate the tragedy of the terrorist acts that occurred in the United States in 2001, for example, or "nice wheels" to compliment a new car purchase.
- *Litotes:* This is deliberate understatement. "Apple is not a bad investment," or "Abraham Lincoln had a few problems to resolve as president."

Some examples of these techniques in action:

- Your new product ideas need escape velocity to achieve separation from conservative cultural restraints. (metaphor)
- Your top salespeople wouldn't be the worst resources to serve as mentors for new hires, which isn't being done at the moment. (litotes)
- The weekly management meetings are like lost people in the desert seeing mirages—nothing substantial is discussed. (simile)
- The customer has been telling you for quite some time that your service standards are not as good as your competition. (metonymy)
- Quarterly pressures are playing too great a role in daily business decisions. (synecdoche)

The language of the sale, as I like to call it, is the prelude to conceptual agreement once trust has been established. The effective use of language will focus the customer on *your* intended goal and prevent wandering.

To control the conversation, you also need to interrupt the buyer. That's right, *interrupt*. Otherwise, with the best of intentions, polite discourse could take you to territories uncharted and far removed from your intended destination.

Here's how to use language to interrupt politely:

- May I stop you right there? You've said something I think is vitally important, and I want to make sure I understand it.
- Excuse me, but I think you've said in three different ways that attrition is the major issue, is that right?

- Pardon me, but can we discuss that last point further before moving on?
- May I summarize what you've been saying, to make sure I'm on the right track?

Note that all of these are what I call "rhetorical permissions," in that you're making a request that really can't be denied and isn't so much a request as a directive! But these are pivot points that will redirect a rambling conversation back toward your destination (keeping within the boat channel).

You are not with the buyer to be polite—you are there to offer value to improve the buyer's condition, and that often requires that you take control of the conversation through effective language to enable that value to be realized.

If you are interested in a practice exercise on language, simply review this last segment and identify all the language techniques I've described that I've also employed.

CONCEPTUAL AGREEMENT

Conceptual agreement can only be attained with an economic buyer. If you're not talking to your true buyer, then don't even attempt to gain conceptual agreement *because it will be useless.*

In Figure 3-2 you can see the central role that conceptual agreement plays in a simplified version of the sales process we examined earlier in the chapter. It is the link from trusting relationship to a successful proposal.

With the economic buyer you want to achieve three basic elements of agreement:

1. Objectives

Objectives are business *outcomes*, never deliverables or inputs or tasks. They are the components of how the buyer's condition is improved. They may be professional and also personal:

- *Professional:* Decrease sales closing time.
- *Personal:* Spend less time refereeing conflicts among teams.

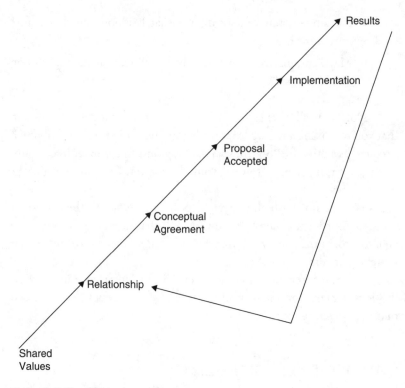

Figure 3-2 Simplified sales sequence

The way to drive a buyer from an alternative to an objective is by asking *Why?*

"We'd like you to run a two-day retreat on sales skills."

"Why?"

"Because our sales are seriously behind forecast."

In this case, the client has a problem (sales are below forecast) but has arrived at an arbitrary alternative as the solution (a two-day retreat). The real objective here is "Restore sales to a level at or above forecasts as soon as possible." The true solution is probably *not* a retreat, but rather an analysis of the forecast, individual producers, product mix, and so on.

> **Expertise: Too many consultants "default" to a classroom or training solution because the client requests it or it's what they know best, even though it's the wrong solution to meet the real objective.**

Here are examples of deliverables or arbitrary options turned into outcomes and objectives:

ALTERNATIVE	REAL OBJECTIVE
Create communications training	Eliminate multiple, costly calls
Run a strategy retreat	Create strategy to improve market share
Coach four subordinates	Create a likely successor to free the person up for promotion
"Mystery shop" our stores	Create best practices to disseminate to maximize frontline sales
Build rapport with IT and others	Utilize technology to reduce repair costs and visits

The left column comprises tasks that might or might not improve the client's condition (most training does not add to productivity or performance, and it's an $80 billion annual industry). The right column can be seen to add demonstrably to the company's (and/or buyer's) results.

Always seek out the true objectives with the buyer by using the right language once trust has been established.

2. Measures of Success

We need to ascertain how we and the buyer will know that progress is being made. (Again, most training does not include metrics for success, so it's a crapshoot as to whether the investment is actually creating a return. Most human resources and training departments shun metrics because they'd be out of business once it was shown that most training has zero impact.)

Every objective requires at least one metric, and more are fine. You and the buyer should agree on how they are measured. *Scientific* metrics rely on data and information gathered by objective means, such as weekly sales reports. *Anecdotal* measures are those you agree will be observed by the buyer.

Here are some examples of objectives and corresponding metrics:

OBJECTIVE	METRIC
Increased cross–product sales	Weekly sales report
Decreased attrition in R&D	Monthly staffing report for R&D
Reduced product complaints	Track weekly call center content
Less refereeing among factions	Personal log and observation
Greater employee satisfaction	Buyer breakfasts with random employees

The metrics enable you to:

- Continually monitor the success rate of the project
- Demonstrate that you are accountable for the success
- Provide good news to counterbalance any bad news
- Agree with the buyer that success is accomplished

3. Value

Value represents the actual impact of meeting the objectives. I pioneered this approach in the early nineties, and it represents the greatest contributor to higher fees that a consultant can create, since fees should be based on value.

Let's take an objective as simple as "profit." You might say that profit is, itself, the value of the project. But if we increase profit, we may also provide for:

- Paying off debt
- Paying higher bonuses
- Attracting top talent
- Paying higher dividends
- Attracting more investors
- Investing more in R&D

As you can see, "profit" has diverse and significant value. We can create that same multiplicity for almost any objective.

Thus, value is the heart of conceptual agreement, which is the sequence of objectives, measures, and value *agreed to with your buyer, pre-proposal.* This is why you should hit at least 80 percent of your proposals, because they become *summations (of conceptual agreement) and not explorations (of negotiations and other options).*

Here is your formula:

- A range of about four to six objectives for your project
- At least one metric for each objective

- At least three value statements for each objective
- At least half of the value statements be monetized

Always take conservative ranges. If the client says, "We could increase our margins by 3 to 5 percent," use 3 percent. If the client says, "We could achieve a savings of $2 million," cut it in half. That way, you can point out that your dramatic ROI is based on highly conservative estimates, which the buyer provided.

Caution: If the buyer doesn't want to give you numbers, then you don't have a trusting relationship and you've rushed the process. If the buyer says honestly, "I don't know what the numbers would be," then use a hypothetical:

> *If you think you're losing 20 people a year whom you don't want to lose, and each replacement costs about $120,000 in search fees, training, and relocation, that's $2.4 million, correct? And what about lost client business that this creates or they take with them?*

We'll return to conceptual agreement when we talk about proposals in Chapter 5.

CLICKS TO CONVERSION

I've always like the phrase "clicks to conversions" because it connotes the idea that no matter how many people look at you, nothing matters until they pay you. I've known too many people who gloat that their website or blog draws "thousands of hits per day," yet their business is in the doldrums.

My reference to "clicks" here is metaphoric. I'm talking about how often people pay attention to you in one form or another versus how often they spend money with you. *The corporate buyers for consulting services do not primarily troll the Internet searching for resources!*[2]

---

[2]Retail buyers sometimes do for services such as realty or insurance, but even for coaching help they will first consult peers for recommendations.

If you consider Figure 2-2, you'll see that the key is to drive prospects down your Accelerant Curve to more valuable and higher-fee offerings. Figure 1-4 shows how to identify your ideal buyer.

When you combine your ideal buyer and your offerings, you have a high potential for high-fee, sustainable business. Here are the best ways to create initial interest that has a high probability of converting to paying projects:

- *Create evangelism opportunities.* Mix your prospects with your clients at events, in virtual communities, and in joint ventures (e.g., surveys, interviews, articles, panels, and so forth).

- *Create provocative intellectual property* that appears in appropriate media. Challenge your buyers with new ideas (e.g., team building doesn't work if you're surrounded by committees) that appear in influential places (e.g., a newsletter from a trade association to which they belong).

- *Speak at events that they attend.* If you were to speak at the American Council of Life Insurers, you could find yourself addressing 250 insurance industry CEOs and COOs, for example.

- *Network where your buyers congregate,* which may well be divorced from their natural environments. Attending charity fund-raisers, awards evenings, political rallies, and so on can place you in proximity to your buyers on a peer basis.

The key is to "convert" these meetings and attention to business. That means that you have to provide the reason to invest. Your mindset must be one of offering value, not "making a sale." That means this type of sequence:

1. You appear on your ideal buyers' radar screens, using techniques such as those above.

2. You offer immediate value in conversation, in writing, in reaction. You suggest "There are three key steps in streamlining supply chains" or "You're better off investing in your all-stars than in your poorest performers."

3. You make an appointment to explore your initial value and more in person. (Criterion for travel: 90 minutes of uninterrupted time with your ideal buyer. You don't close major projects on the phone.)

4. You move toward the conceptual agreement described earlier and a proposal with options.

Expertise: Don't be fooled (or self-delusional) about people paying attention to you—only focus on true buyers with whom you engage.

We can't afford to invest our time in popularity or affiliations or silly metrics like Klout Scores.[3] Here is the formula once again (it's that important) for ensuring a high percentage of conversions (buyers who become clients):

1. Meet with two buyers a week, whether existing or new, whether individually or in groups. (A meeting with 10 buyers would give you five weeks' worth of meetings.) These are in person, not by phone.

2. Of those approximately 100 buyers per year, half should agree to meet again to discuss projects.

3. Of those 50, half should agree to consider a proposal.

4. Of those 25, half accept the proposal (although your "hit rate" should be about 80 percent).

5. Multiply 12 accepted proposals by your average fee (e.g., $50,000), and you have your annual revenue ($600,000). If your average fee is $100,000, then you have a $1.2 million year.

It's that simple. If that's your focus.

[3]A rating of one's popularity on social media platforms.

HOW TO
MAXIMIZE FEES

MONEY LEFT ON THE
TABLE ISN'T THERE
IN THE MORNING

To those of you who turned directly to this chapter to start reading, welcome!

Fees are money paid you as equitable compensation for the value you've delivered. I pioneered the concept of value-based fees for consultants when this book was originally published in 1992. It's the sole method I've ever used, and it should be the sole method you use, particularly now.

THE FUNDAMENTALS OF VALUE-BASED FEES

You are paid a fee in an equilibrium that creates a great deal for buyer and equitable compensation for you. With rare exceptions (a single speech, one day of coaching, and so forth), the fee should be based *on the value you contribute to the success of the project as described in the conceptual agreement on objectives, metrics, and value.* If you are charging by the hour, day, numbers of participants, or any other such measure, you are an amateur. Anyone who recommends that kind of billing structure is an amateur.

When you charge by the hour, you are in an *ethical conflict* with your client. You only receive larger pay for the longer you are there, *but the client is better served by how quickly you can meet the objectives and leave.*

Secondly, the laughable advice to determine your annual financial needs, divide by available working hours in the year, and establish your hourly fee as a result is a recipe for mediocrity. Why limit your income, and why work every available hour? The key is to maximize income and minimize labor. Otherwise, I'd be selling insurance someplace and you wouldn't be reading this book to create a dramatic career.[1]

The "formula" for value-based fees looks like this:
- *Tangible value × annualization +*
- *Intangible value × emotional impact +*
- *Peripheral benefits = ROI*

Your fees should reflect a minimum of a 10:1 investment. That means if you're creating a million dollars in savings or new business or better margins or stress relief—or a combination thereof—your fee would be about $100,000. (We'll discuss how to raise that still more later.)

Remember, in conceptual agreement we've established at least three impacts of value for *every* objective (business outcome), and half of those were monetized. Thus, using the model above, let's say that your monetized value alone comes to $3.4 million as a result of reducing unwanted attrition. The project's value also includes the buyer's reduced stress from board pressure over the departures and internecine fighting over available resources. As a peripheral benefit, not directly related to the objectives, it's likely that less turnover will make it easier to attract top talent and spend less on placement fees and training.

Thus, your total estimated value might actually be about $4 million, and your first option $400,000. (Never forget that most of your accomplishments will be annualized and provide value well into the future with zero cost of implementation.) That figure may be hard to say out loud for some of you, but it's far easier to say than "We can't afford to pay the mortgage this month" or "I hope the kid doesn't get into too expensive a college next year."

Approximately 95 percent of everyone I've ever coached and who has read any of my books *are undercharging and overdelivering.* The good

---

[1]If you would like to read more about the philosophy and more details on practical implementation, see my book *Value-Based Fees* (Pfeiffer/Wiley, 2008).

news is that you're not alone. The bad news is that you want to get out of that herd as quickly as possible.

Case Study

I was speaking to a group of consultants in Reno, Nevada, when one stepped up to the mike in an aisle we were using for questions. I acknowledged him as soon as I finished the points above.

After I brief pause, he said, "Hello, I'm Mike, and I'm an undercharger."

The entire room, about 500 people, responded, "Hello, Mike!"

He went on to explain that while consulting for one of the largest technical firms in the world, he had created and implemented a project that the client's own financial people estimated at $1.3 billion in savings over the next few years. The client was ecstatic. Mike was a hero. I had to ask him twice to speak up about his fee.

"I charged $35,000," he said, and slowly walked back to his seat in a deafeningly quiet room.

Your fee represents your contribution to the success of the client's project as expressed in the value statements and the formula above. If a client were to say, "What's your fee basis?" or "Why don't you charge by the hour like all our other consultants?" you should respond:

> *My fee represents my contribution to this project with a dramatic return on investment for you and equitable compensation for me.*

That's how partners act, and I've explained at the outset that this is a relationship business built on trust. You simply need to learn that simple sentence and believe the completely logical rationale that underlies it.

Never provide a fee while gaining conceptual agreement. If pressed, tell the buyer:

> *It would be unfair to you for me to cite a fee without carefully considering what we've discussed, which I can do quickly and have a proposal on your desk within 24 hours.*

No buyer needs a fee quote that same day! The fees can wait for the complete proposal, which is the place to demonstrate the true ROI.

Expertise: You must have a true economic buyer with whom you have conceptual agreement if you are to establish significant value-based fees.

You must become comfortable with the reality that the formulation of fees is both art and science. You can calculate benefits that are tangible, but you have to assess the true value of the intangible (less stress, better aesthetics, better media relations, a better community citizen, more comfort, and so forth) as well as the power of the buyer's personal objectives underlying the corporate objectives. For example, to be seen as a leader and innovator and top candidate for a key promotion is worth more than mere dollars and cents.

Finally, understand that if you charge $185,000 for a project, it doesn't matter that it might have been $160,000 or $205,000. At these amounts, such worrying is totally irrelevant, because virtually *all* of the fee is pure profit (clients pay for expenses). If you're providing projects for $15,000, then I'd admit that if it were $11,000 or $19,000 the difference would be significant.

But you're not reading this book to create $15,000 projects.

If you were to "leave on the table" $50,000 a year in fees you could have charged but did not, you'd lose a half million in a decade, *a half million that you can never recover and that would have been pure profit.*

RETAINERS

Retainers are fees paid in return for access to your smarts.

Retainers are fees paid in return for access to your smarts.
Retainers are fees paid in return for access to your smarts.

Have I made the point? Retainers in consulting *are not* like law-yers' retainers, which are simply deposits from a client from which they deduct their paltry hourly fees.[2] (Lawyers are among the worst-paid pro-fessionals given their degree of schooling and difficulty of the barriers to entry. The average attorney salary in the United States is about $132,000 per year, gross.)

Thus, a consulting retainer means that a client has the right to access you as a sounding board, trusted advisor, and objective source at any time within the parameters of the retainer. The ultimate goal of the Acceler-ant Curve is to move business into high fee, low labor combinations, and "vault items" which are uniquely your own (therefore, not competitive with anyone else and not price sensitive). Consequently, the retainer is the ultimate expression of high fee and low labor, since it is not project-based.

There is no "hands on" with a retainer, just brainpower that is val-ued by the client.

In Figure 4-1 we repeat the relationship that we work hard when we launch our practice, taking on almost anything to put bread on the table (I was doing $20 résumé assessments at one point). But as our careers progress, the labor should drop as we move toward smarter methodol-ogies, and our fees should rise as our brand grows more powerful. The greater the brand differentiation, the greater that positive "gap" as shown in the illustration.

There are three variables in a retainer:

1. *Numbers.* How many people have access? Is it only the buyer, or three people designated by the buyer? Generally, this number is limited to one to four people. They must be specified so there is no misconception that their direct reports also have access.

2. *Scope.* If you are on the East Coast and the client is on the West Coast (or overseas), what hours of access are acceptable? Are weekends or evenings included? Is communication by e-mail, phone, and/or Skype (or other electronic media)? Is it by appointment? Is it immediate access or rapid response? (Mine is always rapid response, never immediate access, which is too

---

[2]Even lawyers are catching on to value-based fees, and the chief justice of the Western Australia supreme court wrote me to say that he believes lawyers grossly undercharge for their value. The "thou-sand dollar an hour" fees you see in New York or Washington are simply publicity gimmicks.

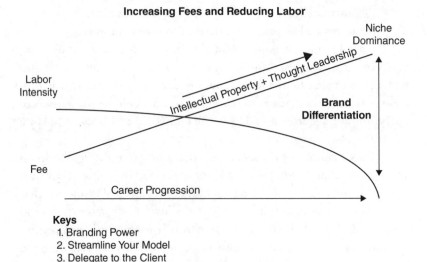

Figure 4-1 Increasing fees and reducing labor

difficult to guarantee.) Are personal meetings involved, and/or can they be requested? These are all important scope questions, and you can see the differences in value (e.g., meetings possible in person, rapid response, and so forth).

3. *Duration.* How long is the retainer to be in effect? I suggest never less than 90 days to give it a chance to be tested well. The client should pay by the quarter, at the beginning of the period.

I want to be clear that retainers are access to you that the client initiates. You don't call in, or check up, or suggest things. You have to have the confidence to know that your mere availability is of immense value, *not* the number of calls made to you. It is reactive, not proactive, more like mentoring than coaching. You contact a mentor when you need help, but a coach actively intervenes when the coach believes it's necessary.

Case Study

A coaching client said to me, "My client is considering reducing or eliminating our retainer because he only accessed me a few times this past year."

> *I asked, "Does he have fire insurance?"*
> *"Of course he does."*
> *"Did he have a fire?"*
> *"No."*
> *"Ask him if he intends to cancel the fire insurance."*

Never agree to conduct projects as part of a retainer, because you will lose your shirt. You will not be able to provide value-based fees, and you'll be called upon to address anything the client chooses.

> **Expertise: Restrict a retainer to advice. Never allow it to include project creation, implementation, or oversight, or you'll be trying to play soccer with a lacrosse stick.**

My suggestions for consultants with fairly strong brands is that they charge at least $7,500 per month (with a three-month minimum) for retainer work in 2016 dollars; for stronger brands, at least $10,000 or more per month. Weak brands are not ready to support a retainer, and creating an inexpensive one (e.g., $1,500 per month) will involve far more work than you'll want to take on.

Generally, the best places for retainer business are:

1. Clients who are very happy with your past work for them who would welcome an alternative to continue to be in touch and situationally use your help.

2. In option 3 of proposals (see Chapter 5) where you're extending your involvement in a project with an advisory capacity longer term.

3. Larger businesses. Small business owners often don't see the value of payments without demonstrable on-site work and will often disregard the agreement of access to demand more laborious work.

The stronger your brand, the more likely you can begin retainer business, but you can attempt it at any time. The usual maximum tenure is a year, since many businesses don't approve professional services agreements that span more than one fiscal year. However, retainer agreements are easy to renew once a buyer utilizes the ability to draw on your expertise just before a board meeting, or to referee an internal turf battle, or to review how to respond to poor media coverage, or to decide how to become the front-runner for an attractive promotion.

Finally, no client or prospect will know you offer retainer work unless you suggest it. The potential of the retainer should be in your conversations and in your proposal options.

RFPS: REQUESTS FOR PROPOSALS

I'm including requests for proposals (RFPs) in fees and not below in proposals because they are a strange duck, so they might as well be in this pond.

Many public sector (government) agencies, nonprofits, and some for-profits prefer to use or are mandated to use RFPs to solicit bids on projects. RFPs are anathema to high-value consulting work because:

- They focus on deliverables, tasks, and activities and not results, outcomes, and value.
- They are issued by low-level people (procurement, purchasing, learning and development, human resources) who also evaluate the responses using the poor criteria above.
- They are notoriously cost-sensitive, not ROI-driven.
- The true buyer (the person who owns the project budget) is far removed and highly "protected" by these minions.
- They are laborious and time-consuming to complete.
- They usually only pay after work is completed, and even then on a basis of 30 days net, or even 90 days net. Their payments and expense reimbursements are bureaucratically and habitually late.

Nevertheless, it's possible to compete in RFP environments *if you are willing to be innovative and "work the system."*

Here are my criteria for effectively competing with others in an RFP environment:

1. *Try to find the buyer.* There are sometimes "public hearings" at which the need is explained in person and questions are encouraged from those considering bidding. The buyer is sometimes present, but there are always people present who could introduce you to the buyer. Befriend one, and ask for the introduction. Alternatively, network within your own lists and see if you can find someone who knows the buyer and will grant an introduction. If successful, form a trusting relationship and work as though you were submitting your own proposal, not merely an RFP response.

2. *Go beyond the RFP with your own proposal.* Once you comply with the RFP, there is nothing stopping you from adding to it. I suggest that you create your own proposal (see Chapter 5) and attach it to the RFP. Thus, you'll show your compliance with the requests (wants) but also show additional value (needs) that just might put you ahead of the pack.

Case Study

I was bidding on an RFP at USA Today and was told I had the inside track. But two weeks went by with no word, and I found that I had lost to another firm.

When I called my contact, I was told that I was favored until the winning firm included in its bid the training of the next level of managers to ensure a sustained growth (and for additional fees, of course).

"But you didn't ask for that," I said.

"Yes," she said, "which is why we knew we had missed something and they knew how to supply it."

That was the last time I neglected to attach my own value-laden proposal.

3. *Study the laws, rules, and regulations.* For example, the U.S. government's Federal Acquisition Regulation (known as FAR) specifies that bids may be accepted not on the basis of least cost but on the basis of most value. Many organizations have that rule as well. This means you need to stress value, ROI, and longer-term benefits, such as annualization of savings or growth.

4. *Befriend key influencers.* If you have met the buyer or even people who will be creating the RFP, they can sometimes "tailor" the document to give you a benefit. (Some are actually designed for only one firm to be eligible.) That may mean they require someone with two books on strategy work, and/or who has worked in Asia, and/or who speaks Spanish, and/or who has a PhD. You get the idea. You can "massage" an RFP so that it is solely the mold for your own profile.

5. *Delegate the boilerplate.* Have someone else take care of the details if you have full-time or part-time staff or a virtual assistant.

> ***Expertise: Don't pursue RFPs or rely on them for a substantial part of your business. If you do accept such bidding, stack the deck in your favor as much as possible. If you don't do this, your odds of a successful bid are highly remote.***

While the RFP process is situationally required by some attractive prospects, it is in the vast minority in terms of securing external resources. You should be prepared to handle RFPs, but you should not involve yourself in this process as a primary way of obtaining business.

If you're bidding on more than two RFPs per quarter, your business acquisition efforts are misplaced.

OPTIONS

In Chapter 5, I'll demonstrate how to provide optional approaches to the project in the proposal itself. But I want to first establish the great utilitarian and psychological aspects of options.

An option is an alternative. It is another means or route to achieve the same objective or goal. Going from New Jersey into New York you can drive, take a bus, hire a car, take the train, use a ferry, fly, or swim. You can also take the George Washington Bridge, Lincoln Tunnel, or Holland Tunnel. In every case you will wind up in New York, *but with varying degrees of speed, safety, comfort, risk, and so forth.* No two options are alike in their appeal or their risk, or in other words, in the eye of the decision maker.

On most occasions we give people a "take it or leave it" option. Do it or don't do it.

- Would you like to go out to dinner tonight?
- Should I buy a new outfit?
- Should we take a July vacation?
- Can you work on the Figby project?
- Can we meet again next week?

I call these "binary" options—yes or no, up or down, right or left, in or out? They are delimiting and dangerous. They are fatal in the business acquisition process because you are flipping a coin hoping for "heads." Despite your excellent relationship and conceptual agreement, *you haven't given the buyer any flexibility.*

> **Expertise: Adopt the habit of always *giving options, even on minor matters, because it's never excessive, and failing to give them can be extremely costly.***

When you provide a binary pair of options, you have a 50 percent chance of the decision you desire. Even with a great relationship leading up to the decision, it may be no better than 60 percent. Those are horrible odds in business. [Famed football coach Woody Hayes was asked once why his teams seldom passed and usually ran the ball. "Only three things can happen with a pass," he counseled, "and two of them are bad (interception and incompletion rather than a reception), so why would I do that?"] Thus, the key is to provide multiple positive options.

If you really want to go to dinner, don't ask "Would you like to go out to dinner?" but rather "*Where* would you like to go for dinner?" That opens up the options hugely and involves the other person's broader self-interests ("Hmmm, what restaurant have I been dying to try?"). Similarly:

- Instead of "Should I buy a new outfit?" ask, *Which new outfit should I buy?*
- Instead of "Should we take a July vacation?" ask, *When should we take our vacation?*
- Instead of "Can you work on the Figby project?" ask, *When can you best work on the Figby project?*
- Instead of "Can we meet again next week?" ask, *What day and time are best for you to meet again next week?*

If you were to provide a client with options to meet again, instead of saying, "Would you like to meet again?" or even "When would you like to meet again?" by saying instead, "I can meet with you again Monday at the same time here in your office, or any morning next week by Skype, or Wednesday and Thursday for lunch—which is best?" you have seriously increased your changes of an acceptance of some sort. Psychologically, the other person has defaulted to "What would be easiest for my calendar?"

Look at it mathematically:

A choice in a binary decision is 50/50.

A choice with three options is 75 percent, because the buyer may choose any one of your three or refuse despite the options. But you've increased your odds of success by half. That's pretty good when you have merely used language and haven't invested a cent!

The options for a proposal include these conditions:

1. The first option must meet *all* of the objectives, because otherwise you have an unethical offer. You can't provide objectives and consequent value to justify your fee and then an option that won't deliver on all of them.
2. Successive options should include those prior. This isn't *à la carte*, but a full-course meal.

3. Fees escalate with the options because they provide more value. Option 1 will meet the objectives, but option 3 meets the objectives and also includes much more value. This is the principle of adding value to an RFP to enhance your chances of acceptance, as discussed in the preceding section.

You will see an immediate increase in every aspect of business acquisition (meetings, follow-up, suggestions, and so forth), and every aspect of your life once you form the habit of naturally offering options.

Why don't you test ways to prove that, and not take it or leave it!

PROPOSALS

NEVER NEGOTIATION, ALWAYS SUMMATION

My definition of a proposal is that it is a *summation* of conceptual agreement, and not an *exploration* (of whether to proceed) nor a *negotiation* (of how to proceed). It is also my contract, since it includes an acceptance segment at the conclusion.

As in all else in this profession: simplify.

THE NINE STEPS

I wrote a book once called *How to Write a Proposal That's Accepted Every Time*, and I meant it. Your "hit" rate following the advice thus far and what immediately follows should be *at least 80 percent*.[1] Many of my coaching clients can demonstrate proof of 90 to 100 percent proposal acceptance.

Here is that royal road:

1. Situation Appraisal

The proposal starts with one or two paragraphs—no more—defining the situation that brings you and the buyer to this point. It has been discussed in the earlier meetings. It *is not* a description of the client's business but rather a description of the client's *needs*.

---

[1] The most recent iteration is *Million Dollar Proposals* (McGraw-Hill, 2012).

Poor Situation Appraisal

The following is a poor situation appraisal:

> *Hewlett-Packard is a hardware, software, and technical consulting firm headquartered in Palo Alto, California, with offices around the world. It has moved from primarily a supplier of technical products (e.g., printer ink) to one of technical services (e.g., consulting). It was founded in a garage by Bill Hewlett and David Packard in 1947 and went public in 1957.*

This is a poor situation appraisal because HP quite obviously knows all this and isn't very concerned about it!

Good Situation Appraisal

Compare the following good situation appraisal:

> *Hewlett-Packard was once able to rely on its strong brand and powerful word of mouth from existing employees to attract talent as an employer of first choice, with low costs of acquisition and very high retention rates. However, after years of erratic earnings, organizational change, and turnover at both executive and board levels, it must derive ways to once again command top talent, which is now far harder to acquire than ever before.*

Once we have a concise situation appraisal, we can go to steps 2, 3, and 4, which are a summary of conceptual agreement: objectives, metrics, and value. I prefer to state these in bullet-point form, like this:

2. Objectives

The objectives for this project according to our mutual agreement are:

- Increase of applicants from 20 designated top schools seeking out HP as their choice of employment.
- The ability to acquire desired talent within company compensation guidelines and avoid "bidding wars."

- Retention rate after one year in excess of 90 percent for such hires.
- Candidates HP seeks engage in at least two rounds of discussions with assigned personnel resulting in offers.

Note that these are all *outcomes*, as described earlier in conceptual agreement. They are not deliverables or tasks or inputs. They have demonstrable improvement for the company.

3. Metrics (or Measures of Success)

There should be one of these, minimally, for each objective to assess progress and your contribution to it.

The metrics for these objectives include:

- During recruiting season (January to May), HP interviews a minimum of six candidates each from at least 10 of the schools on the top 20 list.
- HP receives a minimum of 10 unsolicited résumés from those schools monthly during recruiting season.
- With the exception of special circumstances (e.g., diversity, language skills) 100 percent of new hires are acquired within existing compensation limits.
- After one year, HP has retained at least 90 percent of new hires.
- Candidates HP actively seeks out agree to discussions resulting in offers at least 75 percent of the time.

Note that metrics can be tracked via monthly or weekly reports, anecdotal evidence, and observation. Some reports may already be in place (numbers of offers made) and some may have to be created (offers relative to top 20 schools).

4. Value

The objectives have impacts (we've explained earlier how something as simple as "profit" can have varied impacts) that need to be stipulated here so that the client can appreciate ROI (on your fees).

The value of meeting these objectives includes:

- A net reduction in cost of professional-level talent acquisition of $1 million (half of your estimate).
- A net reduction in attrition expense, including training, replacement, and delayed work, of about $2 million (half of your estimate).
- A reduction of overall recruiting time and involvement by one-quarter, or about $500,000 (half of your estimate).
- An increase in investor appeal given talent stability.
- A return to employee "evangelism" to recruit friends and acquaintances.
- Reduced client complaint and grievance caused by the loss of a familiar and constant contact in the company.
- Improved press coverage and media reports.
- Elimination of current task forces and meetings on the "talent crisis" that currently consume about $400,000 of management time and actions annually (half of your estimate).

Note that we have eight value statements based on our four objectives, and four are clearly monetized, equaling $3.9 million *based on conservatively taking half the buyer's estimate in the conceptual agreement phase.* Thus, a 10:1 return on investment would justify a nearly $400,000 project.

5. Methodology and Options

This is our "choice of yeses" described earlier. I recommend three escalating options, each including the prior.

Option 1: Create and Deploy
We will:

- Interview and assess the techniques of the current main interviewers for HP. We will create a "best practices" protocol based on what's being done well here and with our other clients.

- Interview and evaluate top candidates who were acquired and top candidates who left prior to two years and find causes. We will adjust the process according to these findings.

- Create an overall recruiting system specifically designed for the top 20 schools for both solicited and unsolicited candidates and codify it for all involved.

Option 2: Execute and Oversight
In addition to Option 1, we will:

- Create an advisory board among top schools to assess their students' changing attitudes, needs, and expectations. We will also ensure that HP is presented favorably as a career choice within the counseling environment.

- Create a media campaign to publicize HP's focus on top talent and profound career potential. This will involve articles featuring top people.

- Implement an accountability system so that every senior executive has recruiting and retention as part of his or her personal quarterly evaluation measures.

Option 3: Longevity and Trusted Advisor
In addition to Options 1 and 2, we will:

- Serve as a trusted advisor for a period of six months after Option 2 is completed, enabling an objective, external sounding board to be accessed without restriction and without having to make any investment decision. We will decide who has such access (maximum four people) and under what conditions.

Note that Option 3 assumes that Option 2 is desired, and that we still have not mentioned fees.

You can simply number the options or give them names. For example, a coaching assignment's options might be (1) Backstage, (2) Onstage, (3) Trusted Advisor.

6. Timing

This is a simple statement of approximate times required for completion. Always use sequences, not calendar dates, since you never know when the buyer will actually sign the proposal.

- Option 1: 45 days
- Option 2: 75 days
- Option 3: Six months beyond the end of Option 2

7. Joint Accountabilities

This very important section lists what the buyer is accountable for, what you are accountable for, and what you are jointly accountable for. Here is an example.

You will:

- Provide security clearance for me for all buildings.
- Provide an office with Internet access.
- Allow for use of the cafeteria.
- Serve as project "champion," including leading our informational meetings, making three videos for remote locations, and making this a part of your direct reports' personal emphasis areas.
- Provide access to key documentation and people upon my request.
- Resolve disputes and reluctance to participate among your staff.

I will:

- Sign nondisclosure agreements.
- Personally conduct all interviews and focus groups.
- Debrief with you at least twice a month in person or by Skype.
- Respond to you by phone within three hours and e-mail within one day whenever you need me during normal business hours.
- Conduct informational meetings at your remote locations upon request.

We both will:

- Immediately inform the other of any developments we find that might materially affect the success of this project, whether directly related to the project or not.

Here are a couple of reasons for this last statement. One is that a client hadn't disclosed that the division in the first part of the project was being divested! I found that another client's three key vice presidents all had résumés on the street and were trying to leave!

8. Terms and Conditions

This is *the first time* the buyer sees the fees. The idea is that the buyer has been nodding in agreement throughout all of the prior steps, and will now nod right through the fees! Counterintuitively, these must be kept *very simple.*

- The fee for Option 1 is $380,000.
- The fee for Option 2 is $415,000.
- The fee for Option 3 is $495,000.

Terms

A 50 percent deposit on acceptance of this proposal and 50 percent in 45 days. Alternatively, we offer a 10 percent professional discount if you choose to pay the entire fee upon acceptance.

Expense Reimbursements

Expenses are billed monthly as actually accrued and are due on presentation of our invoice. We bill for reasonable travel, lodging, and dining expenses. We do not bill for courier, postage, copies, phone, or administrative work.

These fees and terms are noncancelable for any reason, and even if the project is delayed or rescheduled by mutual agreement, the payment dates and amounts must still be met. We guarantee the quality of our work in terms of meeting our agreements, conducting programs, providing deliverables, and so forth.

> **Expertise: Never prematurely present or suggest your fees. Leave them until the proposal has already emphasized value and potential savings.**

You may consider this approach very aggressive. It is. Here are points for your consideration:

- Never, ever negotiate fees. *But you can negotiate terms.* You're starting with terms most favorable to you, so negotiating to, say, 50 percent on acceptance, 50 percent in 60 days would be acceptable.
- At these ranges, whether you charge $350,000 or $400,000 for Option 1 doesn't really matter. All of it is pure profit. Fees are art and science. The key is the perceived ROI of the buyer.[2]
- It is helpful to explain what you *don't* charge for in expenses so the expenses seem well defined. I don't believe in including expenses in the fees themselves.[3]
- Important: Many organizations have internal rules that *require* the acceptance of any discount. Hence, the 10 percent offer for full payment often triggers that provision, and you have the entire use of your money immediately.

Note that these agreements are noncancelable *for any reason.* The *quid pro quo* is that I guarantee the quality of my work (not the results, which would be impossible). The client has assurances and I have a firm contract.

---

[2]Obviously, if you're dealing with $15,000 fees, the difference between $12,000 and $18,000 would be significant, but then you'd be reading *Five Figure Consulting* and not *Million Dollar Consulting.*

[3]I travel first class, stay in suites, and use a limo service. I charge the client a rate of the local Marriott, full coach fare, and taxi fare. I don't expect the client to support my lifestyle or to pay for me to travel better than the client's people do.

9. Acceptance

My proposals also constitute a contract, since I want to keep things simple and avoid multiple documents and approvals. The acceptance looks like this:

Your signature below—or your payment—indicates agreement with the terms and conditions above and constitutes the launch of this project:

Choose one: Option 1 ____   Option 2____   Option 3____

Choose one: 50% deposit____ Full fee with 10% discount____

For Hewlett-Packard: For Summit Consulting Group:

_____ _____

Name: Joan Chase   Name: Alan Weiss

Title: Senior Vice President Title: President

Date: _____ Date: _____

That concludes the proposal, generally two-and-a-half pages in length. Note that you don't need promotional material, résumés, or anything else because you have conceptual agreement prior to creating the document.

HOW TO PRESENT

I don't like to present proposals in person. My preferred sequence is this:

- Conceptual agreement is made with client in person.
- Proposal is sent by electronic means and courier.
- I follow up in 24 hours to hear which option is chosen.

When the client reads the proposal in advance, there is still the chance to ask questions and obtain clarification during the follow-up phone call. But since this is not a negotiating document, I see no reason to make the trip for a personal meeting.

If you present the proposal initially in a meeting, the buyer has the (usually taken) option to say, "This has been interesting, but I haven't read it carefully, so let me do that now and call you once I'm comfortable." This just wastes time. There is also the danger of the buyer inviting others to the meeting, creating the possibility of nonbuyers (and threatened people) opposing the proposal.

I suggest that you send the proposal both electronically for speed and by courier so the buyer has hard copies on your letterhead on the table. It doesn't hurt to enclose a return courier envelope billed to your account for the executed copy's return. I don't favor packaging, binders, or any other bells and whistles. You read in the prior section that these are "lean and mean," two-and-a-half-page documents. Send two copies.

You may also want to send some invoices that cover the breadth of your options and payment terms.

Since the proposal is merely a *summary of conceptual agreement* reached prior, along with your options and fees, the delivery of it should be treated like a summation and not a formal presentation.

Expertise: Keep proposals consistent with conceptual agreement, and make the presentation of the proposal and decisions about it almost a pro forma exercise, not a major event.

HOW TO FOLLOW UP, LAUNCH, OR RECOVER

The best way to follow up is by phone at an agreed-upon time and date. Hence, when you are with the buyer gaining conceptual agreement, you should make a statement like this:

I will have the completed proposal to you electronically by end of business tomorrow. Let's talk the day after so that I can learn which option best suits you. What time is best, and which number should I use, your business line or cell phone?

Never leave a meeting without an established time and date. Make sure the buyer agrees to a time and day to talk. Those are negotiable but must be in the short term. Note the "assumptive close," where you want to learn which option to move ahead with (not whether to move ahead, thus, the power of options).

Here is how to follow up, depending on the buyer's response:

1. *The buyer says "Yes" on the phone.* Acknowledge when you will begin, thank the buyer for the trust, and ask how the first payment will be made and when. That is *not* "pushy"—it has a different name: good business.

2. *The buyer has questions.* Answer the questions to the best of your ability. Never commit to arbitrary requests (say, for example, "I don't know how many days I'll be on-site, it depends on the project's progress, but if you need me it will never be a problem.") Once the buyer's questions are answered, ask which option will be chosen. If the buyer is still uncertain, ask "What obstacles or issues do you still see that prevent you from committing right now? Let's discuss them while we're on the phone together."

3. *The buyer wants to involve others in the decision.* Stress that this is a strategic decision that may well threaten others, and that the first step must be the buyer's commitment, after which you can bring in the implementers to establish their roles and accountabilities. Resist this request strongly.

4. *The buyer wants more time.* See response to number 2 above.

5. *The buyer says, in effect, "No."* See the following discussion.

If at this point, with trust, conceptual agreement, a proposal with options, and a follow-up call, the buyer demurs (he or she might say, "Let's talk in six months" or "Let's wait for the next budget cycle," both of which are "No" in other language), then you need to back away. Ask the buyer this question:

What could I have done differently to convince you to have accepted my help? I'd appreciate your candor for my own education and growth.

You can at least learn from the refusal. You may be prone to press harder at this point, but generally, when you're thrown down the stairs the buyer just doesn't want you in there. Learn from what didn't work—and that may just be that the buyer is foolish.

> **Expertise: You should close about 80 percent or more of proposals using this system. Learn, as well, from the 20 percent that you do not close.**

Finally, in the "Go" situation, "throw cement" immediately, and begin the initial project phases, especially remote work such as interviews or surveys. If you haven't arranged for invoicing, do so immediately. Schedule your first meeting with your new client in the next week or so.

THE CONCEPT OF VALUE

Throughout this book (and all of my work), the concept of value is paramount. In fact, when asked about your billing basis or structure (when prospects often expect an hourly rate to be cited), my suggested language is this:

> *My fee is based on my contribution to the project and represents a dramatic ROI (return on investment) for you and equitable compensation for me.*

Isn't that how partners treat one another? The *quid pro quo* is value delivered in return for *equitable* compensation. Hourly fees aren't equitable; they are arbitrary and based on time use. In fact, they're unethical, in that the longer a project takes—inimical to the client's best interests—the more the consultant is paid. That's not equitable and ought to be illegal. Yet that's the basis for a great deal of professional services billing, even today.

ORIGINS

Subsistence farming gave way to capitalism when farmers were able to use human resources (hence, large families) and technology (horses or oxen to pull plows or grind grain) to create an excess of food, beyond the needs of the family. The farmers could now feed others in return for some kind of equitable compensation.

Hence, the artisan or craftsman was born.

People could repair harnesses, thatch roofs, provide entertainment, or supply meat in return for the farmer's food. None of this was done by the hour, but rather by the result. The payment of some amount of peas or tomatoes or corn was negotiated based on the *value* of the service or entertainment provided.

This is the essence of capitalism: private ownership of trade and production owned by individuals and used as the means of transaction to exchange value. When society reached a point of awkwardness due to the plenty (it's tough to accept 40 goats or 100 bushels of peaches as payment because they can run away or rot), specie (coin money) was invented and, eventually, paper money. Now there was a means of storing and saving the value of the transaction.

MEANING

My meaning of *value* today is quite simple: It is the importance, worth, and/or usefulness of a product or service (including ideas, comfort, support, and so forth). *That value is in the eye of the beholder.* Thus, our challenges include:

- Create value.
- Promote the value.
- Create equitable fees for the value.

Everyone knows what he or she wants, but few people know what they *need*. The difference between want and need is what I call the value distance (Figure I2.1).

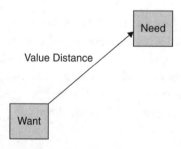

Figure I2.1 The value distance

It's our job to create need if none is apparent or if the buyer is focused merely on wants. The key is the question, "Why?"

> Why do you ask for a leadership retreat?
>
> Because we have no consensus about strategy.
>
> Would it make more sense to first create more involvement about strategy to gain commitment?

By directing the buyer to a larger view, you create needs that weren't appreciated before.

At one time there was a "boombox" rage, when the highest status was accorded to those with the largest boomboxes and speakers. They became larger and larger. Some were so big that they required two people to carry!

Then Akio Morita, head of Sony, decided to create a music device that someone could wear on a belt and listen to through earphones. His engineers pointed out that no one wanted such a player, and his marketing people told him he was not listening to the public. But Mr. Morita owned the place, and he persisted.

Voilà, the Walkman was born—and its great-grandchild is the iPhone. People now listen through tiny earbuds to devices that are out of sight. No one knew they needed this until Sony informed them. (Henry Ford once observed that if he had listened to his customers for business advice, he would have simply bred faster horses.)

You can easily name great organizations that have introduced massive need: FedEx, Uber, Southwest Airlines, Enterprise Rent-A-Car™. On a more localized basis, you can and should relentlessly pursue need within your clients and with your prospects. Not only does this create a larger project, but it also instills more and more value in what you do and who you are.

The somewhat counterintuitive result of increased fees is that people believe they get what they pay for. Not long ago I had to buy a wrench to take care of a minor leak. There were three in the hardware store, undistinguishable to me, except they were three different prices. I chose the most expensive, thinking it must be the best. You may fault my logic, but believe me, *no one attempts to find the cheapest heart surgeon.*

Thus, as your fees have traditionally followed the value you provide, *you can reach a point where value is inputted by how high your fees are!*

The crossover where fees become the driving force of perceived value is usually represented by very high brand power, cachet, and evangelism. In other words, enough people are raving about you that others feel obligated to approach you. In those cases, fee is never an issue. (Today I received what has become a very frequent inquiry for a $17,000 coaching relationship: "Do you have room for me?" That's a far cry from "What can you do for me?"!)

The reason that value and commensurate fees are so important is shown in Figure 12.2. When the buyer is committed to you and your reputation, you provide reciprocal value and merely need to demonstrate a high return to justify a high fee. When fees are high and commitment is low, there generally won't be any sale at all. And when both commitment and fees are low, apathy results.

But the real danger occurs when commitment is high and fees are low, and too many consultants find themselves in the opportunity wasteland. They charge too little for a project and a buyer where more would

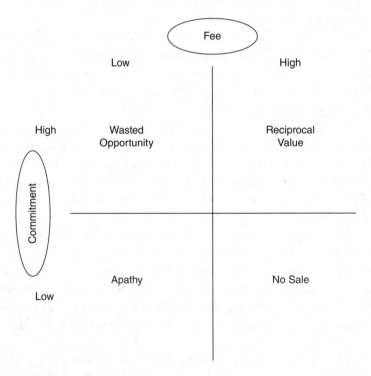

Figure 12.2 Fees and commitment

easily have been paid. (How many of you have ever been told by a happy client, "I'm surprised you were so inexpensive"? That is *not* a compliment you should be proud of.)

CONVERTING TO VALUE

The "must" in the process of conceptual agreement with a buyer is to convert business outcomes into value. Here are some generic questions to use during the conversations:

Questions

1. What will these results mean for your organization?
2. How would you assess the actual return [ROI, Return on Assets (ROA), Return on Sales (ROS), Return on Equity (ROE), etc.]?
3. What would be the extent of the improvement (or correction)?
4. How will these results impact the bottom line?
5. What are the *annualized* savings (the first year might be deceptive)?
6. What is the intangible impact (e.g., on repute, safety, comfort, etc.)?
7. How would you, personally, be better off or better supported?
8. What is the scope of the impact (on customers, employees, vendors)?
9. How important is this compared to your overall responsibilities?
10. What if this fails?

The *follow-up* questions are all about "What would that mean in savings, improvements, revenue, profit?"

If a client provides a project objective (preferably a business outcome) such as "We seek one contact with our major clients, not overlap from differing product and service areas," you ask "Why?" This provides the real reason for the objective.

Answer: "We are spending too much money on multiple, duplicative visits and creating complaints from our best clients who feel 'hounded.'"

Follow-up: "What does a client visit typically entail in terms of time, and how much time of which managers is required to respond to the client complaint?" Another option: "If you had just one person selling multiple products and services during one visit, how much in additional sales do you think would be generated?"

These questions lead you to substantive answers with estimated monetization. Make it a habit to cut the number in half (if there is $500,000 in estimated savings, use $250,000) or take the bottom half of the ranges (if the estimate is a 5 to 8 percent sales increase, use 5 percent). This way you can explain, when the buyer is examining ROI (total benefits divided by total investment), that your numbers are archly conservative and the probability is that the actual return will be much higher.

When you settle for "vanilla" objectives such as "increased clarity," or "more confidence," or "higher commitment" (which I call "human resources objectives" because they are so weak and nonmeasurable), you deny yourself the opportunity to create dynamic ROI, where the client receives huge benefit and your equitable compensation is quite reasonable in light of that improvement.

THE PHILOSOPHY OF VALUE

We've established that our role is to improve our client's condition. That means that the improvement, by definition, must constitute significant value. Value is about enhanced results, not frantic activity.

There is a myth in management that leaders are paid to take action. We idolize and elevate those who are "action oriented." But no one is paid to take action. People are paid to achieve results. No board ever passes a resolution citing the executive team for the number of activities undertaken despite the poor financial results, higher attrition, and loss of market share.

Here are the tenets of value, in your life and in your career, and most certainly with your clients:

- Value is manifest in an improved condition.
- Value is also manifest in maintaining the current condition through effective preventive work and flexibility in managing volatility.

- There is more value in improving performance and raising the bar (innovation) than there is in problem solving and restoring past performance ("fixing").

- Value, like beauty, is in the eye of the beholder. The buyer's perception is the sole arbiter of whether value has been provided.

- Value can be quantified (improved sales, higher market share, less attrition), but it can also be qualitative (improved aesthetics, greater feelings of security, greater comfort).

- Creating value is not time dependent at all. The old dictum, "If it hurts when you do that, stop doing that," provides immediate value.

- Standards of value change. Nordstrom once took back all returns, even dresses with perspiration stains and products not purchased there. Today, it is far more concerned with profit and has abandoned that policy.

Binge watching new TV programs now supersedes merely time shifting programs.

Your value must evolve over time. And, as I have noted, value is often determined by high fee! We would not believe that a Bulgari watch on sale in a street cart for $12 is real. Likewise, people don't believe that a consultant charging $350 an hour is very good.

Finally, the process of demonstrating what the client really *needs*, despite statements of what the client claims to want, is instrumental in creating high value where low value was previously perceived. A leadership retreat of two days is a commodity that competitive pricing may drive to $5,000, but the *reason* it's needed (the *why*) is that there is no involvement or commitment about strategy, which requires a $100,000 cultural change initiative.

And you were the one who demonstrated why that's needed.

EXAMPLES OF MODERN VALUE PERCEPTION

We've become rather inured to value unless the true import is deliberately confronting us. I recall my very first car phone. I made a call to a London client and complained to my wife that there was static on the line.

"Alan," she stated slowly, "you're calling *London* from your car!" Comedian Louis C.K. tells people to stop complaining about crowded spaces in airplanes: "You have a seat traveling at 35,000 feet and arriving across the country in five hours!" A 1930s movie starlet observed, "A private railroad car is not an acquired taste. One gets used to it instantly."

A luxury has a short half-life. Once used or applied a second time, it becomes a need, then an expectation, then barely a blip on one's comfort radar screen. One curses the fates if the automatic garage door opener fails and a walk in the rain is required to open the door manually.

The history of a consultant with an excellent client runs something like this:

> We need Alan Weiss.
>
> We couldn't have done this without him.
>
> Alan was extremely helpful.
>
> Alan had some good ideas.
>
> We could have done this without that consultant.
>
> Who's Alan Weiss?

Thus, we have to deliberately and meticulously keep our value in the eyes of our beholders: clients and prospects.

This has often been done by branding over the years:

- Mercedes: "Engineered like no other car in the world."
- BMW: "The ultimate driving machine."
- FedEx: "When it absolutely, positively has to be there overnight."
- U.S. Marines: "We're looking for a few good men."
- Delta Airlines: "Delta is ready when you are."
- United Airlines: "Fly the friendly skies."
- Las Vegas: "What happens in Vegas, stays in Vegas."

Modern perceptions of value tend to focus on the following:

- *Speed.* The advantage of solo consultants and boutique firms is agility and nimbleness. We don't need to land on the beaches with 300 consultants being paid by the hour while learning the client's business. That's why value-based billing is critical, because our great value is in getting things done fast. The speed limits on most roads rarely exceed 70 miles per hour, but most high-end cars advertise 200-mile-per-hour top speeds and 0 to 60 in three to four seconds.

- *Minimal disruption.* Our clients require their customers to be treated without discomfort and hassle. Today, renovations are often done while the building is fully functional. Businesses can't be shut down while changes occur. We need to work seamlessly wherever possible. If you visit the mansions in Newport, Rhode Island, constructed during the Gilded Age of the late nineteenth century, you'll often find a second hallway, hidden behind walls, which the servants used so as not to inconvenience the residents and guests.

- *Autonomous control.* Most research shows that people at work crave autonomy, and individuals experience far less stress when they perceive that they have control over their work and results. We are best served when we transfer skills to the client. While that might seem as if we are lessening the need for our continued participation, we are actually meeting an important client need—control—which increases our attractiveness for future projects (and which is why we need a variety of value offerings— see the Accelerant Curve in Chapter 2).

We need to continually demonstrate to the buyer what our value is and make it extremely clear that our role was central to project success. If we're serving in an advisory retainer capacity, we have to talk about the advantages and ramifications of our past advice.

We need to continually demonstrate to *prospective* buyers the value they can expect to derive, using testimonials, case studies, and references.

Finally, we must continually create, discover, and present *new* value that the buyer hadn't considered. Remember that behind every corporate objective is a personal objective that we can tap into to create even greater satisfaction:

- Reduce turnover (I'm weary of all these interviews)
- Increase profits (my bonus relies on exceeding profit goals)

- Improve teamwork (I hate playing referee among teams)
- Create remote access for clients (reduce my travel)
- Open new markets (to improve my chances for promotion)

The more we seek and manifest value, the more we can improve the client's condition and, therefore, maximize our fees. This requires a value-based mindset.

THE ESTIMABLE CONSULTANT

HOW TO BUILD YOUR PRACTICE BY BUILDING YOUR ESTEEM

My coaching of global consultants for 25 years has validated that the key variable is emotional and personal—the ability to establish and trust one's self-worth, which is entirely different from efficacy. Consultants fail when they seek merely affection and succeed when they seek respect.

I once thought the problem was undercapitalization. I was completely wrong. I'm always amazed by how stupid I was two weeks ago!

SELF-WORTH, NOT CAPITALIZATION OR METHODOLOGY, DETERMINES SUCCESS

Your self-worth can't be dependent on your last victory or defeat. It has to be constant. Otherwise, you're on the proverbial roller coaster, controlled by events and external influences rather than your own merits.

The importance of this is the avoidance of a "doom loop," in which you're unsuccessful, get "down" on yourself, go into the next situation feeling poorly, are unsuccessful again, reinforce your "down" mentality—you get the idea (see Figure 6-1). Only by having a constantly high degree of self-worth can you avoid the doom loop.

Self-Esteem as a Roller Coaster

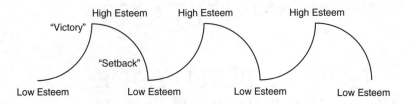

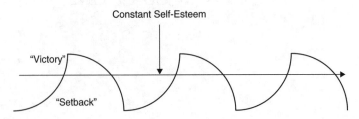

Figure 6-1 Self-esteem as a constant

The opposite situation, the success loop, comes from constantly building skills so that you're able to excel in more and more diverse situations (Figure 6-2).

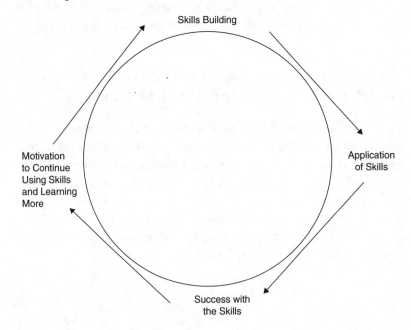

Figure 6-2 The success loop

This is how efficacy—the ability to do things well—is connected to esteem, feeling worthy yourself. None of us always "wins," but many of us lose *without feeling that we are somehow unworthy*. The relationship between self-worth and efficacy, however, is not direct. One can vary in one direction while the other is consistent or varies in a different direction. As consultants operating independently, we have to largely be our own cheerleaders and supporting cast.

I recall my wife saying to me once after a rough night of poor sleep and allergies, "You'd better start building up your confidence, because a little later today you're supposed to build up a client's confidence!"

When both our efficacy (performance) and esteem (feelings or worth) are high, we have a healthy life (Figure 6-3). However, many people feel as though they are "imposters," because they perform well but are afraid of being "found out," not believing they are really good, just lucky for the moment. (Many actors who have received Oscars are worried about whether they'll ever work again. They received their awards, after all, for portraying someone other than their true selves.) Books through the decades have documented research showing that the majority of successful businesspeople, athletes, entertainers, and so forth often feel like imposters.[1]

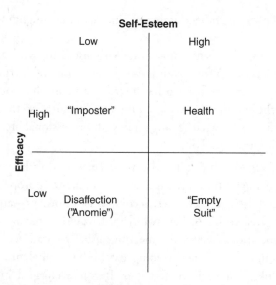

Figure 6-3 Self-esteem related to efficacy

[1]One of the best was by Dr. Pauline Rose Clance, *The Imposter Phenomenon* (Peachtree Publications, 1985).

When you have high esteem but don't perform well, you are the proverbial "empty suit" (in Texas: "big hat, no cattle"). This can easily become narcissism, where pride, arrogance, and talk try to disguise non-performance and failure.

Finally, disaffection results when people feel they are both unequal to the task and unworthy of the task. The French *anomie* means socially disaffected, and there is even a type of suicide called "anomic suicide."

Building your skills will help build your self-worth, absolutely essential to solo consultants and small firm owners. But you can also build a network.

HOW TO CREATE A "PACK" AS A LONE WOLF

You are going to need some "company" in your new company. Some people have major affiliation needs, and they will most likely hire at least a part-time assistant or rent space in a suite of shared offices where there is a common receptionist and there are other professionals around. Those are adequate actions, but overly expensive, and they just complicate things. (For my entire career, I've worked out of my home, through several houses.)

Your "pack" members, with a minimum of fuss, might include:

1. *Family.* There's nothing wrong with discussing work and getting advice—even from your kids—at the dinner table. If you have a spouse or significant other, I strongly advise that you "debrief" at the end of each day, even for a few minutes, so that he or she understands what's going on in your professional life. If you live alone, then read on.

2. *Colleagues.* Find kindred spirits. They needn't be consultants. You might find any kind of entrepreneur appropriate: architects, designers, coaches, accountants, attorneys—anyone who has created his or her own firm. I wouldn't recommend trade associations, where the meetings usually entail everyone lying about how well they're doing. Establish informal meals together, drinks, some leisure activities. If you're engaged in the same interests—a club or charity group, for example—all the better.

3. *Create an advisory board.* Keep this very simple, say, a dinner you buy once a quarter. Keep your attorney and accountant *off* of this board, because those professions are often suffering from lousy business judgment and the use of hourly fees. (They are fine to use for commiseration in point 2, but not as advisors here.) You may call them individually between meetings to solicit advice and counsel.

4. *Volunteer your time.* Develop friends doing charity work, supporting an arts group, or providing help pro bono for a favorite cause. (This also serves the marketing purpose of networking.)

5. *Establish virtual friends.* Use Skype and similar technologies to interact more personally than by e-mail or even phone. Join groups on social media. Join a chat room or professional site, or comment on other people's blogs.

Whatever you do, don't confuse respect and affection. You want affiliations that support you and provide sounding boards, not unconditional love. If you need the latter, get a dog.

You saw the trust pyramid in Figure 3-1, and that trust has many levels. You can be trusted because a trusted third party recommended you. Or others may immediately trust your manifest expertise, as exhibited in your writing, speaking, and word of mouth. Then there is the trust of affiliation needs, where you and the other party look kindly on each other because you have something in common and are comfortable together.

As we go on we encounter intellectual respect, where someone is impressed with our mind, cognitive ability, reasoning, problem solving, and so on. But at the highest level is the trust that is based on an emotional connection.

Expertise: Logic makes us think, but emotion makes us act.

Thus, if you are uncomfortable being completely on your own, I suggest that you use some of these five alternatives based on which levels of trust you want to create among your "pack" members. It might remain purely professional, with common goals and approaches, or attractive based on learning from shared expertise.

Normally, the most trusting relationships are based on emotional appeal, which naturally includes family, but can also include charisma, an exemplar, a thoroughly honest and responsive person.

The dog, of course, is also an emotional connection.

CREATING PEER-LEVEL RELATIONSHIPS WITH TRUE BUYERS

The point of gaining trust is so that you can reach the conceptual agreement about proposals we discussed in the last chapter. People make decisions far more easily when there is trust. That's why brands are so important, because the consumer is confident of what Coke or McDonald's or Emirates Airline represents. That's why executives instinctively called McKinsey for so long when they needed strategic help. And that's why I'm writing this on an Apple computer, whose products I've used for 30 years and that I managed to convert the technical company that handles all my work to, from their PCs, many years ago.

Peer-level relationships are based on the peak of the pyramid in Figure 3-1. They are the heart and soul of emotional connections, which accelerate action and not merely discussion. But most—*most*—consultants, neophyte or veteran, have a hard time acting as a peer of an executive buyer. (And we are talking exclusively buyers here, not HR people or purchasing agents.)

Let's be frank: We've all been intimidated at some point during our lives by the huge office, the mementos on the walls, the secretaries, the *accoutrement*, the titles, and the status. A great deal of this emanates from the fact that most of us are refugees from organizational hierarchies, where we've experienced and been subject to the pecking order. But this changes when we start our own business.

You must picture yourself as a learned expert, contributing value that is not resident in the client's company. Why else is the buyer taking the time to talk to you? The buyer, ironically, vests you with power when you walk in the door, *and you may too easily discard it almost immediately*. You don't have to perform acrobatics to earn the buyer's trust—you merely have to act as the legitimate peer he or she assumes you to be.

Here are my best practices for putting your mind and body in the position of being a true peer of an executive buyer:[2]

- *Dress the part.* Make sure you own well-tailored suits and appropriate accessories. Don't take out a 29-cent hotel pen; buy a good brand name. Have your hair, nails, and makeup neat and cared for.

- *Don't be a pack animal.* If you have luggage for a return trip, a heavy coat, or computer gear, leave them in the closet or with the receptionist. Take only a small notepad and calendar with you to the meeting. People get very nervous when you record a meeting, and it's impossible to type fast enough on small devices to take accurate notes.

- *Know your manners.* Don't sit until offered. Use a firm handshake. Smile. Turn down food and drink because you're not there for the culinary experience, and if you spill them you might as well jump out the window to speed your exit.

- *Be rested.* Do not show up for major appointments right from an airport or with back-to-back meetings scheduled. Have a decent meal at the usual intervals.

- *Check the mirror.* Before you walk into the office, walk into the restroom. Look in the mirror and smile. Make sure that lunch isn't sitting in your teeth and your hair is on the parts of your head it's intended to be on. Women should touch up their makeup. Check your clothes for any kind of detritus.

- *Be calm.* Do not default into "presenting mode." (*Never* use any kind of slides in a one-on-one meeting with a buyer.) Speak slowly. Don't interrupt. (In the next segment we'll discuss how to command the conversation.) Don't act as if you're trying to get the answers right on a test you're taking. Be in a conversation, not a "pitch."

> **Expertise: You don't have to so much create peer credibility as be alert not to forfeit it.**

---

[2]And I include here others based on your market: a small business owner, a government agency head, the executive director of a nonprofit, and so forth.

Ask yourself how peers act. How do you act with people whom you know are you peers (not lifelong buddies, but equals)? You express opinions and listen to theirs. You use a common terminology that both of you easily understand. You share interests readily. You're not concerned about being liked (affiliation) but rather about mutual esteem (respect). You're not overly familiar and you don't assume they share your own interests completely, but you're also not standoffish and aloof, and you easily engage in conversation.

Finally, separate taste and principle. I'm happy for a peer to tell a joke about consultants, just as confident lawyers love humor about their profession. But I won't tolerate derogatory comments about what I do. I'll accept that "Consultants arrive to study a problem and then stay to become part of it," but I won't accept, "You're really in a con game, right?"

Peers respect one another.

THE MARTIAL ARTS OF LANGUAGE AND SELF-TALK

In the martial arts, the objective in most instances is to use the opponent's weight and momentum in your favor. This enables even small men and women to overpower much larger foes.

And it enables small consultancies to prevail in large companies and against larger competition.

Here's an example: I was introduced to an executive in a large, closely held company. He said he was happy to see me as a favor to a common friend, but, "We have never hired outside consultants in this company and never intend to do so."

Well! What would you have said? You could have claimed you could convince him otherwise, just had a nice chat to satisfy the friend, or left to conserve your time and breath. All of those moves are clumsy and inept.

I said, *"You'd be surprised how many of my best clients started the conversation with me in exactly the same way, word for word!"* (No one is shooting at me, and I can't leave poorer than when I entered, that's the mentality that allows this.)

That process is one I call *reframing*. I took his frame of reference—you're in a situation where you can't be hired—and changed it to my frame—you're in company with a lot of people who became my clients.

That is a powerful use of language, the equivalent of an "escape back strangle" in jujitsu.

Case Study

I had been asked, as an experienced consultant working there already, to attend a Hewlett-Packard conference where the company would choose a consultant to help implement the reengineering effort that had just been formulated by Ernst & Young. The other candidate for the job was the Ernst & Young team that had done the formulation, represented by the practice's partner.

The HP team presented its objectives about helping people adjust well, and we were asked to respond. The EY guy said, "Do you want to go first or second?" I pretended to consider it and said, "Second, you be my guest."

He proceeded to show how templates would be used to determine which employees were assigned where in the new structure. Yet this was the company of the "HP Way," where people were highly respected at all levels. I saw eyes looking at the ceiling.

When he was done, I was careful to focus on involving people and supporting them through the transitions. I knew that, so long as I didn't spill coffee on the committee chair, I had the assignment.

All because of one word: Second.

Use language to induce, cajole, and influence. Remember the sequence: language controls discussions, discussions create relationships, relationships determine business. Here are some further examples:

- *When you're asked for your opinion or for advice, use a numbered list.* "There are three reasons why people leave companies, and usually they leave a superior, not the company."

- *Ask powerful rhetorical questions.* Remember that Ronald Reagan beat an incumbent president by asking during a debate, "Are you better off than you were four years ago?"
- *Reverse the objection.* "You're a small firm, and we deal with larger consulting firms." "That's *exactly* why you need me: I only take on a few clients at a time, my fees don't reflect having to support massive overhead, you have access to me, personally, without restriction...."
- *Provide options.* (I discussed this in proposals earlier.) If another meeting is called for, offer, "I can see you on Friday back here at the same time, by Skype tomorrow morning at 9, or by phone at 2 any day this week. What's best for you?"

Using the right language can accelerate your progress and preempt objections. It's the greatest tool in your kit, it's free, and it can be constantly expanded.[3]

Thus far we've spoken of external language, intended for others. There is another kind of powerful language, intended for you: positive self-talk. The field of positive psychology that has emerged over the past decade or so has proven how vital it is for us to monitor how we speak to ourselves.[4]

If we feel "lucky" to get work, we're degrading ourselves. We should talk about our outstanding work and talent. We have to stop saying, "Why would they listen to me?" and start saying, "I know how to get them to listen to me."

The words we use to describe ourselves and our results inform our behavior, and that manifestation influences others—positively or negatively. The person hanging around the periphery not willing to enter the conversation is saying to him- or herself, "I can't contribute much to this discussion. I won't be credible." But the person eager to start talking is the one saying, "Wait until they hear my great idea!"

A great many people do "postmortems" when something fails. They want to find out what went wrong. I've even heard the term used when there was success. What we really need are "post-celebrations." Find out what went right and why, and then tell yourself what your role was.

---

[3]For a detailed study of the power of language in sales, see *The Language of Success*, Kim Wilkerson and Alan Weiss (Business Expert Press, 2016).

[4]The seminal work here is *Learned Optimism*, Dr. Martin Seligman (Vintage, 2006). He was my guest speaker at my first Million Dollar Consulting® Convention in 2015.

> *Expertise: It's more important to know **why** you're good **than** that you're good.*

Positive self-talk is not bragging. It's learned success (as opposed to the very real learned helplessness). It's the antithesis of victimhood. Here's an exercise I recommend to everyone I coach: When you wake up in the morning and just before you get into bed in the evening, tell yourself something powerful about your talents and successes. It may be that you were able to confirm a difficult appointment, or you ran a successful meeting, or you gave your spouse help with an important project.

If you focus for just 30 seconds, twice a day, on these issues, you'll have a much more positive view and self-talk.

Case Study

I was helping Joan, an expert in improving bank brand performance. Despite a track record of success, she wasn't charging enough and was terrified that the next buyer would find her inappropriate and an imposter. I asked her why.

"I never graduated from college," she explained, "I'm even younger than I look, and banking was an accident— I have no specific financial background."

"How do the buyers know that?" I asked.

"Oh, I tell them," she said.

Watch your language, to yourself and to others!

And make sure that as your business progresses, you allow yourself to progress by making the necessary changes.

SEALING WATERTIGHT DOORS

As we grow through the stages of our careers, we have to adjust our habits, behaviors, and beliefs. If we don't, we won't make the best of the new landscape, like having a beautiful lawn that we don't want to mow because of the price of a mower.

I've dealt with wealthy people who search for deals when deals are inappropriate, or who view a dinner check among friends as if it's a cobra about to strike. I had dinner with a multimillionaire developer who bragged that the wine he was serving cost only $1.80 per bottle (it tasted like it) and demonstrated in his huge home how he avoided replacing the worn-out and tired furnishings. He died in a freak seaplane accident years later—I'm convinced never having really enjoyed himself and coming to grips with his own station in life.

It's a shame when the adjective that people most often bestow on someone is "cheap."

But the progression I'm talking about isn't merely about money. It's about being "estimable" in your conduct and bearing. It's about being *seen* as a success by others.

Let's understand the steps in Figure 6-4:

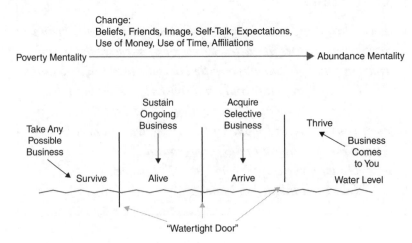

Figure 6-4 Watertight doors

1. Survive

This is equivalent to the basic needs in Maslow's famous hierarchy.[5] When we begin our careers (I was fired to begin this one), we often have

[5]See his book *Motivation and Personality* (Longman, 1987).

as our immediate concern the need to "put bread on the table." We will take any business available or possible. I did résumé reviews and critiques for $20 per hour. I figured that if I were struggling, there must be others struggling whom I could help!

When we are trying merely to survive—no money in the bank, rent due, no steady clients—we do whatever we need to in order to provide sustenance for our families.

2. Alive

At this step we have established a business with clients, we are post-start-up, and we can sustain ourselves, though we still have little in the way of reserves or discretionary funds. The accountants might call us a going concern, where the bills are paid, the inevitable debt is manageable, and we are able to create longer-term client relationships and find and acquire new business.

> *Expertise: You have to make significant, deliberate changes if you want to move toward an abundance mentality.*

3. Arrive

When you "arrive," you can acquire selective business. You identify your ideal buyer and attract the kind of business that best suits your passion and your expertise. You have begun to establish reserves, credit lines, and financial security. Your business is often from referrals, and you are beginning to become known in your niche and your home geography. You are a known competitor to others and an influence in your field.

4. Thrive

You are now a thought leader, an object of interest, someone whom others seek out. You no longer have to say, "I'd love to work with you," because prospects are asking, "How can I work with *you*?" Fees and credibility aren't issues because your repute is so significant. Think of IBM with hardware years ago, or McKinsey with strategy more recently. You can name your own price and people come to you.

These are the various levels you can achieve as your business progresses. But unless you change your friends, colleagues, memberships, beliefs, behavior, and so forth, the "watertight doors" aren't secured, and you slide back to prior, more scarcity and poverty-minded behavior.

Case Study

When I was fired by a horrendous, tyrannical owner from the presidency of one of his companies, I said to my wife that I wanted to go out on my own, never to be fired by a narrow-minded moron again. She said fine, but I had to get serious.

I told her that there was an important provision. I would only fly first class, use limos, and I had to buy two very expensive suits. She reminded me that we had little money and asked why this was so urgent.

I explained that if I were to interact with the sophisticated, high-level buyers I had in mind, I had to feel good about myself, not arrive rumpled and tired, and not show up in a rental car or taxi. I wanted to adopt an abundance mentality even before we had the abundance.

She agreed, we never looked back, and now you're reading this book.

You have to slam shut and batten down the watertight doors. You can't revert to prior levels of accomplishment. It might have behooved you to cut back on luxuries when you were in survival mode, but that no longer suits you.

Michael Vick was a fantastic quarterback, earning millions, when he was jailed for the heinous act of staging illegal dogfights. He never changed his friends, and he still associated with the people from his meager origins who continued to practice these things. Although gifted and wealthy, he slid back past the unclosed watertight doors to behavior both inappropriate and illegal.

You can't afford *not to change*.

If you want to possess and benefit from an abundance mentality:

- Develop friends who possess an abundance mentality and decrease your time with those who do not.
- Treat yourself well at all times.
- Determine not where you will withdraw money in time of need, but where you will *generate* money.
- Above all, remember that *you can always make another dollar, but you can't make another minute.*

THE CYBERSPACE CONSULTANT

HOUSTON, LET'S NOT HAVE A PROBLEM

No, this isn't a chapter about IT consulting. It's a chapter about the reality of being a consultant with a great deal of marketing connected to the Internet. In the 25 years since the first edition of this book—in fact, in the prior six years since the fourth edition of this book—nothing has changed in our lives as much as cyberspace.

It's not my intent here to try to keep you abreast of the latest developments, since they will be obsolete tomorrow.[1] It is rather my intent to provide you with pragmatic and profitable practices that you can use with existing and future technology.

TRUE PERSPECTIVE: THIS IS A RELATIONSHIP BUSINESS

Technology is an augmentation, not a substitute. I maintain as of this writing:

- AlanWeiss.com
- AlansForums.com
- ConsultingSociety.com

---

[1] I become giddy over "reviews" that point out that a cited Internet address has been changed. This isn't Wikipedia, where I suggest you go if you want to find out what's happened since last night.

- ContrarianConsulting.com
- AlanandtheGang.com

The first is my website, the second my 24/7 Forum of global exchanges, the third the site for my Society for Advancement of Consulting®, the fourth my blog, and the fifth my restricted site for my most active and important clients.

I also publish:

- The Writing on the Wall® (monthly, free video)
- Alan's Monday Morning Memo® (weekly, free newsletter)
- Balancing Act® (monthly, free newsletter)
- Million Dollar Mindset (monthly, free newsletter)
- Million Dollar Mindset Pro (quarterly, paid video)
- The Power of Personal Worth (weekly, paid video/audio/print)
- Mentor Newsletter (monthly, free restricted newsletter)

At various times I've had another six paid subscription videos, and I currently have two YouTube channels and a huge subscription access to my entire body of work in all media (http://www.alanweiss.com/store/online-learning/alans-million-dollar-consulting-growth-access/).

We've done streaming video sessions, interactive webinars, teleconference series, and podcasts, and I use Skype for my global coaching. We've converted all of our historical recordings to digital downloads.

It's fair to say I've been highly active and present in global technology and Internet impact. I've used an expert firm in the business, chadbarrgroup.com, to support all of this multifarious and constant content.

However.

As an analogy, compare Internet use to publishing. Publishers want us to write books to create higher book sales. But we want to publish books to help attract new clients to our business. Those are dissimilar objectives.

Similarly, technical experts and gurus want us to use the web because it's there (and it will earn them consulting fees). We should want to use the web to the extent that it helps us attract new clients.

A website, for example, for corporate consultants (not realtors or insurance people, who sell "retail"), is a credibility statement. It is usually visited by a buyer only after the buyer has heard us, or read something by us, or been referred to us. It is *not a sales tool* for corporate buyers. Corporate buyers make most professional services acquisition decisions based on peer referrals. Thus, that buyer *might* want to read your bio or see what kind of clients you've consulted with, but that's it.

The home page on a website is *the* most important aspect of it, and it should contain the following:

- Your name or company name and photo
- A brief list of typical client results (10 to 12)
- Testimonials, preferably video and brief, from buyers
- Your value proposition

As you read this, there are a thousand others who have read it and are prepared to march against me with pitchforks and torches to deal with the heretic. Others are writing to my publisher or tearing me apart with reviews on Amazon.

I don't care. I'm here to help you be successful, not to please the Internet gods and their acolytes.

Later in this chapter I'll discuss specific practices that help and hurt, and make recommendations. For now, I'm merely emphasizing that this is a relationship business that is most affected by human interaction and not technological gimmickry, and that you shouldn't take out a second mortgage to build or constantly update your website.

Most buyers will never see your website. I've worked with consultants making in excess of $5 million who don't have one. I've seen thousands of consultants who do have one—and are making very little money.

> **Expertise: You should use the Internet to market and to deliver, but not to sell to new clients.**

As we all know, there is a difference between marketing (creating need) and selling (providing alternatives to meet that need). The most effective marketing is evangelization, the word of mouth that creates the peer-to-peer referrals I referenced above. This can be stimulated by your presence on the Internet. But the sale itself will occur when you personally interact with the economic buyer.

There are too many people giving too much advice about the Internet that is irrelevant to corporate consultants, such as using pop-up menus to build lists, buying lists from cheap sources abroad, prominently asking for newsletter subscriptions, increasing SEO (search engine optimization, which I call "seriously, eternally obnoxious"), and other such nonsense that only creates a market for . . . the people giving you lousy advice about the Internet.

SOCIAL MEDIA PLATFORMS

Note that these are not called "business media" platforms. (We'll talk about what those would look like in the next segment.) The risk one takes in debunking the claimed "marketing power" of social media is being branded some kind of Luddite. However, just because technology exists doesn't mean it's right for your marketing needs.

I wouldn't suggest you use a billboard to market your consulting (and I actually had to talk a guy out of that $25,000 investment recently). Nor would I recommend skywriting, nor cable television infomercials, nor inserts in newspapers, nor a video game. I would urge you *not* to look at your Apple Watch during a meeting with a buyer, and restrain yourself from trying to call up needed information on it. Pecking away at an iPad is never a good idea at an initial meeting, even if it's with Apple!

So, anticipating the outrage, let me start with the benefits and bounty of all social media platforms and alternatives, from YouTube to Facebook, LinkedIn to Twitter, Instagram to whatever is being invented as I write this. (I'm waiting for Inside Elon Musk's Brain.)

Benefits

- On some platforms, most notably LinkedIn, you have direct access to whomever you are linked with. Consequently, there is no secretary, assistant, or other filter between you and the person you're contacting.
- It is easy to ask for referrals from mutual friends and contacts, and easy to find such connectors.

- The discipline, for example on Twitter, of confining value and promotion to under 140 characters (and far less if you want to be retweeted) is a great trait to develop, as is the habit of doing it every day.

- If you are in the "retail business" (e.g., selling to individuals, not corporations—which I would consider to be "wholesale"), you can dramatically extend your reach via postings, targeted advertising, and endorsements. I believe that realty, insurance, design, home services, accounting, law, auto sales, and so forth are ideal here. So are coaching, counseling, career development, image improvement, and so forth.

- You can automate placements so that you don't need to take time every day to post.

- You can find kindred spirits and potential alliance partners, especially remotely and globally.

- You have mobile access from almost anywhere you're traveling.

- Groups are quite popular, some with a dozen members, some with 30,000, and they can be helpful and informative if they provide value for your development (and don't serve merely as chat rooms and ego halls).

Now let's look at some of the downsides.

Disadvantages

- Corporate (wholesale) buyers do not use the social media platforms to find consultants—they overwhelmingly use peer reference (of course, they might access those peers over the Internet, but that's neither here nor there).

- The pure hokum about the power of social media promotion *irrespective of the kind of services you provide and buyers you seek* is overwhelming. There are thousands of "Internet marketing experts" and "social media authorities" whose sole claim to fame is that title, never having successfully sold or marketed anything else themselves. They are hammers seeing everything else as nails (to paraphrase Abraham Maslow). Search engine optimization, about which you receive a dozen e-mails a day from India, is totally irrelevant if your buyers are not using the Internet to find your services.

- The potential time dump is severe. We are all easily distracted on social media sites by videos of alligators jumping into boats, dumb debates about dumber statements by vacant politicians, and pictures of someone's new baby or near-death experience.

- You are lost in the noise. Everyday on LinkedIn there are hundreds of repetitive and duplicate articles on the same subjects (e.g., "Five steps to better listening"). *Everyone publishing articles on LinkedIn seems like part of a herd of similar beasts.* There is no differentiation. There is no validation. There is no credibility inherent in participating in any social media platform. *The people who do it well and are instantly followed, supported, and believed are those with preexisting, market-dominating brands:* Seth Godin, Guy Kawasaki, Marshall Goldsmith, Dan Pink, me. Social media created Justin Bieber, but they don't create strong brands for consultants.

My recommendations, in light of this, are to use the social media platforms to your advantage, not to your detriment. Here's an example of what I post on Twitter, three times every morning, requiring about 60 seconds:

Alan Weiss @BentleyGTCSpeedB2h
2 hours ago
Deliverables (facilitation, training) are inexpensive commodities. Results are high value outcomes. Which are your fees based on?

Alan Weiss @BentleyGTCSpeedB3h
3 hours ago
If you don't blow your own horn, there is no music. —Alan Weiss
No one can promote you like you can.

And here's an example of a promotional tweet:

Alan Weiss @BentleyGTCSpeedB2h
2 hours ago
Listen to the best language just before you make that critical phone call:

If you want to provide an example of your value, IP, and independent thinking, you can do so quickly and painlessly in that manner.

Expertise: Your ROI on social media will be small if you invest a lot of time, but it could be large if you invest just a little time.

Alan's 10 social media guidelines

1. Severely limit your time to less than an hour a day on *all* sites combined, except for pure pleasure and entertainment, which should not occur during your hours set aside for work.

2. Do not look to these sites for validation. Don't care at all about how many people follow you, or are linked, or are friends, or view your video. And for heaven's sake, ignore your Klout Score.[2]

3. Test and experiment with your intellectual property and new ideas. Ignore those who critique everything they see, but listen to those who have reasoned responses and suggestions.

4. Use the appropriate platforms for introductions to corporate buyers when you find someone who is capable and willing to introduce you.

5. Pause before posting. Never print anything out of anger or pique or resentment. It's astounding how viral things can become when they are embarrassing or unpleasant.

6. Don't think you're separating your private and public life. There are thousands of examples of business connections being ruined by posts on social media that the originator never dreamed would be seen by business colleagues and clients. Assume everything you print or post will be seen by everyone.

---

[2]A vague and elitist attempt to show your "popularity" using metrics such as retweets, visits, responses, and so on. Try paying the mortgage with your Klout Score and see what kind of clout it provides at the bank.

7. Ruthlessly block, unfriend, unlink, and so on. If you find rude, profane, loud, or otherwise obnoxious people, remove them. Don't be embarrassed to do so. I routinely remove those who use obscenity as adjectives, those who see a government conspiracy behind every tree, and those who are insulting and rude. I also remove all attempts at advertising and promotion.

8. Watch others' YouTube videos to learn about the best production techniques, subject matter orientation, length, value, and so forth.

9. Consider creating your own groups, especially if you have a specialty or narrow focus. If you provide enough value and attract some successful people, you may be able to convert group members to business media efforts (see below) or even actual business.

10. If you do advertise and promote, carefully monitor your expenditures and conversions. The number of "views" or "clicks" are irrelevant, only actual business counts. The platforms have an annoyingly common characteristic of perpetuating your advertising and upselling "improvements," and the costs increase dramatically over time, so it's up to you to track your actual ROI.

BUSINESS MEDIA PLATFORMS

There are a lot of social media but precious few business media platforms. You will find business discussed randomly on social media, and you'll even find dedicated groups. But these are strictly informal adjuncts to the social dynamic surrounding them. LinkedIn has thousands of articles appearing every day, but they are mostly boring rehashes of what everyone already knows ("Six Myths About Employee Motivation") or boring ("Why Your Meetings Are Boring").

When I Google "business media platforms," the first entire page has "social media" in the entries. There were 46 million hits, but a random search through scores of pages shows "social media" overwhelmingly predominant. What does this mean?

It means that the Internet has not adapted well to purely business needs. People may boast that on LinkedIn, for example, you don't have to go through secretaries, screening, and assistants to reach someone with whom you're linked, but that's like bragging upon finishing medical school that you can identify the proper Band-Aid to apply.

There are, of course, business subscriptions online, but those merely re-create hard-copy news media. And then there are the blogs, such as *Forbes*, or *Huffington Post*, or *Harvard Business Review*. The problem here is that they're mostly awful. There are professional bloggers who do nothing but write for pay for these organizations. They are not learned business people. Then there are hundreds of consultants and others who rotate as bloggers, but the predominant number of them are thankful to have the opportunity to have their name associated with the source. They are usually not thought leaders or experts.

These blog entries are not vetted, not peer-reviewed—they are simply opinions of people who often have less experience than the reader who is seeking new opinions.

Thus, the advantage here is that you have to define your own business media for your parochial purposes. This might be your own blog (mine is at http://www.contrarianconsulting.com) or an interactive site you create for dialog and debate (mine is http://www.alansforums .com). My advice is that you can seize the opportunity here to build your own ballpark.

Here are the prerequisites for creating your own business media platform that will attract others who in turn attract others (the "app" principle):

1. The site must be readily navigable and linked to your other endeavors, such as websites. Keep the interface clean and the instructions simple for transactions such as posting, search, saves, finding other members, and so forth.

2. Ensure that you can easily post text, video, audio, photos, and graphics on the site. You don't want to have to go through your technical people every time you want to make an addition or change.

3. Allow for comments from all members, but retain the right to edit and delete any entries. Arrange the interface so that you can deny entry if necessary to anyone who has deserved expulsion (for profanity, theft, and so on).

4. You must visit daily, preferably three or more times. Post articles, questions, tests, case studies, and so on. Respond to others' posts and questions. You must insert IP and value on a daily basis.[3]

5. Allow debate and argument, but never rudeness.

6. Don't feel that all must agree with you, but do confront poor advice and insufficient examples.

7. Create various topics "boards" (marketing, fees, global business, and so on) to keep related "threads" together. (I even have one called "sex, religion, and politics.")

8. Provide free entry to your clients and/or high-potential prospects. Otherwise you can charge for annual or lifetime membership.

9. Don't allow it to become a chat room or gossip column.

10. Try to maintain a certain level of participation. Senior people don't enjoy interacting with lower-level people.

11. Provide massive free value daily. Even when you're not present, credit will accrue to you as the person who makes it possible.

Expertise: Keep your business platform focused mainly on business and make certain that visitors can find pragmatic, valuable ideas daily.

Here's an example of one such thread on my Forum that I began about internal briefings:

I had a coaching call this morning and mentioned something I had done as a matter of course, but apparently it created quite a splash, and I began wondering if, in all my billions of words, I had ever bothered to describe it.

---

[3]Recently my Forum had a server problem and went down for a few hours. That morning I received e-mails from around the world alerting me and telling me that people were missing their daily "fix."

I was asked how to ensure you can meet the successor to your current buyer, or successors to other potential buying positions, from internal candidates. My response:

Hold internal, free briefings. Tell your buyer that it would be great to brief his direct reports and/or colleagues on what's happening and your basic approaches. It's "free." (Don't mention this in your proposal.) I used to do this at very large clients where the buyer was astounded I'd do it, we'd do it sometimes after hours or after a shift in a hospital, and once word spread about how informative/entertaining/humorous/charming I was (choose any four), everyone wanted to take part.

Just a thought, rather simple, but maybe I never mentioned it. Consider it an "internal breakfast" session by analogy.

Alan Weiss

Alan,

Just so I am clear, when you talk about debriefing internal people, what would be the content of this meeting and what was your most successful format for doing this?

Thanks,

Andrew

You debrief on the project, your approaches, progress. Small group: a conference table. Larger group: classroom seating. Huge group: auditorium.

Alan Weiss

Brilliant. Thanks.

What is the added value for the EB?

Bragging rights? Ego?

Or is it more about internal education to create buy-in and good will?

Jeffrey Scott

What would you think?

- Gaining commitment
- Providing education/growth to others

- Showing how excellent the resources he/she brings in are
- Finding out levels of questions and ideas
- Inspiring contributions and innovation
- Gaining volunteers
- Unearthing any unforeseen risks

Thanks Alan. This is brilliant.

I feel like this is something that Kim talks a lot about in our growth cycle meetings . . . helping our buyers be internal stars by sharing results from their initiatives. It's a great way for us to be known by others in the organization and I can think of two projects right now where this would be a great thing to do at the end (both for my buyer and for me).

Do you mention this after you're in the organization or before?
Simma Lieberman

After. You want to position this as a real unexpected benefit to the buyer (see above) which also will introduce you to people who can be very helpful, now and in the future.
Alan Weiss

This is great Alan. I can recollect just two instances where I've done this, and both times it's been a hit. One time definitely led to considerable visibility within the client organisation and led to more work. This thread prompts me to make this a more conscious, deliberate offering.
Andrew

This is very timely for me. I am seeing a couple of years of work come apart because of a transition in top management (my EB and project sponsor is leaving the company–project was complete). I have seen similar circumstances (not involving me) in two other large companies over the years. Great results were undone by the new people trying to make their own marks. Perhaps using Alan's approach I can help my clients avoid that.
Rick

I've traditionally done a good job of this which has been responsible for a significant amount of repeat business for me. It never fails that someone leaves, is promoted or something else happens that has the potential to derail the project (if not paid in advance) or impact future business. I've been surprised by how often this has occurred. Actually, it came up again yesterday in a situation I would not have predicted.

Before I realized how valuable it could be to business, I followed this path anyway as I see it as a good way to gain alignment and ensure implementation success.

Lisa

On this highly practical thread we had people from four countries, in five disciplines, "time shifting" the thread globally. Once you're at the center of these types of exchanges, you are at the center of your business universe.

PRIORITIES AND WASTES OF TIME

Here's an idea of what happens with intelligent use versus undisciplined use of social media sites.

This is an unscientific, undocumented, and probably unpopular analysis of what I'm learning from coaching thousands of people who are active at various levels of social media and conventional marketing. Call me "the king of social media." (I'm reminded of a great review of a leading actor in *King Lear* by Eugene Field: "He played the king as though under momentary apprehension that someone else was about to play the ace.")

Here are my anecdotal observations.

If people visit LinkedIn twice a day for 15 minutes each time, that's 2.5 hours in a five-day week. (I'm discounting weekends, though I shouldn't, because social media wandering is clearly a full-time avocation, but I want to be conservative here.)

If they visit Facebook four times a day for 10 minutes each, that's roughly 3.3 hours.

If they use Twitter six times a day for five minutes each time, that's 2.5 hours. (Or 12 times at 2.5 minutes each—you get the idea.)

Lets' not even think about YouTube or Instagram or dating sites for the moment!

If they post on their blogs three times a week (rather important to keep a blog active and interesting), and the creation and posting of the item takes 30 minutes (and I think I'm really lowballing this one), that's 2.5 hours.

And now I'm going to add just two hours to the week that accommodate reading others' blogs, replying to commentary, following up social media stuff offline, updating profiles, uploading photos, and so on. (You could include YouTube, et al. here.)

Drum roll, please: We now have a five-day week on a conventional 40-hour basis with about 13 hours engaged in what is somewhat inappropriately termed "social media." I understand that those hours may well extend into evening or early morning time. On the basis of a 40-hour week, that's 33 percent devoted to this stuff; but even on the basis of a 12-hour day, the percentage is 22 percent.

If you were devoting less than half of those 13 hours, say, 6 hours, to other professional marketing pursuits, I estimate you could do any one of the following during that week:

- Write two or three chapters in a book
- Create and post 10 to 12 position papers on your website
- Call, at a moderate pace with follow-up, 30 past clients and/or warm leads
- Send out a dozen press releases
- Engage in a full day of self-development or a workshop
- Create three speeches or a complete multiday workshop
- Create a new product to be sold on your website
- Create and develop a marketing plan for a teleconference
- Create and record three podcasts
- Create and tape a brief video
- Contact 30 prior clients for testimonials, referrals, or references
- Attend two networking events
- Create and distribute two newsletters
- Complete at least half of a professional book proposal for an agent
- Respond to 50 or more reporters' inquiries on, say, PRLeads.com

- Seek out two high-potential pro bono opportunities
- Contact and follow up with five trade associations for speaking opportunities

You get the idea. Don't forget, in my unscientific analysis, I've halved the hours I think are really being invested in full-fledged social media activity based on an already conservative estimate of what they truly are. And I'm not even counting other networks or platforms, just the few I've mentioned.

And over the course of a couple of months, you can easily do *all* of the bullet points, if you have a mind to do so. I'm just allocating six hours a week, just over an hour a day.

My current evaluation is this: Don't confuse occupation with avocation. I've never said that "social media" are evil or will not help someone find a buyer somewhere at some time. Heck, I've become an avid blogger, and I visit Facebook and Twitter daily. Yet I can still do all of the bullet points above and work only 20 hours a week in total.

If you're serious about corporate consulting and coaching—and the blog you should be reading is located at www.contrarianconsulting. com—then I'd continue to advise that you're not going to find those buyers on social platforms. Is it impossible? No. Have some people done it? They claim so. But if you're engaged in social browsing at the *expense* of those bullet points, then that's not a good disposition nor apportionment of time. If you can do both and still live a balanced and fulfilling life by your terms, then go for it.

I'm posting intellectual property, for free of course, on Twitter, just as I'm doing here, where you've paid for the book (I hope). I do find that these platforms present a great way to pay back, to contribute, and to share. You have to be judicious in your selections, however, since some people just want "air time," and you only have so much air.

EXAMPLES OF IMPACT

If you use cyberspace intelligently, since you'll be active within it every day, you can achieve these types of results:

- Effective delivery of remote work
- Passive income

- Remote marketing
- Mass marketing
- Rapid responsiveness to all requests
- Daily promotion

Effective Delivery of Remote Work

You can interact with clients on Skype, Google, and a host of other platforms that allow for a more intimate, visual sharing. You can deliver a lecture to a classroom, conduct a webinar, hold a teleconference, conduct interviews, perform surveys, complete 360-degree assessments, and so on. While there is always a need to be on-site in person (presentations to your buyers, observation of performance, investigation of processes), many of the other demands for your time can be obviated through technology.

Passive Income

You can offer on your website products, manuals, procedural lists, videos, newsletters, podcasts, text downloads, and so on. You may choose to have a shopping cart with the ability to accept credit cards (e.g., 1ShoppingCart.com), or you might use a service such as PayPal.

Case Study

I coached an attorney who offered free forms for small businesses on issues like interview questions, evaluation forms, termination procedures, retirement plan funding, and so on. They became so popular that he began to charge for them, increasing their diversity to cover the expertise that small businesses usually lacked (human resources, benefits administration, legal, and so forth). Finally, he created a yearly membership, allowing as many forms as needed to be downloaded on demand. He made so much money with so little work that he abandoned his legal offices.

Remote Marketing

You can deliver free teleconferences, webinars, Q&A discussion groups, podcasts, and video on your site, your blog, or email to your lists.[4] You can appear as a free guest speaker at others' events and be projected onto large screens. Especially effective are brief (30-second) video testimonials from your own clients, who act as "evangelists" by allowing others to listen to their endorsements of your work and examples of your accomplishments with them.

Mass Marketing

If you diligently develop your lists and use social media judiciously, you can market to tens of thousands around the world on a regular basis. My free newsletters always contain "soft sell" promotions for my events and experiences. While most authorities feel that a positive 1.5 percent return is highly desirable on mass mailings, mine average over 10 percent because I keep lists of people who have purchased something from me before, and send special offers to them. If you put out a free newsletter with great value for your ideal audience, you'll find that your lists will grow weekly.

Rapid Responsiveness

I return all my calls within 90 minutes during Eastern U.S. business hours, and all my e-mail within about three hours. People are astonished by this, yet it's very easy with the use of a cell phone and/or tablet or laptop. Texting can create real-time help for people. I don't believe in a "work life" and "personal life," but simply "my life." I don't mind hitting the pool at noon or taking a business call on the beach. Usually on the first afternoon of our vacation, my wife will say, "Have you paid for the trip yet?"

Expertise: People don't expect instant access to you today, but they greatly appreciate rapid response.

---

[4]Large files are easily sent today with services such as YouSendIt.com.

Daily Promotion

You send thousands of e-mails a year, probably scores a day. In every one your signature file should carry a brief promotion for your new book, new service, latest IP, upcoming trip—whatever it is you want to keep in front of prospects and clients. You can alter your website and blog daily to create constant reminders for fresh offerings. Social media platforms offer the opportunity to launch new IP regularly.

This is the marketing business, so you should be spending at least 50 percent of your time marketing. You can do that daily, effortlessly, and inexpensively on the Internet and with technology.

DELIVERING THE GOODS

TAKING THE
EXPRESS LANE

There is nothing illegal, immoral, or unethical about marketing while you are delivering. They are parallel endeavors. Yet many consultants "shut down" when delivering, some of them even refusing to respond to voice mail and e-mail. There is a name for this mode of operating: stupid.

SUSTAINING BUSINESS

It is *far* less expensive and far less labor intensive to sustain and perpetuate existing business than it is to acquire new business. In fact, the acquisition of new business is one of the hardest endeavors for anyone without a very strong brand and market gravity (which attracts clients to you). One of the reasons it's so easy to find subcontractors to help you deliver business (and free up your time) is that there are so many people who love to, and are excellent at, delivery but who can't market.

Hence, they are dependent on those of us who can market for their income. They are a commodity resource, so they can't demand high fees (though they will claim that the quality of delivery is the key element, it isn't—acquiring and sustaining business is).

In Figure 8-1 I've created the simple relationship between existing products and services, new products and services, and existing and new clients.

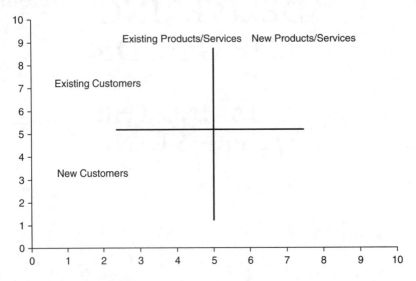

Figure 8-1 New and existing products and customers

You might think that the easiest route here is to sell more existing products and services to existing customers, but it's not. *Note that this segment is called "sustaining business," not sustaining customers!* The best way to sustain your business is in this sequence:

1. *Offer your existing products and services to new customers.* Reason: You have a track record and testimonials for them, and therefore it's easier to make a high value case for others to accept them.

2. *Offer new products and services to existing customers.* Reason: You have a strong, existing relationship, but your clients can weary of the "same old, same old." Introducing new value will keep your worth fresh and is an easy entry point.

3. *Offer existing products and services to existing clients.* Reason: There may well be additional populations, additional buyers, and reinforcement needed, especially in larger organizations.

4. *Refrain from offering new products and services to new clients.* Reason: You sacrifice the advantages of successful existing offerings, *and* you don't have the advantage of an existing relationship.

This is the worst place to apply your energy and resources. An example of people who try this are those who make cold calls, or buy lists, or make mass mailings. It is the area of your least leverage and least advantage.

Expertise: Never lose sight of the difficulty of acquiring new business on a consistent basis. Not many people are excellent at it.

If you find yourself allied with someone in acquiring and delivering business, here's an objective formula to apply so that all parties are treated equitably:

Acquisition = 50%   Methodology = 30%   Delivery = 20%

This means that if I acquire the business (50 percent) and we use your methodology (30 percent) and split the delivery (20 percent), then the total fee would be split like this: 60 percent me, 40 percent you. This reflects the various importance of the three elements involved in sharing business. Note that this *does not apply* to people who solely deliver. They should be paid a daily rate plus expenses. At this writing, excellent delivery people (training, facilitating, focus groups, assessment work, interviewing, and so forth) can easily be obtained for $1,000 per day.[1]

We'll get to specific tactics later. But the strategy I'm suggesting is to look at your offerings, your existing clients, and your potential (ideal) clients and make decisions about how you appear in the marketplace. Remember that "build it and they will come" works only on those occasions *when you tell them you've built it.*

On average, you should be seeking about 80 percent repeat business annually, and 20 percent new business. To accomplish that, some existing business will correctly run its course and end, but some must be

---

[1]If you were a subcontractor working just 10 days a month, you'd gross over six figures a year, which is pretty good for someone who can't generate business on your own. I think you can see the symbiosis here.

jettisoned. Every 18 months or so, try to drop the bottom 15 percent of your business (based on amount of profit). The business most eligible to be abandoned:

- You've had it since you were struggling to survive, but it no longer represents your ideal client.
- You're no longer learning anything.
- You margins are too low (too much delivery is required).
- There are troublesome client individuals.

You can't reach out unless you let go. You have to make way for new and better business—just as you don't keep every car you've ever owned, you keep trading them in for newer and better models.

FOSTERING REPEAT BUSINESS

Repeat business in my lexicon means business acquired with a current or past client, but if the latter, within 12 months. Otherwise, it's new business. Repeat business does not necessarily mean "more of the same" but can mean different value purchased by the same company or entity (not always the same buyer). Figure I1-2 in Interlude 1 demonstrates the wisdom of offering new products and services to existing clients.

Repeat business emanates from these activities:

- *Never lose contact with your buyer.* Provide debriefs and updates regularly, at least weekly at the outset, in person, by Skype, or by e-mail. Bring good news so that when there are problems they don't constitute the sole reason you talk to your buyer. Never allow yourself to be delegated (to HR, a subordinate, purchasing, a committee, or whatever). Always have regular discussion with your buyer.
- *Meet new buyers along the way.* In large companies there are scores of potential buyers—remember that repeat business is with an organization, not necessarily the same buyer—and nurture those relationships.

> **Case Study**
>
> *I worked for Merck for 12 consecutive years, working with around 20 buyers in five divisions and four countries. I worked with Hewlett-Packard for 10 consecutive years, working with six buyers in three countries.*
>
> *You can call this "internal referral business" if you like, but I think it's a matter of making a significant impression with the quality of your work.*
>
> *One buyer at Merck, a division president who had worked with me prior in another area, introduced me to his top team with, "This is Alan Weiss, an excellent consultant. Like all good consultants, he will insinuate himself like a virus into our systems and then stay to become a part of us!"*

- *Be vigilant for new opportunities to help.* You'll see issues not related to your own project but holding tremendous potential impact for your buyer or other buyers. Don't take it on for free (which I call scope seep), and don't ignore it. Instead, use this language: "As a consultant I often come upon issues not related to my project but having great potential import for you. I would be remiss if I didn't bring a couple of these to your attention, and while you may choose to handle them on your own, I'm also willing to help if you would like me to do so."

- Use best practices you've seen elsewhere to make suggestions for improvement, using similar language to that above. "Many of my best clients are now doing this . . . ."

> *Expertise: If you're not acquiring more than 50 percent repeat business from existing clients, either you're not doing a superb job, the client doesn't realize you're doing a superb job, or you're not asking.*

Finally, here's a methodical way in which to view new business potential. The various routes aren't purely repeat business, since they point you toward the client's customers and trade associations. But you get the idea: create what today people are wild about calling "genealogy charts," and you can see clearly the potential directions you can pursue for repeat business.

You can't regard a client engagement simply as a snapshot in time. It's actually part of a moving picture, and you can help create its direction and outcomes.

When you become proficient and methodical about securing repeat business, you lower your costs of acquisition, thereby improving your margins. You diminish your need to learn new details about a client, thereby decreasing your labor intensity. And you have no need to create trust and credibility, which are already present, thereby speeding up the next sale.

My admonition to you is to "think of the fourth sale first." That is, consider your long-term business with a client, not just your current project. If you don't plan for it, it won't happen.

REFERRALS

Referral business is the "second half of the sale." When you acquire a new client, you will receive a check to cash. But the second check comes when that delighted client provides more business at other organizations through referrals.[2]

Why don't consultants receive more referrals? Surprisingly, it's not because their work quality is poor—it's because *they don't ask*.

Never wait to ask for a referral until the project is completed. Wait until it is about two-thirds completed, then use this language:

> *Referrals are like the coinage of my realm. Almost all of my work comes from referrals from delighted customers. I think we're both ecstatic about our results to date, so I'd like to ask a favor: Can you introduce me to three people who you believe can profit from the same type of value?*

[2]For an entire book on this one segment, see my *Million Dollar Referrals* (McGraw-Hill, 2012).

Or, even better:

> *Can you introduce me to Betsy Taylor at your main supplier, who I think would be ideal?*

And a backup:

> *If an introduction isn't convenient, may I use your name as a delighted client?*

There are some professions—auto sales, insurance, realty, medicine, accountancy—where referrals are the absolute lifeblood. You've probably referred people consistently to your doctor, dentist, attorney, and so on as a thoughtful gesture of win/win/win. Yet how many people have they referred to you?

Not many, if any!

That's because *they don't know what on earth you do!* Your dentist has probably had someone in the chair who is in need of personal coaching, or strategy work, or supply chain management, but simply listened empathetically because your name did not come to mind. And that's because you've seldom if ever asked for referrals or reminded the dentist, whom you probably see at least twice a year professionally and perhaps more than that at social events.

There are two basic types of referral business: solicited and unsolicited.

Solicited

You should make a list, using simple software such as FileMaker Pro or an Excel spreadsheet, of everyone you know. (Observe how dumb it is to purchase lists from Bangladesh when you have your own, far higher quality and personalized list if you put your energy into it?) Then, divide the list into three unequal parts:

1. Those people you suspect can either purchase from you or provide referrals for you
2. Those people you're unsure of for the first group
3. Those people you're sure don't belong in the first group

Call the people on your first list. Note that they may be past clients, current clients, professional associates (that dentist), friends, acquaintances, family members, civic contacts, and so on. I'd suggest you call just two a day so that it's not onerous, but that means 40 contacts a month. Ask each one for three names. That's 120 potential leads monthly. (Even if only half comply with two names, that's still 40 leads monthly.)

Write to the people in category 2. Use the same language, but send an e-mail, personalized if possible. (Say things like, "Did your daughter enjoy her first year at school?")

Include the people in category 3 on your mailing lists: newsletters, podcasts, promotions, and so forth.

If you follow these rules monthly, you will obtain leads and eventual business. (See Chapter 2 on trusting relationships and conceptual agreement.)

2. Unsolicited

You may feel that "unsolicited" means you can't control these referrals, but that's not correct. If you do an excellent job and are constantly visible—even ubiquitous, you'll draw the proper attention. At one point I worked for six different newspapers concurrently, one referring me to another despite sometimes being in competition. I had five pharmaceutical clients at once, through the same means. People talk. They change companies. They want to do a favor for others.

Case Study

When I was young, newly married, and poor (very frequently the trifecta of young life), I worked at Prudential. An agent named Hal Mapes—I still remember his name—would visit new employees and suggest that the way to show loyalty to Prudential was to purchase a policy. I bought the cheapest I could—I think the burial provision was to throw me off a train.

Hal visited every six months and asked for three referrals. He wouldn't leave until he got them. Literally,

> *wouldn't leave. He'd suggest former classmates, working companions, social contacts.*
>
> *If Hal had even 60 clients, quite reasonable, and he visited them twice a year and acquired three names a visit, that was 360 names. If half were relevant, and he was able to sell to half of them, that would have been 90 new clients. And the next year he had 150 clients to ask for three names.*
>
> *Hal retired a wealthy man.*

Referrals are a prime source of lowering labor intensity and increasing margins, since they entail *virtually no cost of acquisition.* You should be mining and drilling for these referrals at every opportunity, no matter what stage of your career you're traversing at the moment.

Here is the way to follow up on a referral:

> *I'm Jim Hutton, and Sarah Ward has introduced us by e-mail. I don't do this often, but in the past her advice to meet with someone has always been extremely valuable. I'll be in your area on several occasions and wondered if we might spend 30 minutes together. I promised her I'd contact you and get back to her.*

What we've done here is ensure that we follow up promptly, mention that we're due to get back to the referral source, and suggested a very brief meeting. Never try to "sell" anything on the phone; you merely want the next "yes," which is a personal meeting.

> *Expertise: Never allow anyone to represent you, with your materials, to someone else. Others don't have your passion, can't answer certain questions, and will easily be turned away.*

New business acquisition is difficult if done "cold," to the point that you can die from the cold. But you warm it up considerably when you leverage your current contacts—not solely clients—to provide you with likely new sources of income. They provide the flow in your "pipeline" for short-term business.

If you're not asking for referrals daily, then you're not serious about marketing. And as I've mentioned before, this is not the consulting business, it's the marketing business.

NEW SERVICES

If you consider the Accelerant Curve presented earlier in the book (Figure 2-2) and repeated in Figure 8-2, the ongoing market need is to add services on the right—lower labor and higher fees, culminating in the personal vault, services unique to you. New services are the catalyst for consulting growth.

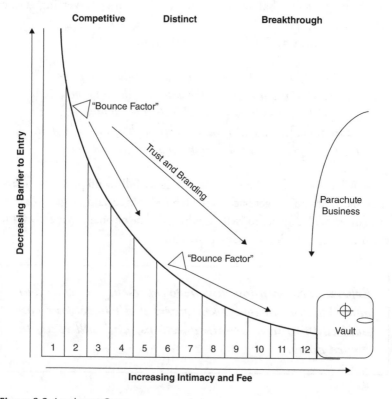

Figure 8-2 Accelerant Curve

Where do new services originate, out of what alchemy do they emerge, from what source do you gain inspiration? Counterintuitively, there is a process to this creativity!

The sequence shown in Figure 8-3 depicts a simple, single product as an origin point. This could be a booklet, an audit,[3] coaching, and so forth. We can then repurpose this: the booklet becomes a video, the audit becomes a podcast, the coaching becomes a remote intervention.

We can then look at a series: a subscription to your leadership practices via a weekly video, or your team improvement techniques via a mobile application, or your executive decision making via quarterly Skype call.

We can move on to more personal interactions of higher value and fee—remember, moving right on the Accelerant Curve is intended to personalize while lowering labor and raising fees. For example, a tailored, private executive coaching engagement for $40,000 a month, three-month minimum. Or a monthly, interactive phone call for no more than a dozen executives on current economic events and implications for

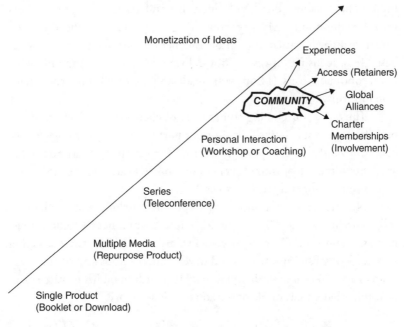

Figure 8-3 Process of new services creation

---

[3]I'm going to use "product" and "service" interchangeably from this point on, since the process holds for either.

talent acquisition, for a $15,000 annual subscription. Or access to your entire body of work (video, audio, print, electronic, whatever) for $5,000 per person per year.[4]

I'm sharing a sequence here to build services as your career progresses. You may feel it's too early in your career, but all long-range plans have to start today. Moreover, if this is at all attractive, you're in a position to begin to target your creations that will result in the "body of work" I allude to. If you create only one podcast, one video, and one article per month, which is extremely low volume, you'll nonetheless have 36 items of value annually. Take each one through the sequence in Figure 8-3, and you're going to have a wealth of valuable material and services.

Finally, the apotheosis of the sequence is "community." I believe strongly in client communities. Seth Godin, a respected colleague and brilliant author, talks of "tribes." We part company on this particular subject. A tribe is a distinctively close-knit group, striving for commonality and homogeneous membership, acknowledging "totems" and exclusivity.

A "community" is a heterogeneous group of diverse people sharing common values, but highly inclusive and readily accepting others into the community. My own consulting community around the globe is extraordinarily varied, but all of us concur about, for example, value-based fees, focusing on results not deliverables, and working only with true economic buyers. (I hope your readership here will constitute inclusion into this community.)

Thus, your developing community of clients (buyers) serves as the basis for your vault items, but more important *as the laboratory for the development of these ever-growing services.* The very people most desirable as clients at the top of your sequence are those who are also the most valuable as sources for still more services.

Not that the community concept can't include global alliances, official memberships, "inner circle" elites, common experiences (e.g., retreats), and special access to you. I've always admired the marketing savvy of Tony Robbins, though I'd never walk barefoot on hot coals. He charges $50,000 for an individual to fly to visit him on his private island near Fiji. That's an example of the top of this sequence.

---

[4]Before you scoff, consider that I do all of these, and so can you. See for example http://www.alanweiss.com/store/online-learning/alans-million-dollar-consulting-growth-access/.

No matter where you are in your career, you should keep this sequence in mind as your guide to new and more valuable services, to your trek to the right of the Accelerant Curve. Otherwise, you'll find yourself, by default, producing *more of the same services for the same fees.*

> **Expertise: You have to have a plan to continually offer new and more alluring services, or your growth will sputter and eventually stagnate.**

This chapter is about "delivery"—becoming not merely more proficient at delivery, but rather more selective in delivery. You can always outsource and subcontract the volume of the mundane. But you will retain the uniqueness and the high fees of the select. The point of the Accelerant Curve is to *move* clients who like your basic work toward more and more unique and high-fee work.

Delivery should diminish as your career flourishes. People will come to you, your work will be remote, a great deal of your income will be passive. Ultimately, excellent consultants *who are also excellent business people* become trusted advisors and are valuable by dint of the potential access to them.

The million dollar consultant will always have retainer business.

RETAINERS

It's worthwhile to revisit retainers here, because they are a vault item.

Retainers in consulting are not retainers in their most popular usage: with attorneys. An attorney's retainer is nothing more than a *deposit*, meaning that the attorney will deduct his or her hourly fees from that money, not trusting you to pay them when due, and when it's exhausted will ask for another retainer or will cease work.

This is the dumbest billing system in the history of the world. But, then again, the national anthem was written by a lawyer, and it's almost impossible to sing, hard to decipher, and isn't original—the music is based on an old English drinking song.

In consulting, *a retainer is a fee paid in return for access to your smarts.* Big difference.

A client may pay you $10,000 a month to have unrestricted access. Your value is in your advice, suggestions, ideas, and/or service as a sounding board. But it is not to become involved in client projects, and it is almost always an off-site relationship. You may be contacted three times a week or never. The value is in your being available if and when needed.

Retainer value is not based on frequency of use but rather on guarantee of response. It has these three variables which help determine the amount of the retainer:

1. *Who has access?* If it's one person, there is less value than if there are three people. But it's generally unwise to have more than a few people with such access from one company.

2. *What is the scope?* If I'm on the East Coast and you're on the West, are we talking about your business hours or mine? Are any personal meetings involved? Is it by phone, Skype, e-mail? What about weekends or evenings?

3. *What is the duration?* I suggest that no retainer be for less than three months, since we should allow time for it to be used. A month is not enough. A quarter is minimum, a half-year is good, and a year is excellent.

If you're a veteran with a decent brand, your retainer should be for a minimum of $10,000 per month, perhaps with a discount for payment in advance—for example, $25,000 for a quarter, $50,000 for six months, $100,000 for a year. Otherwise bill at least quarterly, and at the beginning of each quarter.

> **Expertise: Clients don't actually need instant access—they need fast responsiveness.**

As opposed to a deposit, this retainer is a guarantee of access and response. It's a vault item on the Accelerant Curve, because your retainer is unique to you and your practice. Retainer relationships generally require only a few contacts a month of relatively brief duration. If you have six of these, we're talking about roughly $600,000 annually just from retainer work and requiring a few hours a month at most. This is the apotheosis of high fees and low labor. And, of course, when your brand generates the interest, you could easily have a million dollars of retainer business alone, still leaving plenty of time for more convention work or the beach.

You can have projects with a client with which you also have a retainer, as well. But never include project work in the retainer: always use a separate proposal, or you'll lose your shirt.

Case Study

After a series of projects with high success at Calgon, the CEO was happy to put me on retainer. He would sometimes call me during halftime of Monday Night Football, not because he liked football, but because he knew I did.

Monday night was often important because he had Tuesday morning board meetings. He'd pass a few things by me that he couldn't resolve himself and test his presentation on me, asking for suggestions. This took about 20 minutes—the duration of halftime.

How do you best acquire retainers?

1. Always offer them as part of option 3 in your proposals (see Chapter 5). An example:

   In addition to Options 1 and 2, I will serve on retainer for a period of six months to provide feedback and serve as a sounding board without restriction whenever you need me. This way you do not have to make an investment decision every time you may need some advice or analysis.

2. Go back to past clients or mention to current clients who have not originally opted for a retainer that you offer them, reminding them of the value:

   I'd be remiss if I didn't mention again that my best and most successful clients have requested a retainer approach to ensure the continued application and evolution of the original work.

3. Elicit testimonials about your retainer work and place them on your website, in your collateral, and in your conversations.

4. Encourage clients who place you on retainer to mingle with clients and prospects who don't have you on retainer at common events (evangelism).

5. This is a tad tricky, but suggest a retainer in Option 1:

> *For the new talent acquisition project your own people initiate, I will serve as a trusted advisor to your three-member steering committee, offering advice and counsel when requested and without limit or restriction.*

Many consultants don't realize they can use this "Option 1 retainer." They would receive more fee, probably, by actually implementing the project themselves, *however, the possibly lower retainer fee is offset by the near absence of any labor at all.*

Remember, wealth is discretionary time, money is only fuel. You can always make another dollar, but you cannot make another minute.

You will not acquire retainer business if you don't make it known that you offer it and you don't ask. It's as simple as that. I know consultants in the business for 20 years and more with zero retainer business because they just don't think to offer it. They think their value is in their *presence.* It is not. Their value is in their *expertise.*

True story: Entering the fourth year of what would be five years of six-figure retainers at Calgon, I entered the president's office one November as I always did to shake hands on the next year's retainer, which he paid with a discount, $100,000 on January 2. But he said, "Alan, we're changing the agreement."

I wondered what on earth I had missed. Had I become complacent or deficient in value. "Why?" I stammered.

"Because you're more valuable than the agreement, and we're raising it to $130,000. Have a great holiday."

THOUGHT LEADERSHIP

IT'S FINE TO STAND OUT IN A CROWD SO LONG AS YOU LOOK GOOD STANDING THERE

"Thought leadership" can be an empty, banal concept unless you view what people like Marshall Goldsmith, Jim Collins, Seth Godin, Marcus Buckingham, and I have done with it. Here is the blueprint for how to create and maintain thought leadership, obviating all worries about competition.

WHAT OR WHO IS A TRUE THOUGHT LEADER?

The natural extrapolation of unique expertise is what we colloquially call "thought leadership." (I've often thought a more valuable phrase is "results leadership.") Thought leadership (TL) is about being *the* acclaimed and recognized generator of intellectual property and pragmatic approaches in a given field.

Peter Drucker was the TL in strategy. There are many other fine strategic sources and practitioners, but he was the one who set the standards. I always looked to Walt Mossberg, the one-time *Wall Street Journal* columnist, as the thought leader in technology. (Among his gems:

We don't talk about "plugging in" to the electric grid, why do we say we're "going on the Internet" when we're on it constantly?)

Here are the traits of thought leaders:[1]

- They are cited by others in their field.
- They publish prolifically, including multiple books.
- They speak frequently at public and private events.
- They produce new intellectual property regularly.
- They are acclaimed as thought leaders by others.
- They have powerful brands in their fields.
- The are often hired as trusted advisors (retainer).
- People come to them.
- Fees are never an issue.
- They are global in their appeal, not solely local.

I "own" the solo and boutique consulting niche. That's why you're reading this book or any number of others I've written, and I've written more books on consulting than anyone, ever. Yet, at a civic event, someone might say, "Oh, a consultant . . . are you out of work?" Or, at an extended family event, someone will inevitably say, "How does he make his money?" (usually somewhat astounded).

Thought leaders needn't be well known outside their niche. But if you're in the coaching profession and don't know who Marshall Goldsmith is, or in the performance improvement world and don't know who Marcus Buckingham is, or in consulting and don't know who I am, then you're an amateur. You may not agree with us, may think we're arrogant or wrong, but it's impossible not to have heard of us if you're serious in your field.

That's true thought leadership (Figure 9-1).

You base your TL on the Accelerant Curve, market bell curve, and market gravity we've spoken about earlier, combined with a growing number of testimonials and maximizing your impact through technology, as we've discussed. Fueling all of this is your IP factory.

---

[1]I run an annual Thought Leadership Conference in Palm Beach, and these are the typical responses of participants. My guests have included James Carville, Robert Cialdini, Marshall Goldsmith, Dan Pink, and others.

TL SCAFFOLDING

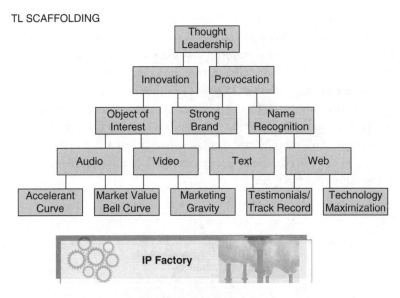

Figure 9-1 The scaffolding of thought leadership

At the next level, you employ delivery mechanisms to broadcast your talents. At the third level, you've developed the brand and recognition to become an object of interest. You can then leverage this repute to be provocative and innovative in your field, resulting in true TL.

- Where are you deficient at the moment?
- What is needed to remediate the deficiency?
- Can you do so yourself?
- If you can't, who can help you?

It's wise to keep TL as a goal because it maintains your focus on being distinct and constantly creative. You don't have to become *the* thought leader, being one of many is fine. In a field like leadership, for example, you could point to many: Warren Bennis, John Gardner, Seth Godin, Patrick Lencioni, et alia. But if you don't at least point the ship in that direction, you will wind up being derivative, and the 455,000th person to talk about commitment instead of compliance.

That brings me to my final point about true TL: it is often contrarian, counter to the mainstream, bringing people to a screeching halt.

I began my career as a contrarian, arguing that one could have too much quality (tolerances that were too tight), too much teamwork (most organizations actually have committees, as does Congress), and too much growth (nonprofitable growth). A true thought leader can point out the reverse of conventional wisdom and invert the tried and true.

As you can see in Figure 9-2, our experiences, education, talents, and knowledge can lead to true wisdom. But we need the courage of our convictions if we are to bridge that last gap, make that last step. Like anything else, there is a methodical way to create TL, and to garner the courage to claim that top spot.

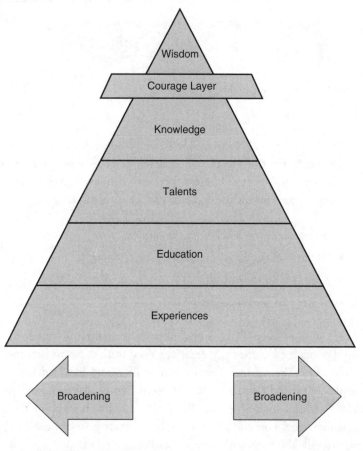

Figure 9-2 The wisdom pyramid
This first appeared in *Business Wealth Builders*, Phil Symchych and Alan Weiss (BEP, 2015).

THE STEPS TO CREATING THOUGHT LEADERSHIP

While it may seem that people in the forefront of their field, by acclamation, arrived there through some natural gravitational pull of raw talent, I've found that to be rare. In fact, most arrived by methodical means. They may not all be able to articulate—or choose to articulate—the means, but there are common steps, nonetheless.

Marshall Goldsmith, the preeminent coach, told me that he learned to "hang out" with thought leaders if you want to be like them. He used to, literally, carry Peter Drucker's briefcase. He met a great many influential people while at Drucker's side, and was identified with him. Not long ago, Marshall was awarded the top award from a leadership institute that was once called the Drucker Leadership Institute.

I'd add that Marshall is relentlessly generous. He provides help, testimonials, endorsements, and advice to peers on a constant basis, and this also establishes him in my mind as an avatar.

First, ask yourself this question: How well known are you in your field at the moment?

10: Widely acclaimed in your niche or specialty
7: Acknowledged by many within your group of influencers
4: Rarely identified
1: Can't get arrested

This applies to your national or global standing in your particular field. The average of all the people who have responded to this question in my Thought Leadership Conferences is 3.4!

> *Digression: The familiarity and respect for your contributions must be outside of your community, not because you're known well there, but because of the observation of St. Mark's Gospel (6:4):* **A prophet is not without honor except in his native place and among his own kin and in his own house.**

Second, you need "aerodynamics." You must have a recognized field, specialty, point of focus. Mine is boutique consulting. Dan Pink's is sales. Nessim Taleb's is decision making and risk. Otherwise, you have a flying barn, not a sleek arrow. I've found that you can't teach goats to fly, even if you strap wings on them and throw them off a building. What you will have is an angry goat.

What is your niche or focus? _____

Third, you should "stair step" your public exposure in any variety of media. This is what Marcus Buckingham or Seth Godin or Malcolm Gladwell have done (again, whether deliberate or natural or accidental). This means that you begin locally, build regionally, target nationally, and eventually have an impact globally.

In Figure 9-3 you can see a "stair step" of publishing, from your own newsletter to a trade association newsletter, on to a column in a larger newsletter or magazine (or online), then to national publishing and finally a commercially published book.

Every thought leader I know of publishes widely, and almost all have a multitude of books, usually in several languages.[2]

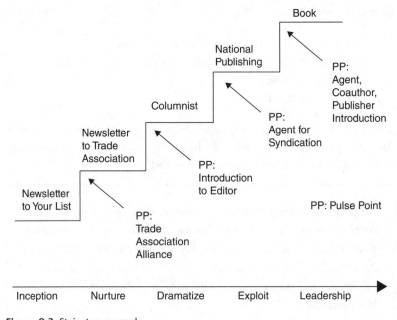

Figure 9-3 Stair step example

---

[2]I advise the most successful people in my coaching programs to plan to publish a book every two years and, preferably, every year.

Fourth, you need to adopt the traits of those who have been successful in achieving thought leadership. This doesn't mean trying to become them, but rather adding what has proven to be effective to your personal repertoire.

These include:

- Producing IP weekly, in print, audio, video, and/or public events.
- Taking controversial views and not trying to conform with expected metrics. (I follow no one on Twitter, which enrages some people, even though I have over 7,000 *actual* followers.)
- Continually evolving and changing. There is nothing wrong with increased learning changing your view, methodology, and approaches.
- Making predictions. They don't all have to be right, but people expect predictions and ideas for the future from thought leaders.
- Staying above the fray. It's not appropriate to get into debates with people who disagree or snipe. They are entitled to their opinions, so long as they are not libelous.
- A certain relish is people taking offense because you are disturbing comfortable nests. I've never placed any worth in audience "smile sheets" (approval sheets), only the satisfaction and delight of the person who hires me.

Why is thought leadership a consideration, no matter where you are in your career? Because TL creates a tropism toward higher fees. It draws people to you: call it "super" market gravity.

Here's now to capitalize on it:

1. Abandon normal market ranges. Your speaking, consulting, coaching, retainer, product, and other fees should be well above others in your field, because it's expected.

Expertise: Fee follows value, until thought leadership and branding enable value to follow fee. That is, the more you charge, the more people think you're the best.

2. Accept "losing business." You have to let go to reach out. Seal the watertight doors and abandon your low-end business.

3. Continue to insert strong IP into the marketplace, and never rest on your laurels. (If you blog and you haven't posted anything in three days, you're slacking off.)

4. Focus your clients on ROI, not fees, not deliverables, not tasks.

5. Aggressively build your brand.

6. Aggressively build your viral and word-of-mouth buzz.

7. Create a constant presence in the public square: publishing, op ed pieces, speaking, leadership positions, and so forth.

As a reminder, there can come a point where perceived value follows the increases in your fees (Figure 9-4). That gap is created by thought leadership and consequent brand power.

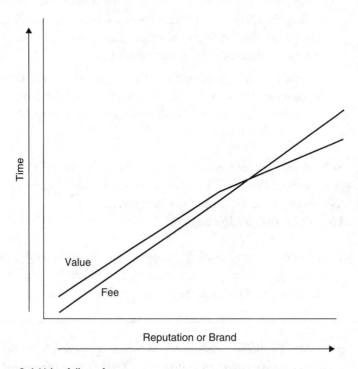

Figure 9-4 Value follows fee

Case Study

Not long ago I went to the hardware store to buy a wrench to fix an outdoor tap. I haven't purchased a wrench in forever, and I have no idea of brands or quality. I saw four in the size I wanted from different manufacturers.

How was I to choose? What would you have done? I purchased the most expensive, assuming it was the best. It has not let me down. That's how people should look at you and your fees.

HOW TO OWN A MARKET SEGMENT AND AVOID COMPETITION ENTIRELY

Most competition that challenges consultants is *internal*, that is, within the prospect organization. It is not something else *external* to the organization. Hence, the earlier part of this book has dealt with convincing buyers that it's faster and more efficient to use you than it is to use internal resources.

We hear frequently, "We can do that ourselves," to which I've had two standard replies:

1. "Then why haven't you?"
2. "How's that working out for you?"

The reasons that a project doesn't make sense to try to accomplish with resources on the payroll include:

- No matter what you think, these people are now doing *something*. Asking them to take on an organizational intervention will result in either less of that *something* or a halfhearted attention to the new project or, more likely, both.

- The people assigned will be "available," meaning that they aren't currently the best people, who are simply untouchable, yet those are exactly the ones you want, not those who aren't performing well now.

- Internal people have internal biases and cultural inculcation that is hard to change, let alone replace.

- There are turf issues, politics, and private agendas that will be competing across team members and departments.

- The expertise in change management and project implementation do not exist to any great degree in organizations of any size (don't even consider the human resources people, who, by definition, are those not wanted elsewhere).

- Internal people aren't about to place their status and career potential on the line for someone else's project.

- When management creates a project that fails, it's the implementers, not the formulators, who are blamed, and everyone knows this.

- People on the inside cannot force their own superiors to make tough calls and serve as champions.

- There will be investment squabbles.

I could go on, but I think you can see there's really no need. Keep these reasons handy in case you have to convince a wavering buyer that "doing it internally" is the equivalent of spending money to not do it at all.

Expertise: You only have to overcome two types of competition, and that's a lot easier than you may suspect.

This leaves the occasional external competition and how to deal with that. First, some guidelines:

- You are seldom competing against *the* thought leader in your field, if there is one, because he or she is unaffordable (or unthinkable) for the client in front of you. For small business, that's about a 100 percent proposition, as it is for most divisions and departments of larger organizations.

- The fact that you are present and talking to the buyer is virtually never a "fishing expedition" but rather a true interest in your capacity to help. Therefore, you have a direct line to the decision maker (assuming you're committed to meeting economic buyers) and the ability to influence and convince in person. (Most "fishing expeditions" are conducted by lower-level people who ask about price over the phone or in e-mail.)

- Using the processes described in this book (and other of my works) will give you a clear and decisive advantage over others who don't focus on the true buyer, who quote hourly fees, and who simply try to respond to requests instead of building relationships.

- If you've been following my advice, then you have a body of work, you have a brand, and you are known to some degree or at least can produce testimonials and references that are convincing and far superior to others.

My position is that if you can readily overcome the 85 percent of prospects who are considering internal options, and can outperform the competition in the 15 percent of cases where other consultants are being considered, you should win 100 percent of the business! But let's be reasonable: we are talking about a vast majority simply by preparing effectively.

So if you want to be lead dog (because the others have such a terrible view), then here is your battle plan against external competition to own your market segment:

1. *Be contrarian.* Don't provide people with better ways to accomplish team building—tell them they actually have committees and team building can't do anything for a committee.

2. *Always try to go last.* If given a choice, be the last one to present to your buyer. Despite what you may fear about fatigue, it's often the last thing people hear that they most remember.

3. *Use colorful metaphors and examples.* I told a hospital CEO that strategy has to be "organic" (in use and not sitting on a shelf), and he kept repeating that for days to all of his staff.

4. *Suggest radically different views.* I told executives of a water treatment company that they should stop trying to catch up with competition over the horizon, which they'd never managed, and "take a sharp right turn" to rebrand themselves as an "environmental effluent management firm." You can see the visual that closed the sale in Figure 9-5. It was that simple.

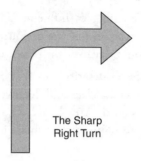

The Sharp
Right Turn

Figure 9-5 The sharp right turn

5. *Find the buyer's personal objectives.* Behind every corporate objective is a personal objective. The CEO of an animal health company told me he wanted better communications and fewer turf battles. I found out that he was worn out by acting as referee all the time, so one of our metrics was that he could record fewer than three occasions to settle a dispute monthly. We brought it down to zero.

All of this makes sense and is simple if you can identify the half of the Michelangelo Factor that accounts for what you're really great at doing.[3]

IDENTIFYING YOUR "SWEET SPOT" AND KEY FACTORS FOR DEVELOPING IP

Figure 9-6 shows how we portrayed the sweet spot earlier. Intellectual property originates with those components that constitute your major talents. Most consultants are bright, energetic, and intellectually curious. These are stellar characteristics.

Except when they're not.

We tend to chase shiny objects.

My German shepherd, Bentley, will chase anything he sees in motion. It may be a squirrel, a ball, a leaf blowing in the wind, or a shadow. Predators tend to chase moving objects. The phenomenon,

---

[3]When Michaelangelo was asked how he carved *David*, he supposedly replied, "I carved away everything that didn't look like David." In your career, carve away everything that doesn't match your passion and competence and you'll have the artwork of your life.

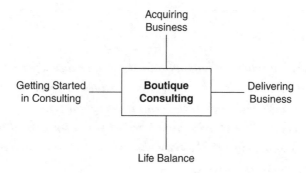

Figure 9-6 The sweet spot revisited

studied by scientists, is called predatory drift. This urge can easily overwhelm what's happening at the moment: a game, eating, sniffing a trail. In the case of our own behavior, it can disturb our focus, our intent, the project in front of us, even relationships. (Have you ever seen people simply tune out of a conversation or use their cell phones in the middle of a meal?)

The factors around the sweet spot—and the reason I urge that they be relatively few in number—are meant to keep us focused and insulated from predatory drift. Our drift is toward the bright, shiny objects of new learning, discovery, experimentation, and even perfection. This drift is at first glance an asset, but it turns out to be a detriment, because we wind up *producing irrelevant intellectual property.*

> ### *Expertise: Not every idea is a good idea for your business.*

The key is to look at the IP you develop as motive forces, propellants to drive the elements around your sweet spot. This focuses your IP on your occupation and your value proposition. I happen to adore electric trains, and I build plastic models, and I drive exotic cars—just to name three of my hobbies or avocations. But I'm not about to develop IP around these things because they aren't part of my sweet spot or value proposition. *In fact, when I seek to get better at train layouts or model building or driving sports cars, I seek out those who have made these things occupations and who have relevant IP to sell to me.*

Case Study

I had a coaching client who told me one day that he was prepared to write a book proposal on the tragedy of 9/11. He is a marketing expert—and a very good one.

I asked if he was in New York at the time or had some direct connection to the tragedy, other than the pain all of us felt as Americans.

"No," he said, "but I want to write the book."

"So this will be a hobby, not for your business," I told him.

"Oh, no, I'm sure it would help my business," he assured me.

I talked him out of a book no one would have published and, if he self-published it, no one would have bought, and if anyone did buy it they wouldn't have thought for two seconds about his business.

You should be developing new IP every week. This sounds daunting, but it's not. The tough part is *directing it toward your sweet spot and critical elements*, and not simply developing anything that intrigues you or pleases you.

In other words, you can't allow your IP development to be undermined by intellectual predatory drift!

It's okay for Bentley to drop what he's doing and chase a chipmunk, but it's not okay for you to stop your relevant creativity to chase an irrelevant idea.

As for developing IP weekly, here are some easy examples. In these three different illustrations (Figures 9-7 through 9-9), you can see IP that consists of relationships among variables, sequences, or timing. There is nothing new about the words, but there is about the combinations, and all of them pertain to my work (moving without waiting for perfection, integrating learning, and ethics).

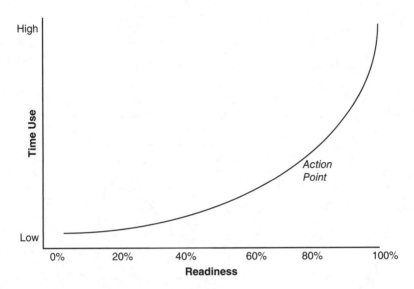

Figure 9-7 When you're 80 percent ready, move

You can create intellectual property daily, but weekly is fine. The point, however, is that they must have a point—relative to your own work and sweet spot.

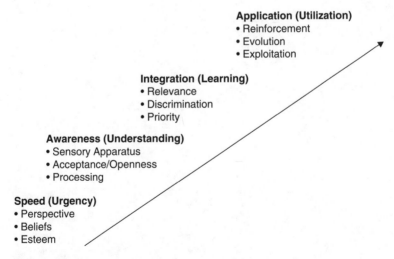

Figure 9-8 Integrated learning and speed

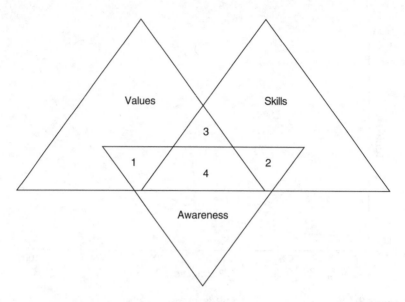

1. "Would act" but can't, because of lack of skills
2. "Should act" but won't, because of lack of values
3. "Could act" but doesn't, because of lack of awareness
4. "Will act" because all elements are present

Figure 9-9 Ethical dimensions and relationships

THE ETHICAL CONSULTANT

HOW TO DO WELL BY DOING RIGHT

Consulting has drawn all types because there is no barrier to entry. That's wonderful for the honest entrepreneur, but it's also an unguarded gate for the shyster or lazy or unknowing. A palm reader on the boardwalk of Atlantic City requires more licensing than a solo consultant. Think about that.

ETHICAL ISSUES

As you achieve multidimensional growth and your practice prospers, the nature of the problems and challenges you face evolves. At the outset of your consulting career, you are typically concerned about cash flow, marketing, and developing the expertise required to complete more diverse assignments.

In midcareer, during the firm's dramatic growth, the issues become those of finding the right alliance partners, developing long-term relationships, and establishing proper fee levels. Once you are a prominent expert, the priorities become the unique issues related to your very success.

Million dollar consulting generates some million dollar ethical challenges. How would you respond to these 11 challenges?

1. Can I simply charge the highest fee possible and not even worry about perceived value? If I'm in demand, isn't the guideline "whatever the traffic will bear"?

2. I choose to travel first class, stay on the concierge floor of the best hotels, and take limos rather than taxis. That's my travel style, and I'm worth it. As long as I'm honest about it, shouldn't the client be billed for my normal travel preferences?

3. There is nothing new under the sun, and I'm a recognized name and a sought-after figure. There's nothing wrong with taking some ideas espoused by other consultants and authors and using them in my work or writing as long as I put my personal spin on them. You can't copyright ideas, so I can use what I wish to, right?

4. I'm seeing three clients on this trip. I know that if I attempt to prorate expenses, their accounting systems will question the charges. However, if I simply bill each one for the entire airfare and lodging, there won't be a single question. Shouldn't I make it easier on myself and on them and bill each of them for 100 percent, since I have to visit each one anyway?

5. In doing my research within a client organization, I'm told by a midlevel manager *on a strictly confidential basis* about an internal leak to competitors and ongoing employee theft. If I divulge this to the president, it will be clear that I was the source, and my value to the client within the organization may suffer. Isn't it better—and even ethically necessary—to maintain the confidentiality and continue to be a valuable resource within the organization for the client?

6. A client offers me first-class airfare to visit its European offices. I can use my free airline mileage to take my entire family and, by cashing in the first-class tickets, pay for all our food, lodging, and recreation. There's no reason to explain all this to the client, is there, since it's my personal business?

7. A competitor of one of my largest clients wants to hire me because my reputation has been associated with my client's success. Is there any problem with taking on competitive organizations?

8. A client asks me to conduct an anonymous employee survey by mail, but asks me to use a hidden code to differentiate by unit—though not by person—the source of the feedback. This is because the client is sincerely interested in the quality of the unit managers and wants to isolate those whose people are

unhappy with their treatment. Is this a legitimate goal to justify the subterfuge?

9. I am asked to write speeches and articles for the president of the organization, who is my client. He confers with me on topics and critiques the final work, but the actual writing is totally mine. The president gives no attribution whatsoever, publishes some of the articles in the trade press, and gives the speeches at business conferences to great acclaim. Is this a service that I should continue to provide?

10. Through an alliance partner, I develop a client contact with the alliance partner's blessing. After a three-month, highly successful assignment, the client asks me to take on a long-term project in place of the alliance partner, with whom the client has been unhappy for some time. Can I ethically accept this project?

11. The prospect is the antithesis of "green" and environmentally friendly. The firms observes the laws in theory, but not in practice. Can I use my opposition to its wasteful ways as justification not to do business with this firm?

Expertise: Always ask yourself, "Would I be proud of this if it appeared all over the Internet tomorrow?"

Most of these situations have happened to me, and the rest have happened to colleagues. There are no magic answers to ethical dilemmas. Ernest Hemingway observed, "What is moral is what you feel good after, and what is immoral is what you feel bad after." Of course, no one ever recorded that Hemingway tried his hand at consulting; otherwise, *For Whom the Bell Tolls* might have been called *An Analytic Report on Bell Cacophony, Causation, and Demographic Probabilities*.

You can't do much better than to try to do the right thing consistently.

I'd rather go with the credo that I've heard virtually all managers at Merck articulate when they are asked what to do in ambiguous situations when policy and precedent don't apply: do the right thing. Here's what I consider the right thing to do in each instance.

1. Should You Charge the Highest Fees You Can Get Away With?

Why shouldn't you listen to those who claim nothing stops you from charging what the traffic will bear. If you are charging on a fee basis and the client is aware of and accepts the fee, the client obviously has determined that the value is worth the investment. However, I would emphasize two caveats:

- It is never advisable to overpromise and underdeliver. Consequently, if you are justifying the high investment through extravagant promises and providing only marginal delivery, you are certainly not building long-term potential. Which is better: a single $150,000 project that results in no further work, or an ongoing series of $75,000 projects, the results of which send the client into fits of ecstasy?
- If you are charging a per diem or a fee based on some other fixed standard, despite the strictures of Chapter 4,[1] there is never an excuse to charge for anything other than actual hours performed, on-site or off-site. Padding days goes beyond an ethical transgression—it's theft.

2. Should You Travel First Class and Bill the Client?

You can make a case for the fact that if the client approves of a sybaritic travel style, there is no problem. However, your primary charter is to improve the client's condition. Do you help fiscally through this kind of expense (which has nothing to do with your value or expertise), and do you help your credibility with the client's people through this kind of image?

I doubt it. There are some high-flying organizations in which this mode of travel is the status quo, and in such circumstances, the luxury makes sense. I've also found that most clients offer first-class transportation overseas, and many do so for domestic coast-to-coast trips. (However, these tend to be terminated quickly in a poor economy.)

---

[1]Frankly, if you are charging by the day, I doubt that you'll ever need the advice in this chapter, and I wonder why you've even read this far.

Nevertheless, my rule of thumb is simple: if the client doesn't offer it, I don't abuse it. I travel first class and use limos and the best hotels, but I charge clients for coach, taxis, and standard Marriott-type rates. And I won't use limos or other frills if their visibility raises questions about the "high-priced outside help," even if I am paying for them myself. And don't pull a fast one: take the difference in the cost of luxury travel out of your pocket as a decreased margin; don't pad the fee to make up the difference.

3. Should You Borrow Others' Ideas and Present Them as Your Own?

It's true that you cannot copyright concepts (you cannot even copyright book titles) and that there are few breakthrough ideas. Most of the really good ones are merely old ideas reapplied in new ways. However, your clients are smart. People recognize ideas that were formulated by others. Since it's your *application* of the idea for your client that is novel, why not give credit where credit is due? It's the mark of a successful, self-confident consultant to say, "This is a technique developed by Sally Smith and written about in the *McGoo Review of Management*. I've developed an adaptation for your situation that I believe we should implement."

You are not expected to be a rocket scientist or the director of a research and development factory. You are hired to provide pragmatic consulting interventions using the best ideas in existence. Since this is what you are being paid for, it makes sense to reveal the sources of all ideas and techniques.

4. Should You Bill More Than One Client for the Same Basic Expenses?

Never double-bill (or, in this case, triple-bill). I've seen every excuse under the sun for doing this, and none of them passes muster as "doing the right thing."

Send a cover letter with your expense statement explaining why you are charging the client only one-third of the full amount on some of the receipts (for example, airfare) and the full amount on others (for example, meals during the days you are working exclusively for that client). Turn the procedure into an opportunity to demonstrate your fiscal responsibility toward that client.[2]

5. Should You Pass on to the Client Confidential Information Given You in the Course of Your Assignment?

Who is the client here? You were brought onboard to help improve the client's condition, and it's up to the client to determine what the most useful role is. In this case, you're ethically bound to inform the client about what you've discovered and allow the client to decide whether to take action immediately or to preserve your current role by not taking action.

You cannot make these moral decisions *for* the client, only in collaboration *with* the client reserving the decision-making prerogative.

By the way, I never ask for information in return for a promise not to reveal it, and I *never* agree to accept information on the condition that I not reveal it. Once you do this, you are ethically compromised on the spot. When someone tells you, "This is confidential, but ... ," you are free to listen and use the information as long as you haven't acknowledged that you will respect the confidentiality. Good consultants find out what they need to through intelligent questioning and keen observation. Relying on informants isn't consulting—it's spying.

Case Study

I was asked to coach the president of a bank's retail lending division. One of his direct subordinates had sent alarming reports about his behavior to the president's corporate boss.

---

[2] I once had two clients whose accounts payable bureaucrats both demanded the single, original receipt for the airfare. Since there was only a single original (which I like to keep for my records), I gave them each a choice: I would send the original to whichever wanted to pay the entire air bill and a copy to the one who would pay a 50 percent share. Both quickly accepted copies, and I had examples of internal policies that, when followed blindly, create waste to show to my buyer.

As I conducted my work, the subordinate continued to send confidential messages to the corporate officer and to me, reporting transgressions but demanding that the information and source not be revealed. I quickly ended this by telling the corporate officer and the subordinate that he was compromising the organization. You can't say, "I know where we're losing money, but you can't do anything about it."

The subordinate was furious at having been "sold out," but I merely pointed out that his behavior was as destructive as his boss's and maybe worse because his was with premeditation. Confidences are not more important than the health of the organization. Period.

6. Should You Use Tickets Supplied by Your Client to Bring Your Spouse Along?

This might be your personal business, but the tickets are the client's. There's nothing wrong with this practice if you inform the client of your plans. You can never be too candid or err on the side of excessive honesty.

I've taken my wife on many trips using the tons of free air mileage we all acquire, and I tell the client what I'm doing and that I'll simply charge the equivalent of coach airfare. I also pay any difference in the room rate.

I've never had a client say anything other than, "It's always a good idea to take along your spouse whenever you can; I always try to myself."

As for "it's only my personal business," here's what happened to my own personal physician, who consults on medical computer applications. The client provided a first-class ticket to Paris on British Air. The doctor cashed it in to pay for two business-class tickets for a subsequent European vacation with his wife, and he booked a coach fare on another carrier. Just before his departure, he received a fax informing him that the client's limo would meet him at the special first-class arrivals area!

> *"Innocent" falsehoods can develop into complicated and unnecessary questions about your ethical standards. Either tell the client what you're doing, or don't do it. (If you're uncomfortable telling the client, the chances are strong that what you're doing is unacceptable.)*

As for my doctor, he had to fess up, which is why he's a full-time physician and only a former consultant.

7. Should You Accept an Assignment from a Client's Competitor?

This is a tricky one, and I've found the following criteria to be sound in determining whether to accept or decline an assignment:

- I will not do anything that reveals confidential information, directly or indirectly. A direct revelation: "Tell us how they plan to promote in region X." An indirect revelation: "Design a succession-planning process that is similar to theirs." Acceptable conditions: "Evaluate our field-force management personnel and tell us what developmental work is needed in light of our business goals." (No competitive revelation is necessary at all.)
- I will try to assign different personnel (subcontractors) to each project. If I am personally demanded, I will make the provisions in the first criterion clear at the outset.
- I will inform my present client of the competitor's request and the tentative project and ask if the client wishes me to decline.
- If the new assignment is accepted under the preceding criteria, I will not divulge anything learned to the current client either.

There is nothing intrinsically wrong with working for several clients within the same industry. After all, many buyers use "experience in our industry" as a hiring condition. The critical ethical consideration is this: Are you being hired for your expertise and your ability to improve the client's condition, or are you being hired for what you happen to know about the competition? Revealing confidential data is never itself a confidential process, and once it is inevitably discovered, it will propel you back to a nine-to-five job very rapidly.

8. Should You Agree to Use Secret Identifying Codes on a Confidential Survey?

Sorry, but ends do not justify means. Despite the client's pure thoughts on the matter, the action is unethical. Anonymous surveys are supposed to be exactly that. You are committing an unethical act as soon as you tell people that their responses are confidential and then provide a document that exposes them by area.

If the client's need for information makes sense, as it does in this case, there are other options. You could tell people that the responses are sorted by unit. Or you could provide a place for the unit to be recorded at the respondent's option. Or you could suggest other alternatives altogether, such as focus groups or direct observations.

There are always pragmatic reasons for doing the right thing. I've found that any attempt to disclose respondents' feedback by unit or person despite promises to the contrary is always found out by the rank and file. There are no secrets in organizations. There are simply some facts that take longer to surface than others.

9. Should You Continue to Write for a Client Who Passes Off Your Work as His Own?

No problem here. The president is paying you for your expertise, you have agreed to the arrangement, and the president is acting with your permission. (Presumably, this service is also specified in your consulting contract with the client.) The only trouble with plagiarism arises when permission is not obtained. If you don't like someone else taking credit for your pearls of wisdom, don't open the clam by accepting such assignments.

10. Should You Agree to Supplant an Alliance Partner Who Introduced You to the Client?

Well, yes and no. Improving the client's condition certainly justifies the project, since the client, having worked both with the partner and with you, is convinced that you can better meet current needs. However, you also have an obligation to anyone who has introduced you to a client that you won't steal her revenue.

In these cases, I tell the client that I can accept only after I speak to the partner, explaining my obligations and my ethical concerns. This usually raises my esteem in the eyes of the client. I'll then explain the situation to my alliance partner, encourage the partner to contact the client to talk about it, and offer assurances that this initiative was the client's, not mine. Having done all this, I will accept the assignment. The client has made an objective choice, my expertise is deemed appropriate, and I've been honest with the partner organization.

Of course, engaging in any action whatsoever to supplant a partner at your initiative is unqualifiedly unethical. If you feel comfortable informing your partner of the situation and inviting the partner to discuss it with the client, you probably have acted well. If you accept without providing this opportunity, you have no doubt acted badly.[3]

11. Are You Justified in Turning Down Business from a Firm Whose Practices Are Reprehensible to You?

Absolutely. There is no law requiring you to take on all prospects. You are neither a public conveyance nor a public accommodation. You can refuse to work with people to your heart's content, providing:

- You're not being capricious or biased. ("I'm not working with men!")
- Your whims don't adversely affect your income. (Whims are not values.)

One of the benefits of building a successful consulting firm is the opportunity—and the necessity—to ponder on, develop criteria for, and take action on ethical issues with clients and colleagues. I've described composites of 11 of the more common ones that I've encountered, but you'll undoubtedly be faced with some unique quandaries of your own.

---

[3]I have a short list of consultants whom I would never use as subcontractors because I have seen evidence of their theft of business from former employers or other consultants. I freely tell my partners and colleagues about them. A pox on their houses.

Therefore, in conclusion, here are the guidelines that I find useful in determining whether I am doing the right thing:

1. Does the activity improve the client's condition or merely my own?
2. Is the activity something that I am comfortable explaining to the client?
3. Is the activity something that I am proud of and would publicize as a trait?
4. Is there harm being done to anyone without his knowing it and/ or being able to respond?
5. Is this treatment something that I would willingly subject myself to?

There are no simple yes or no answers. In fact, the very act of putting the question to the client often may be sufficient to help you avoid ethical compromise. Ultimately, the client will be thankful that you asked.

THE GLOBAL COMMUNITY

THE WORLD IS
NEXT DOOR

The only reasons not to pursue foreign clients early (or later) in your career are the problems of lack of focus and lack of funds. It takes more time and certainly more of an investment to develop relationships abroad. However, I've found that foreign organizations are very receptive to consulting help, particularly if you target your efforts carefully. Once your firm is well established, with both its repute and its resources in larger supply, international expansion is a logical and practical consideration. And since I first wrote this book in 1991, it's become far easier and cheaper to do business abroad.

TRAVELING FOR THE CLIENT

There is a hierarchy of requirements when picking targets for foreign concentration. These criteria apply irrespective of whether you are pursuing a target or opportunity or an organization is pursuing you. I've seen many situations in which what appeared to be a lucrative overseas consulting assignment turned out to be just the opposite because funds couldn't be taken out of the country (one poor soul wound up investing his consulting fee in local baskets, which he tried to import and sell in the States), or because a key client manager demanded a bribe (they're often listed on the books as "commissions" in Latin America), or because the client, after hearing all the consultant's ideas during the proposal process, decided to handle the issue internally.[1]

Here are some criteria to consider in seeking foreign clients:

Language

1. English as a first language: UK, Australia
2. English used as a business language: Germany, Hong Kong
3. English common: Italy, France
4. English spoken by elite: fourth world

Sophistication

1. Information-based, knowledge oriented: Japan, Korea
2. Emerging markets: India, Brazil
3. Labor-intensive: Indonesia, Malaysia

Currency

1. Stable and simple to convert: European Union
2. Uncertain fluctuations: Philippines
3. Difficult to exchange: Russia
4. Highly unstable: fourth world

The best way to acquire overseas clients is through strategic alliances. I've worked with people in Singapore and the United Kingdom whose skills and approaches are complemented by my own. They will often underwrite a trip for me, during which we make joint sales calls after I help them on a particular project. In this manner, I've developed work with Shell Singapore, Citibank in Singapore, and the *Singapore Straits Times*, and with Case Communications, Lucas Engineering, and

---

[1]In the Republic of China, all management ideas are considered the property of mankind, and thus belong to everyone. In Indonesia and the Philippines, plagiarism of published work from even major authors and publishers is widespread and tolerated, and copyright laws are virtually unenforceable. I'm finding entire books made available free online through "clubs" you can subscribe to run by people around the world. And in India, you're promised a share of the profits—but like the motion picture business, there are never any profits!

the British Standards Institute in the United Kingdom. These alliances are extremely productive because they combine current, fee-paying projects with the opportunity to develop new business.

> *Expertise: The globalization of economies combined with ever-advancing technology makes this the best and easiest time ever to work globally, whether in person or remotely.*

A second effective method is to pursue international work through existing multinational clients based in the United States (or based elsewhere with a U.S. operation as your primary client). Through an international division of Merck, I've had the opportunity to work and develop a reputation in the United Kingdom, Costa Rica, Hong Kong, and Brazil. (Note that when you pursue this avenue, some of the difficulties involved with the lower-priority targets are mitigated. For example, I don't worry about currency restrictions or instability in Brazil because I'm paid in the United States by the parent company.)

State Street Bank sent me around the world, first class, because it didn't want to give its global management team the perception that it was getting anything less than what the home office got (me).

Still another way to market internationally is to write for international publications. There are management journals in most countries, and they will usually accept articles written in English, and this is exceptionally easy online. (Many publish in English as well.) I've generated many contacts from writing for such publications in the United Kingdom, Brazil, Mexico, Singapore, Switzerland, Germany, and Hong Kong. As a rule, foreign clients place a much higher value on written papers and research than do Americans. I've published in a major German-language publication based in Switzerland. I was sought over the Internet and wrote and submitted the article via e-mail.

Finally, you can market overseas by seeking speaking opportunities at international conferences. This is no different from seeking domestic speaking assignments, except that you will often be asked to pay your own way. This is one reason why I advocate such tactics only after you have established yourself. The greater your reputation, the more likely it is that your expenses and fee will be covered, but even if they are not, the greater your growth, the more you are able to underwrite such marketing opportunities yourself.

Case Study

Perhaps the most effective way to acquire overseas clients is through a commercially published book, even when that book is solely in English. My books on sales acquisition, proposals, and fee structure have attracted clients in 20 countries in the last five years alone.

Several of my books have also been translated into German, Italian, Spanish, Korean, Arabic, Japanese, Russian, Polish, Portuguese, and Chinese—12 languages in all.

As noted earlier in this book, there are few marketing devices as powerful as a book that promotes your expertise through the force of your authority as an expert and thought leader. The allure of having the author work with a client in person overcomes any problems in terms of expense, currency translation, fees, and so on.

Given the increasing globalization of business, there may well be more opportunity for dramatic growth abroad than at home for entrepreneurial consultants. Million dollar consulting is just as lucrative when the components are pounds, euros, yen, and pesos. And once you've worked internationally, you have a tremendous marketing opportunity at home for your business literature, proposals, interviews, speeches, and articles.

You are now an international consultant who has worked in *x* number of countries. If you don't think that this carries instant credibility, try it out yourself. The first time a client asked me what I could possibly contribute to its benchmarking plans and I replied, "Let me give you an example from my work on innovation with the British Standards Institute, anticipating the expansion of the European Union," there wasn't a sound in the room other than the client's pen sliding out of his pocket to sign the contract.

> *Digression: The Internet and its peripherals—online communities, Instagram, Skype, webinars, teleconferences, discussion groups, and so forth—have made global consulting not merely available, but perhaps mandatory.*

In diversifying your client portfolio, international business now is a virtual "must." Make yourself known through publishing articles, blogs, newsletters, interviews, and so on.

No consultant who aspires to seven-figure status—anywhere in the world—should be focusing merely on domestic prospects.

DESIGNING YOUR OWN FUTURE

TAKING CONTROL OF YOUR FATE

My experiences in the consulting profession have led me to establish a very simple philosophy:

1. This is a relationship business.
2. Multidimensional growth provides for high-quality, enduring relationships.
3. There is no limit to the firm's—or your own—income from those relationships, and you must help yourself if you are to help others.

BEING NUMBER ONE ON YOUR OWN TERMS

At this point, you may be asking, "How can it be that simple? After all, if everyone is trying to establish those relationships, aren't we all back in the old competitive-commodity ball game, trying to prove that a relationship with me is somehow superior to one with the other consultants?

"What about all the people reading this book? Won't we all look the same going out there to try to do the same thing?"

> **Expertise: It's what not life deals you, it's how you deal with life.**

I'd like to respond to these concerns by drawing on a consulting assignment as an avatar. I had been working with a large specialty chemicals firm that found itself a diminishing "number three" among its competitors. Whereas it had once had hopes of overtaking its two much larger rivals, it found itself facing the possibility of smaller organizations chipping away at some of its traditional business. The firm's strategy team was divided: Do we invest the substantial resources needed to make a run at the leaders, or do we solidify our position as number three, fighting off challenges to that spot? Neither position was terribly attractive. After all, overtaking the leaders would take years, flawless performance, and a great deal of luck. However, to remain number three was to manage an "also ran," and it's hard to attract, retain, and motivate people in an acknowledged "loser."

The answer, of course, was breathtakingly simple: to be number one on the company's own terms. The company redefined itself in terms of what it did better than anyone else in the industry—including its larger competitors—and established a vision and mission of being number one in the market and under the conditions it had defined for itself.

I call this "taking a sharp right," discussed in Chapter 9.

Strategically, it's quite simple: You don't allow the competition to define the playing field or to write the rules. You redefine and reinvent yourself.

When I began my own practice leading up to my current firm, I was told unequivocally that I couldn't generate over $300,000 in income and that I would have to add people and facilities, probably using outside investors. I was also advised that I would be swallowed whole unless I specialized in some market segment as protection against "the big guys."

> **It's extraordinarily difficult, if not impossible, to break the paradigms when someone else is defining the paradigms.**

Now listen up: those pieces of advice probably were accurate for someone who chose to play by the existing, conventional rules. However, I defined what I wanted to become. Under my rules, such as the three listed at the beginning of this section, traditional conditions didn't apply. I wasn't competing with anyone because I was going to be *numero uno* as a unique, boutique-type consulting firm that did business with Fortune 1000 organizations and their brethren.

If you use the other person's equipment, play on his field, use his rules, and employ his officials, you're going to lose the game.

The key is *not* to outthink your competitors, because doing so is unlikely and overwhelmingly tiring. The key is to *have* no competitors because you have defined your own playing field and written your own rules (taken the sharp right). The specialty chemical firm did this, avoiding the suffering of myriad organizations in similar straits that have vainly tried to play by others' rules.

I did it, made a fortune, and emerged to write this book (and this fifth edition) because I determined how I would play the game. However, the idea itself isn't mine. It's practiced by the most successful business people and entrepreneurs in the world.

> *Don't worry about being smarter than your competitors, because any competent competitor will be working just as hard to be smarter than you. The trick is to have no competitors.*
>
> —Warren Buffett, CEO, Berkshire Hathaway[1]

Once you've established who you are and how you'll play, concerns about the competition and "Isn't everyone doing this?" evaporate. You'll always need to be cognizant of what your competitors are doing, but you'll never need to be *concerned* about what they're doing.

Another consultant and I were with the CEO of a company that is a client of both our firms. We were returning from a daylong fishing trip off Montauk, Long Island, with two of our kids. There were five tuna in the hold, and Bob and I were very contentedly reflecting on the lives we had carved out in this business.

---

[1] An "oldie but goodie," quoted in *Emory Business Magazine*, Emory University, Atlanta, GA 30322, and cited in *Boardroom Reports* 20(16) (August 15, 1991), p. 2.

I remarked that client relationships didn't get much better than this. He pointed out something that never ceases to astonish me: "The relationship is one thing," he said, "but it's exploiting the opportunity it presents that sets people like us apart. Most consultants I know are pretty good at scrambling around and overcoming setbacks, enabling them to survive. But very, very few know how to exploit success, and know how to prosper."

Maybe out there off the continental shelf we were suffering terminal male bonding. However, Bob's observation makes just as much sense to me here on dry land.

Each of us has to transcend the mere survival reflex and understand that surviving is not the point. *Prospering*, to me, is the ability to meet personal and family goals through the income, wisdom, and experiences generated by a thriving business. The multidimensional growth I've been espousing doesn't pertain only to your professional life, which is why I advocate life balance so strongly. As you grow personally, you grow professionally, and as you grow professionally, you grow personally. This is why this business is so wonderful.

As you prosper, you will begin to create what I call a *body of work*.[2] By this I merely mean that the combination of the types of projects you are best known for, your publishing and/or speeches, your pro bono efforts, and your general visibility will represent those facets of your business at which you have become most adept. Nearer to the beginning of your career, you will have had to deliberately establish your unique, number-one-in-the-field brand and strategy. As your career blossoms, your body of work will speak for you. By the very nature of what you've accomplished, you will be considered the best at what you do, and your clients and prospects will see you in this distinguishing light.

A FLEXIBLE FUTURE

The future of the firm then becomes whatever you wish it to be. What will become of Summit Consulting Group, Inc.? I'm still not sure. My kids won't be going into the business, apparently, because one, after majoring

[2]When a different publisher expressed interest in one of my books, the acquisitions editor told me that I had "a nice shelf." After a stunned moment, I learned that she was referring to the solid sales of my other books. I didn't know whether to be disappointed or relieved. I'll try not to be so obscure here.

in broadcast journalism, was an Emmy Award–nominated producer at MTV and is now an independent producer, and one, after majoring in drama and gaining a master of fine arts to teach as well, is adept both in front of and behind the camera.

I don't plan to retire because I can do what I'm doing—consulting, speaking, writing, and being *the* thought leader in my field—without age constraints, although I can become more selective, into the indefinite future.

Will a larger firm buy me out? Possibly—I'm sure there's an amount of money somewhere that constitutes an offer I can't refuse. Perhaps people with whom I work or even clients will take over the firm. *Frankly, it's a matter of no great importance to me.*

My firm is and always has been a means to an end. That end has been the well-being of my family, the pursuit of our interests, and what Maslow cryptically termed "self-actualization." You see, the future of the firm isn't so important; it's the future of the founder that's crucial! Your body of work defines more than your company's projects and positioning. It defines your values and your contribution to the environment around you. I have since completely lost the source, but I remember Peter Drucker saying once, "An organization is not like a tree or an animal, successful merely by dint of perpetuating the species. An organization is successful based on the contribution it makes to the outside environment."

> *Expertise: Remember that money is fuel for life and that the real wealth is discretionary time.*

For an individual to establish a consulting firm that contributes to the improvement of its clients' conditions, to the enhanced productivity and quality of their people, to the increased profitability of their operations, and therefore to the increased well-being of their customers and stockholders is an ultimate contribution to the outside environment. And if, in so doing, you personally achieve success through the realization of your personal life goals, then you are in rarefied air indeed.

How many of us are in a position to meet our personal and professional goals—and to amass true wealth—through a constant process of helping others to meet *their* personal and professional goals and enhance *their* wealth?

Professional consulting isn't just a wonderful profession; it's a wonderful way of life. And if, in that pursuit, you make millions, who can object?

CHAPTER 13

CREATING A COMPANY

BUT WHAT KIND?

I will leave the technical aspects of creating a company—and they are important, I'm not dismissing them—to a separate chapter. For now, I want to focus on one of the most important decisions you'll have to make about your future: Will you be a solo practitioner, or will you employ resources?

I mean "employ" in the true sense of salaried employees with health benefits, retirement plans, sick days, expense accounts, and so forth. (I've discussed subcontractors, alliance partners, and outsourcing elsewhere.) Some people believe that a staff is the default position for growth. It ain't necessarily so.

SOLO VS. HERD

There are only two models for creating and growing your business. As I've been saying, the key to consulting is to simplify!

Solo Practitioner

The solo practitioner is the person who works alone without aid staff. He or she may utilize others via subcontracting or outsourcing, but there is no payroll other than for the principal (and, occasionally, a spouse or children whom it may make sense to "hire" for benefits purposes—check with your tax accountant for best practices).

> *Expertise: The goal of a solo practitioner is to extract all the money possible annually from the business, to maximize payments with pretax money, and to maximize personal income and well-being yearly. There is no intent to sell the business, although intellectual property may be sold separately.*

There are both benefits and disadvantages to a solo life.

Benefits

- You don't need an office outside of your home.
- Expenses are tightly controlled—no one else can spend money in the business.
- You have far less paperwork and reporting.
- You can design a retirement plan (e.g., SEP IRA in the United States) that is tailored for you and doesn't have to be shared with or funded for others.
- There are no personnel issues, such as theft, poor productivity, or internecine warfare.
- There is no training requirement.
- There is no turnover that threatens account maintenance or even retention.
- There are less peripheral costs: insurance, equipment, and so forth.
- There is far less distraction.

Disadvantages

- If you have high, ongoing affiliation needs you will get desperately lonely.
- There is no one intimately involved in your business to act as a sounding board or counterpoint.
- You will have more difficulty trying to handle concurrent projects.

- You must do the menial and trivial tasks yourself if you can't outsource or subcontract them.
- If you become ill—or just don't feel like getting out of bed—you will probably lose business and definitely lose momentum.
- Travel will be higher for you, personally, until you develop a strong brand.
- You may suffer insecurity (though a client seldom cares about this) by having to admit that you're an independent and not head of a larger entity.
- You will often work at home where there can be major distractions.

Owner of a Firm with Employees

This is someone who builds infrastructure and staff and invests in the business with the intent of eventually selling it or handing it off to family as a legacy. The staff will usually include sales, delivery, and administrative people and will add layers of management if the company becomes large enough.

> *Expertise: The goal of a business owner with employees is to someday sell the business for a multiple of its revenues, profit, or EBITDA.*[1] *Hence, the owner must reinvest in the company each year for growth, often limiting his or her own income to such needs.*

Having a company with employees also has both benefits and disadvantages.

Benefits

- You don't have to do trivial work, you can delegate.
- There are resources to cover multiple concurrent projects.
- You don't have to be physically present.

---

[1]EBITDA is earnings before interest, taxes, depreciation, and amortization.

- Others, presumably, can generate new business.
- There is diverse expertise around you.
- Others may be impressed by the number of people.
- Creativity and healthy debate are stimulated.
- Mutual learning and best practices emerge.
- Personal travel is lessened.
- You can grow rapidly if properly staffed.

Disadvantages

- There will be arguments, envy, jealousy, and issues requiring your intervention. You will often have to be "referee."
- You must "share the wealth" via competitive salaries, bonuses, and benefit plans.
- You can be sued for anything from wrongful termination to sexual harassment, and from unfair work practices to discrimination.[2]
- There can be theft of intellectual property, material, and even clients.
- It is often very difficult to fire nonproductive employees, and expensive to do so. (This is especially true in Europe and some parts of Asia.)
- You may well wind up to be the sole rainmaker, because it's very hard to hire people who can generate new business, since those people would normally do so for themselves.

All right, you should get the idea. Basically, the solo practitioner is putting enough away yearly to satisfy lifestyle needs and provide for retirement when the firm will have no intrinsic worth without the solo's continuing it. The owner of a staffed business will sacrifice each year to build an eventual salable entity that will take care of a retirement with a wonderful lifestyle.

Obviously, I've made my choice. But I'm going to go into depth on each option in order to help you make an informed decision. The key is this:

[2]I didn't say you'd be guilty of them, just that you'd be sued, which happens with alarming frequency and costs a fortune in defense.

You can't act one way and build the other model. That is, you can't have a firm with employees and try to solely maximize your personal income annually, and you can't be a solo and expect that you can sell the business in X year. Picture either of those with one leg on each side of a crevice that is rapidly becoming a chasm as your option to switch to the other disappears.

THE SOLO SUPREME

Having described the cases above, my unequivocal recommendation for those starting out and for veterans assessing their future is to go solo. I'll admit that in some cases and for some content you need staff, but that is not the default model for growth and happiness.

I've run my Million Dollar Clubs for years, and 80 percent or more of the participants have been solo practitioners, and from the other 20 percent we hear about 90 percent of the grievances. A key person has left, the principal is the only rainmaker, the staff is overdelivering, the bureaucracy is too thick, opportunities are overlooked—it is a litany of woes.

The reasons for this are twofold:

1. The aforementioned Michelangelo Factor (see Chapter 9). You should so what you love doing and are great at. The entire staff is not going to be as passionate as you about what they are doing, and many are just looking for a reliable paycheck or the passion of a minor part of the business (e.g., delivery). The staff members don't have "skin in the game" and don't act with an owner's mentality. Hence, slacking off when you're not watching (and many of these people are on the road or work at home) or failing to follow up promptly have little impact on their income, and in fact the infractions may actually improve their day. You would never do that because your name is on the door.

2. Excellent rainmakers, vital to a staffed, growing business, are exceedingly rare. Those who are adept at both sales and delivery are already trying to run their own entrepreneurial practice. Why would such people work for you when they could be landing business for themselves and simply subcontracting delivery? Consequently, the probability is that you will have to continue generating new business while returning home on weekends to "feed the baby chicks."

Case Study

A good friend of mine bought out his firm's founder and built a $6 million dollar consulting business. When it was time for him to get out, he was overjoyed to get an offer from the huge KPMG consulting firm.

However, since he was the sole rainmaker, they asked him to sign a contract to stay for two years and become part of KPMG. Several of us warned him not to do this, but he said, "They're making me an instant partner, I'll go through some training, and in two years I'm free, it's a great deal."

Two months after the sale, he was miserable. He was a "partner" with no staff and a tiny office, and he had to go through training as if he were a rookie MBA. No one thought of him as a peer in management, and the heat was on for his old firm to generate increased business.

He had a heart attack not long after, fortunately survived it, and even more fortunately was able to get out of his contract.

Expertise: The only thing worse than shedding sweat and blood for your business is shedding sweat and blood **for someone else's business.**

I work regularly with former boutique firm owners who have shed staff the way someone would shed weight in an exercise regimen and brag to me about how freeing it is (as if I hadn't recommended it)! There's nothing wrong with a part-time administrative assistant or researcher, but with subcontracting and outsourcing and work streamlining, you can live without full-time staff.

Warning: Don't kid yourself by using subcontractors for 100 percent of their time. The IRS in the United States has very strict rules about when someone is a full-time employee no matter what you call them or how you treat them. For example, they can't make more than 80 percent of their annual income from you as a single source. You can learn more about this to protect yourself on sites such as this:

> http://www.irs.gov/Businesses/Small-Businesses-&-Self-Employed/Independent-Contractor-Self-Employed-or-Employee

As solos, we need three elements—market need, competency, and passion—to ensure success, as you can see in Figure 13-1. The problem with having a staff is that not only does their passion and competency differ from yours, they are not as adept at developing and fulfilling market need. There are three kinds of need:

1. Preexisting need, typically in "evergreen" areas such as strategy, leadership, sales, and so forth.

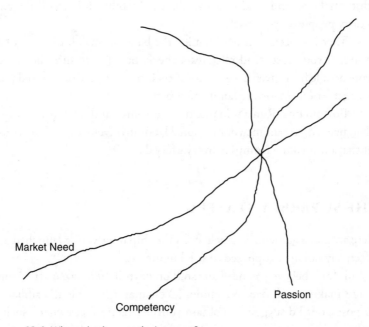

Figure 13-1 Where do these paths intersect?

2. Created need, which is identified by asking "Why?" when a prospect exhibits a "want." For example, the client says, "We want a strategy retreat," and when you ask why, the real need is revealed, which is "more consistent decision making globally within our strategic framework," which is not solved by a retreat.

3. Anticipated need, meaning that you suggest that factors such as globalization, shifting demographics, and changing social mores will alter the prospect's thinking. An example would be making targeted efforts to sell to the growing Hispanic population in the United States or the advent of telehealth, where diagnosis and treatment can be done remotely.

If you have market need and passion, but no competency, you'll lose to competitors. If you have competency and passion, but no market need, you're irrelevant—no one wants to hear your message. If you have market need and competency but no passion, you have a nine-to-five job.

When two or more partners start a business, that's one thing, with common "skin" in the game and common passion and competence. But even partners often split up as a company grows. For an individual, taking substantial risks and seeking, above all, sustainability, it makes little sense to carry people on your back.

That is especially true of family, the bane of small businesses of all nature. If you must, send relatives a check, but do not hire them. Too many people have given away a part of their business and/or created poor management by involving family members.

Bottom line: Run a solo practice, outsource and subcontract wisely when needed, streamline your personal labor involvement, and never forget that rainmaking trumps delivery every day.

THE SUPERBLY STAFFED

Here are some guidelines to help even the ship once you're launched and effectively sailing, as opposed to still building it.

I don't believe you need any staff on payroll, full- or part-time until you're making well over $2 million. You may need this for affiliation purposes, but I'd suggest you obtain your interactions elsewhere, such as health clubs, civic activities, sports, professional associations, and so forth.

Or, get a dog.

You only need an outside office if there are too many distractions and too little space at home. Turn a spare bedroom into a formal office if you can, and don't expect it to do double duty when the relatives visit on holidays. Otherwise, you can rent space in commonly shared offices for very small amounts monthly. They usually include a receptionist, conference room, copier, and so on. (Some people, even with space at home, work better by "going to the office" regularly, and that's fine, and even provides some of those affiliation needs.)

Here are the resources you need for not merely staffing your office but creating your independent life:

1. Financial

You need three kinds of financial help, from tactical to strategic, never found in one person and seldom found in one firm:

- A bookkeeper, who will take monthly deposits, pay stubs, check stubs, bank statements, and similar documents and reconcile your checkbook, provide a general ledger, and show you income and expenses by category. I suggest you code your income categories to track performance—for example, consulting, coaching, speaking, product sales, and so on.
- Tax professionals who complete your annual taxes on federal, state, and local levels, as needed. They will take the inputs from your bookkeeper and advise you of potential deadlines, penalties, and escrow needs. These days all filing is electronic.
- Financial planning. You will need people to apprise you, often in conjunction with your attorney, about estates, wills, powers of attorney, investments, and similar matters. They should never have products to sell, only advice.[3]

All of these people charge by the hour (tell them never to read my books), and you can usually acquire referrals from one to another in the field.

---

[3] If you ask an insurance expert what to purchase for long-term security, he or she will tell you insurance, which is usually ridiculous, and will then try to sell you a policy.

> *Expertise: Do everything legal to avoid high taxes, but never, ever try to evade taxes.*

2. Legal

As opposed to the finance area, try to find a single firm (*not* a lone wolf like you working solo) that can handle all of the following. Lawyers also charge by the hour, and they are not expensive if you're not in court.

- *Corporate.* This is someone who can create the type of business you need legally (I suggest an LLC or subchapter C in the United States, which flows through your personal tax return.) You basically need this attorney only at start-up or if you make later changes.
- *Patent and trademark.* This lawyer helps gain federal protection for your intellectual property, as in ™ or ®, and is essential to protect these assets. *Do not* attempt to do this online for $60! That's like making investments with a guy on the corner in a raincoat.
- *Litigator.* Occasionally you will be sued in a litigious world, or feel the need to sue someone. More commonly, you'll need a legal letter as a "shot across the bow" to some offender who is plagiarizing, not paying you, or being slanderous. This calls for a shark.
- *Estate planning.* As mentioned earlier, your financial and legal experts usually collaborate with your wills and estate needs.

I think you can see why there's a synergy when one firm has the capability to represent you in these varied areas.

3. Insurance

You will need the following, for which you may or may not need to utilize separate agents. (I'm omitting the obvious, such as health, life, property.)

- *Errors and omissions insurance, commonly called malpractice.* This is essential in case you are sued over bad advice or implementation. Some firms will not accept a proposal from you without evidence of an in-force E&O policy.
- *Liability.* In business, this insurance covers you when you use a projector and someone trips over the cord and sues the conference organizers, the projector manufacturer, the hotel, the people who set up the room—and you. It is vitally needed.[4]

Also consider long-term care (LTC) insurance, which is least expensive when you are young and can provide for home care should you require it in the future. Also, disability insurance is a must because it, too, is least costly at younger ages, *and you are much more likely to be disabled than you are to die during your active career.* Make sure you obtain a disability policy that pays you *until you can return to your regular and current work, and not until you can return to* **any** *work.*

4. Office and Business Needs

- *Visuals.* Find superb people who can provide:
  Graphics and design for books and products
  Video for products and marketing collateral
  Still photography for publicity shots
- *Printing and publishing.* Find a good local shop or a chain such as Kinko's or Sir Speedy or Staples that can provide high-speed, fast creation of hard-copy needs. Many resources can print on demand locally so that you don't have to ship. (This can be very important when crossing borders.)
- *Transportation.* Find a limo company that can drive you to the airport, pick up visiting clients, or take you around town. (I know many of you are thinking Uber, which I often use, but not when I want a car waiting. My feeling is the limo should wait for me, I shouldn't wait for the limo.) Internationally, Carey Limousine provides great service and will centrally bill you. If you have several

---

[4]The combination of a formal corporate entity plus proper insurance will protect your personal assets with a "firewall" in almost all cases.

appointments in one city, it is far easier to have a single car at your disposal—one that you don't have to drive and park—rather than trying to catch taxis or Uber repeatedly.

- *House or office sitters.* If you live alone, or if you take your family on some of your trips, you'll need dependable people to watch the pets, get the mail, tend the garden, and so forth. We prefer a "lived-in" house while we're away, so we have people who move in while we're gone. This provides tremendous peace of mind and far more security. I've actually had them ship me material that I had forgotten to bring with me.

- *Shipping.* Create a FedEx and/or UPS account for urgent shipping. *Note:* We send our luggage ahead of us via FedEx rather than risk it being lost and waiting in line at the baggage carousel. We also avoid weight restrictions, which even apply to first class on some airlines (especially internationally).

- *Miscellaneous office help.* You will need people on occasion to ship large quantities, or to do some Internet research, or to move things. Hire students by the hour.

5. Internet and Electronics

In our profession, with ideal buyers being corporate executives or smaller business owners, websites are credibility statements but not sales tools. I know that's heresy, and every "Internet marketing expert" in the world (there are approximately 4.7 million or, as the Australians are fond of saying, "Every man and his dog") will tell you otherwise. Ignore SEO (search engine optimization) and overly elaborate sites *assuming your idea buyers are those mentioned.* They buy through peer referral and public IP (books and speeches). Find a website you like, ask who designed it (it's often on the bottom of the screen), and choose a reasonable option. All of these people charge by the hour. I'd advise *not* to use someone in Bangladesh or the Philippines, but rather someone more local and subject to U.S. (or your local) laws.

You may want a blog, as well, as part of your marketing gravity, and you can set that up with the same people. Just ensure you can make all entries yourself: text, photos, video, and audio.

That is your superbly staffed company without a single employee! It's a lean and mean wealth machine.

THE RAINMAKER AS ENDANGERED SPECIES

It's important to appreciate just how valuable it is to be able to generate new business, a phenomenon often termed *rainmaking*.

Virtually everyone who is successful as a solo practitioner is a rainmaker. Eventually our old contacts dry up, our retainer with the company we left runs out, existing clients exhaust their potential, and serendipity deserts us. At that point we have to generate new business.

If you examine most boutique firms with full-time employees, over 90 percent of the time you'll find a sole rainmaker—the founder and owner—creating new business while the staff (the farmers) implement. No matter how much incentive or training you may provide these farmers, they are not going out hunting for animals that possess teeth and talons—they are going to irrigate the corn and reap the wheat.

You will find multiple rainmakers in larger firms due to size and growth needs. But for every rainmaker in a McKinsey or Bain or Deloitte (and they are usually the partners), you'll find dozens of implementers dependent on their rainmaking and paid far, far less.

Case Study

I was coaching a man named Phil who lived in the Midwest. He had a firm of eight people. He told me that he couldn't buy the Mercedes he desired because the prior year's results were less than forecast and he could not pay full bonuses to his eight employees and, you guessed it, he felt guilty buying an expensive car under those circumstances.

Mind you, the investment and risk were his, yet he felt beholden to these eight people. Phil was 48, smoked, was about 50 pounds overweight, and traveled 75 percent of the time. Whenever we talked, he was in a hotel room or on the way to or from one.

> *At one point he owed me some money for his next ten-*
> *ure with me, and he hadn't paid, so I called his personal*
> *number. His wife answered and told me that Phil had*
> *died of a heart attack—in a Boston hotel room.*

If you need help delivering business, fine: subcontract or outsource, or hire the minimum staff needed to fulfill delivery needs. But never staff up beyond those needs, and try never to have permanent staff. If you do intend to grow as a firm and eventually sell, *you must have successful rainmakers on board to demonstrate that the business is not dependent on you as the sole rainmaker.* I would estimate a ratio of 1:10—one rainmaker creating business sufficient to keep 10 farmers busy in those fields.

But as stated earlier, rainmakers are hard to find and harder to keep because, like you, they are capable of making their own way. If anyone tries to tell you—or lay a guilt trip on your new car—that delivery is the key to client success, I'd remind you and them that delivery people are more common than garden weeds, and rainmakers are rarer than a Sasquatch.

We need to examine why this is so that you don't make these foolish mistakes:

- Thinking you can train delivery people to become salespeople
- Thinking you can generate sales by good work and waiting by the phone
- Thinking you can readily find and hire rainmakers
- Thinking you can easily create remuneration for rainmakers
- Thinking you, yourself, are a natural and don't need further skills to sell new business

> *Expertise: This is the marketing business, not the consulting business, and it requires the creation of need amongst ideal clients* **and the sale of your particular services to fill that need.**

The behaviors required for sales in this business are shown in Figure 13-2: a high degree of assertiveness, a slightly lesser but high degree of persuasiveness, moderate patience..., and slightly below average attention to detail. Underlying this is a relatively high but not fanatical ethical standard.

The rainmaker needs high assertiveness to ask for the sale, higher than persuasiveness, because asking for the sale may jeopardize relationships, and the sale has to be seen as paramount over the relationship. (Achieve the task, and don't worry about being liked.) There is a need for some acceptance of repetition, or patience, because many aspects of a sale are always the same (e.g., see my proposal template in Chapter 5). But each client is different, requiring agility (the content in the proposal template changes by client). We don't seek too much attention to detail because rainmakers have to be "big picture" thinkers. The details can be left to the delivery people.[5]

Underpinning this is an ethically strong base so that the individual is seen as neither slickster nor zealot.

Thus, in addition to what we regularly think of as sales skills, traits such as closing language, relationship creation, product knowledge, and so forth, we also have these behavioral essentials. They are hare to find in that precise profile, *and almost impossible to find in people who are excellent at delivery*, which requires low assertiveness, high patience, and high attention to detail.

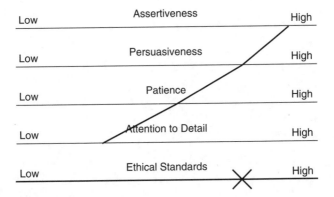

Figure 13-2 Ideal sales behaviors

---

[5]By the way, this is why it's ludicrous to promote the best salespeople to sales manager, or the best athlete to manager, because the behaviors required are substantially different.

That's why I eventually got out of the training business because, while I could do it, I wasn't crazy about it and never passionate about it. I enjoy the thrill of the hunt far more than the cultivation of the fields.

Once you have a strong brand, you're a thought leader, and there is viral talk about you, rainmaking declines in importance because people are regularly coming to you. If that's where you are today, fine.

But if you're starting a business, or intend to dramatically grow your business, or expect to change markets and buyers, you need to be your own chief rainmaker, and the skills, which can be taught, need to be augmented through coaching for the behaviors required.

You'll know whether you or anyone else is successful in this pursuit because you'll be able to see the rain.

LEVERAGE

MORE OUTPUT FOR
LESS INPUT

Leverage: Using something to maximum advantage.

Give me a lever and a spot to stand and I can move the world.

—Archimedes

The need for solo practitioners (and boutique firm owners) to create leverage or scalability (to easily change in size) is conspecific to growth. That's because of the S-curve (Figure 14-1).

As you can see in Figure 14-1, organizations and practices achieve dramatic growth once the basics are mastered (seeing only economic buyers, writing proposals with options, populating the Accelerant Curve, and so forth). However, eventually growth slows, threatening a plateau. Plateaus, because of the laws of entropy, will eventually erode.

Expertise: The time to leap to the next stage of growth is prior to plateauing in order to build on current acceleration.

The X marks the spot where you should take off, because it's far, far harder to gain the next level from a plateau when you are coasting, not accelerating, and when you have a far longer distance to traverse.

I call the false comfort of the growth plateau the success trap. You believe you're successful, right into decline. (A buddy of mine from college

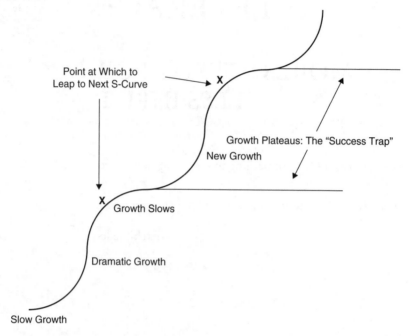

Figure 14-1 S-curve dynamics

told me at the end of his four-year marriage, "I was a happily married man until she told me she was leaving.")

ALLIANCES

Alliances are formed with equal partners (despite the size of the other firm) where the formula looks, metaphorically, like this: 1 + 1= 150. If you would have created a project for $100,000 and your partner would have as well, then taking on a joint project for $200,000 makes no sense, but a $400,000 project does.

Remember Cuba Gooding in the old movie *Jerry McGuire* constantly demanding, "Show me the money!" He didn't believe that other party was sincere or real until he saw the money. Now combine that with a classic commercial for fast-food giant Wendy's that demanded, "Where's the beef?"

These are superb criteria to apply when considering an alliance partner.

Most alliances are fairly brief, created for a single project or single client. They occur most naturally when two noncompeting sets of skills and/or behaviors are required to best meet client needs and create a competitive edge. The longest alliance I ever had was with brilliant speaker and coach Patricia Fripp, with whom I created The Odd Couple® franchise and ran workshops and created products for about a decade.

Don't allow yourself to become embroiled in theoretical alliances and conceptual constructs. These are liminal, never quite proceeding to the starting line (let alone the finish line). They are intellectual games in which both sides speculate about who would do what to whom *if a proper client came along for an alliance.*

"Show me the money."

"Where's the beef?"

Here are the rules for alliances. For methodology about how to share fees when these come to fruition, see Chapter 4 on fees and the formula therein (50 percent for acquisition, 30 percent for methodology, 20 percent for delivery).

1. Make sure you are both professionally and personally compatible. You needn't be close friends, but you need to respect the other party and trust him or her with your wallet (and vice versa). The other party's values and operating beliefs must be similar to your own.

2. Never, ever make the relationship legal. Do not comingle funds. Don't change logos, share trademarks, or jointly create intellectual property. The alliance may be short-lived, or your partner may sell the business or retire. Breaking business legal entanglements are as hard as divorces on the body and soul.

3. Commit everything to writing: fee apportionment, who collects, who delivers, who handles client inquiries, who pays expenses, and so forth. You don't need an attorney, just a letter of agreement you both create and sign. Make clear how repeat business, testimonials, and referrals will be handled.

4. Apply the alliance strictly to the matter at hand, not open-ended. You can always renew it if it's needed, which is a lot easier than abrogating one you no longer want or need.

5. Have at least four meetings in person with your alliance principal, and one or two with his or her people if the person has employees. It's valuable to interact in very different circumstances, such as meals, beginning of the day, end of the day, and so forth. Call the office, visit the website, kick the tires.

6. Don't share more information than is needed for that particular client. There is no reason to share client lists, or bankers, or prospects. Alliances in this business are for *specific, short-term needs*, not forever. Don't give away what you may some day live to regret.

7. Check on your partner. Don't assume that the partner's part of the project is going swimmingly. Ask the *client* how the entire project is going—that's the litmus test of how your partner is doing.

You can create tremendous leverage through partners if you are judicious in selecting them and crisp in organizing and monitoring the relationship.

Two further issues:

- Don't allow the partner's fee practices to undermine your own. If the partner is using hourly billing, either arrange to bill separately or convince him or her to do it your way. Never partner with anyone engaged in hourly fees or you'll lose money.

- Don't allow your brand to be subsumed in the partner's. Retain your business cards and logos and use them throughout. Even if you're allied with a far larger operation, retain your image and brand integrity. Have your name on all key documents, from proposals to collateral, from reports to expense reimbursement.

In 30 years, I've had perhaps three worthwhile alliances. You may have more, but don't expect these—in reality, not conceptualization—to be plentiful if they are good ones.

SUBCONTRACTING

Subcontractors are excellent sources of leverage. They usually always work by the hour or the day (don't mention my books to them). The love the delivery aspect of our work, so their motivation and performance are usually quite high.

Try to build up a "bank" of these people. Here are some best practices:

- Use familiar people whom you can trust. Direct most of your work to them as a reward for their quality and dependability.
- Always have backups. Your primary people might have conflicting job requests or personal priorities.
- Apprise your client that you'll be using subcontractors so there are no surprises.
- Brief the people you use thoroughly on both the client's business and the needs of this particular project.
- Always give *specific and clear* tasks and assignments. Never request that subcontractors "set up and run focus groups," but rather to run a group from 9 to 11 on April 14 at the client's office with a particular client contact.
- Prohibit your subcontractors from engaging in any sales or marketing discussions on their own behalf with the client's people, including asking for references and contacts.
- Create a clear agreement on how expenses will be charged, reimbursed, for what kinds of expenditures, and the timing thereof. (One of my subcontractors had a nasty fight with her boyfriend on the opposite coast and ran up hundreds of dollars of phone charges that she promptly passed on to me.)
- Create a clear fee and payment schedule. If the fee is by day, specify whether it's for an entire day of work or partial. If it's by the hour, specify the maximum number of hours you'll accept for any given aspect of delivery.
- Make it clear that the IP, trademarks, copyrights, and so forth remain solely in your ownership, and that any materials provided for the subcontractor's use must be returned immediately upon request. (You may choose to let your frequently used people retain certain items for convenience.)

If you are not prudent in selecting subcontractors, you run the risk of spending more time than you're saving by using them on such matters as reviewing their work, correcting their errors, and worrying about their honesty. Subcontractors have been known to solicit business for themselves. (I've often had Carey Limousine drivers who give me their cards and offer a better deal if I don't go through their central booking function.)

Here is a sample contract you may want to consider:

Subcontracting Agreement

The provisions in this document will govern our relationship while Joan Larson conducts work on behalf of Summit Consulting Group, Inc. at the Acme Company.

1. You will identify yourself as a subcontractor for Summit Consulting Group, Inc. You will not hand out personal business cards or talk about your personal practice at any time.

2. You will do no promotion for your personal business at any time.

3. You will implement according to instructions provided by Summit Consulting Group, Inc., and will not agree to any altered, modified, or new conditions with the client. Any such client requests will be passed on to Alan Weiss for decision.

4. You expenses will be reimbursed monthly, within 10 days of receipt. You will turn in expenses on the last day of the month. Reimbursement will include airfare at discounted coach rates, taxis, meals (not to exceed $75 per day), hotel room at the Marriott Downtown, and tips. All other expenses, including phone, recreation, laundry, etc., are not reimbursable.

5. Your payment rate will be $1,500 per day on-site, and $750 per day off-site, as directed and approved by Summit Consulting Group, Inc. You agree that the work assigned to you will be completed within 60 days with a cap of 15 actual days on-site and a cap of 4 days off-site. You will complete the work below, even if it requires additional days, but payment will cap at the levels noted:

    • Conduct 12 focus groups as assigned for 90 minutes each

    • Analyze and produce reports on each group in progress

- Analyze and produce a report for the total group experience
- Meet with Alan Weiss at the conclusion to discuss the final report

Fees will be paid within 10 days of the submission of your time reports at the conclusion of each month, providing that all individual focus group progress reports have been submitted.

6. All work created and all materials provided you are the sole property of Summit Consulting Group, Inc. You may not cite this organization as your client in conversation or in writing, and all communications with Summit Consulting Group, Inc. and Acme are confidential and subject to the nondisclosure agreement you have signed.

7. You will conduct yourself professionally, observe business ethics and courtesy, and meet the work requirements above. Failure to do so in the opinion of Acme and/or Summit Consulting Group, Inc. will result in termination of this agreement and cessation of payment.

Your notarized signature below indicates full agreement and compliance with these requirements:

_____ Notary, including signature, date, and seal:

Joan Larson

Date: _____

There are three certain ways to decrease your labor intensity: streamline your business model, transfer work to the client, and use subcontractors. The intelligent and frequent use of high-quality help at sensible rates might create slightly less monetary profit for you but will create far greater wealth: a dramatic increase in your discretionary time.

Be aware that a subcontractor who derives more than 80 percent of his or her income and who works at the direction of a sole manager is usually considered an employee by the IRS, thereby subject to withholding tax, sharing in benefits, and so forth. You can find the criteria on the IRS site on the web, at this writing:

> http://www.irs.gov/Businesses/Small-Businesses-&-Self-Employed/Independent-Contractor-Self-Employed-or-Employee

Now let's look at another excellent type of external help that you might be taking for granted.

OUTSOURCING

What I'm calling outsourcing is actually a network of profession services providers upon whom you can rely. As a solo, they are vital to your ability to leverage by reducing your time and providing good ideas.

Here are some of the areas you should consider for ongoing relationships. Note that you're only paying for performance, not engaging anyone who requires cash flow considerations.

1. *Internet.* You need someone who can set up your website, blog, and other Internet needs and make changes as needed on a quick and efficient basis. If you heed my advice about not needing a world-class site, then you don't need a world-class web company. Just make sure you can have adjustments made quickly and you can add text, audio, and video to your blog at your convenience. If you try to design and create these yourself, even if you have knowledge in the area, it will suck all the oxygen out of your office! Hire someone—they all charge by the hour. Just ask for references and work samples.

2. *Design.* On occasion, you'll need graphics created for some writing you're doing, or slides created for a presentation. Have a good designer take care of this. Just send your ideas over in rough form. Someone told me that I could get "incredible slide software for just $500," but the time it would take for me to master it and use

it well would be prohibitive, and the result *still* wouldn't be as good as the professional's.[1]

3. *Printing.* Use a firm such as Sir Speedy, or Print Shops, or Kinko's (or even Staples), for your hard-copy printing. Most will print at another store if it's closer to your intended distribution point. They can keep your masters on file electronically. All of my letterhead and business cards have been provided by these sources.

4. *Limousine.* Even in an "Uber world," there are times you want a car waiting to pick up guests, or fetch you from the airport, or take you around town on a rainy day. I use a local company for airport and train stations trips and Carey International for other cities around the world. All of them will bill centrally once a month. If you have an account, the reservations are expedited.

5. *Shipping.* I'd suggest having both a UPS and a FedEx account, so that you can ship inexpensively if time isn't urgent, and reliably nationally and internationally if it is. Your requests can be handled online quite easily. I even ship my luggage ahead of me when I travel for business or vacation. I can track it and there are no baggage claim waits or lost luggage.

6. *Bookkeeping.* Try to arrange for someone to pick up and deliver, and to coordinate with your tax professionals what's needed and in what format. You do *not* want to mess around with software and reconciling your own accounts. This type of help is very inexpensive and will save you tons of time every month, as well as minimize errors.

7. *Travel.* While there is a plethora of automated travel sites, dealing with the airlines and hotels is a huge hassle. It's great to have a professional who knows your preferences and can anticipate things. My strong advice is American Express, using the Platinum Card. It has terrific travel help, can bill right to your card (which you'll need anyway), and is accessible 24/7. It can change your plans when needed in the midst of a trip, and can coordinate travel, hotels, limos, dinners, events, and so forth. It even

---

[1] I create a weekly comic strip, *The Adventures of Koufax and Buddy Beagle*, on my blog (contrarianconsulting.com). I send dialogue and crude drawings to an artist who creates the finished product for me.

offers its own airport lounges and expedited trips through an international airport in many cities. (I have a Black Card, and American Express was able to get us home from Capri to Manhattan in one day on short notice when we had a family emergency. That included private cars, ferries, connecting flights, and a suite awaiting us in New York.)

8. *Maintenance.* Most of you are working out of your home. It's not merely important, it's *vital* that your driveway be cleared of snow in the winter, or your yard be cleaned of debris after storms, or your pavement be kept in safe shape, and so forth. Find people who will do this automatically so that you don't spend time on it, you can get to appointments in all kinds of weather, and people visiting you see the proper image.

You may have other areas where outsourced help makes sense in terms of regular use and ease of access.

Expertise: Always pay local, outsourced help first, because they have strong cash flow needs and you may need them at times to allow you to "jump the line" for preferential treatment in an emergency. If you owe them money, that's not likely.

You may consider bartering (trading services) an effective way to engage these services without hurting cash flow, but that's seldom a good idea.

First, when you barter, you need to find what the equivalent values are. Is two days of coaching worth two months of doing the books? Is business advice over the phone worth a round trip to the airport?

Second, you damage the client/provider relationship when you barter. Now you "owe" something to the other part beyond mere payment. What if it is deemed insufficient or inaccurate or unhelpful?

Third, bartering demands your time. So while you may be saving money, you're expending wealth—your discretionary time. That's a bad deal in my book.

Fourth, the IRS deems bartered services taxable. If you receive free rides, or travel advice, or yoga lessons, they are, legally, taxable. If you don't report them, you can be fined. So your cash flow savings may not be what they seemed to be.

My advice is that you get what you pay for. If you want to leverage your business, invest in a lever that works in your favor and is of high quality.

CREATING AND SUSTAINING YOUR ENDEAVOR

CATHEDRALS LAST FOR HUNDREDS OF YEARS

LOGISTICAL, FINANCIAL, LEGAL, UNUSUAL

To run your business smoothly you need to routinize the normal. That means you have to get into a groove about and with issues that surface regularly and require attention periodically.

Here are my suggestions for the actual administration of your business so that you can run it alone, with outsourced help as needed but without any employees, full- or part-time. Employees can kill your business. They require paychecks no matter what your cash flow, benefits, sick days, personal days, help with issues they can't handle, monitoring to ensure quality and honesty, and tolerance when they are obviously goofing off—on your dollar.

They can be stressful as well as expensive, so here's how to run your own show and avoid the tyranny of the employee.

When you arise in the morning at home, after your ablutions, workout, dog walking, paper reading, meditation, or whatever your regimen is (and regimens are great, part of the routinization), check the overnight e-mail. There are three things to do with it:

1. Respond quickly to those you can. Say "thanks," or provide information, or answer a question, or agree to an appointment. Then delete them.

2. Place in desktop folders those that require more thought or work on your part. Get to them before day's end if they are important. Don't delay your morning by trying to respond to them now.

3. Place stuff you want to keep, such as client summaries, directions, or background information, in appropriate client or project folders.

4. Delete everything else.

Expertise: At the end of the day your physical and virtual desktops should be clean with nothing on them. No one wants to face a desk of leftover "stuff" in the morning.

You do *not* have to keep every scrap of client or prospect correspondence. If you're uncertain, keep a "chron" (chronology) folder, and within it a folder for each month. Place monthly correspondence, incoming or outgoing, in there if you're not sure what else to do with it.

Check your daily calendar to remind yourself of your priorities. You may have client calls, prospect follow-ups, writing, referral calls, project reviews—whatever. These should be written with times allotted. People procrastinate because while they would never blow off a client appointment at 3 p.m., they think nothing of overlooking the writing they had planned since there is no allotted time to do it. Hence, you need times for major priorities.

This is counterintuitive, and perhaps Luddite, but I strongly recommend a physical planner, such as a Filofax, over an electronic calendar. Physical planners allow you to see a full day, week, month, and even year at a glance. You don't have to scroll. They will stay open on your desk with your priorities and times. You cross things off as they are completed. Whenever I make an appointment with four other people to meet and we're looking at dates, I'm always the fastest with my Filofax while they are clicking like demented woodpeckers on their tablets and phones.

Every day you should have no more than three or four personal and professional priorities, combined. These are the issues that *must* be done. Make sure to "chunk" your projects. For example, you don't sit down and write a book chapter, you write 5 pages of a 20-page chapter in four separate sessions. You don't follow up on 10 referrals at one time, you follow on two a day for a week. This is equivalent to the lines at Disneyland: they are very long and have mileposts ("You are 30 minutes from the ride"), which creates constant motion and a feeling of progress.

Don't allow interruptions. Tell your kids and partner that when the door is closed, you can't be disturbed. Don't check your e-mail again until after lunch. (There is no such thing as "urgent" e-mail. If it's urgent, the person would call.) Keep your phone forwarded unless you have phone appointments, and the same for Skype and similar vehicles. Note: *People don't expect instant access, but they are thrilled by quick responsiveness.*

Check your voice mail twice in the morning and twice in the afternoon and return appropriate calls. Don't check voice mail or e-mail in the evening unless you are doing business globally and reasonably expect clients from overseas to be in contact.

Have a good lunch. Take a walk, sit outside, do some personal errands. Try to wrap up your work day by 4 p.m. That gives you an hour's leeway until the iconic 5 p.m. I work 20 hours a week when I'm home and try to be at the pool by 2 p.m. No, that's not the way I always did it, but I didn't have the technology then that we do now. Once upon a time we all had to fly in order to meet with clients!

Now for some other routinized approaches:

- Pay your bills twice a month, on the fifteenth and last days of the month. They will never be overdue, and you won't have to fuss with them daily.

- Never meet with anyone who just wants to "explore" working together, or to "pick your brain." These are always attempts to get free help or to have you help them market.

- Any magazine or periodical, hard copy or electronic, that you don't read before the next issue comes out, get rid of and unsubscribe. It's just not that important.

- Don't surf the web on your "company time." Do it in the evening, if you must.

- Go very light on social media platforms. You can get dragged into a huge time dump. If you're posting with business intent (e.g., trying to connect with a prospect on LinkedIn), that's fine, but posting (or responding to) requests to "prove" that posts are being read, or responding to the latest conspiracy theory or political nonsense, is frustrating, stressful, and a waste of time and energy. Don't kid yourself—social media use is *not* marketing in the corporate marketplace, where decisions are largely made based on peer referral.

- Don't give out your cell phone number readily. It makes sense for very important clients, close friends, and family, but not much beyond that. Don't keep it turned on—it's capable of taking messages! You shouldn't be discussing private matters in public, and you should *never* take a nonemergency call when talking to someone else. And if you're walking around with a blinking blue, metallic gizmo in your ear, you might as well be wearing a pocket protector. Executives don't wear earpieces.

- Have hard-copy business cards and stationery, you never know when you'll need them, and put your physical address on your website—some people just might want to send you a check! (If someone really wants to stalk you, he will find a way whether or not your address is on your website!)

- Use intelligent backup for your files, either an external hard drive, or cloud space, or whatever. Don't obsess.

Finally, spend money on a comfortable place to work. Turn the spare bedroom into a real office. Have modern wiring, lighting, and desk space. I had a designer watch me work and create an office around me given my routines. That was money well spent with immediate ROI.

ADVISORY BOARD

Many solos use an advisory board to provide objective advice and to help with any affiliation needs. It can also be good sources of referral business, if chosen carefully. An advisory board is most successful when the members see it as a win/win relationship, rather than having to do a favor for you.

Here are my criteria for a highly successful, strongly committed advisory board, in terms of both protocols and people:

Protocols

- *Don't meet too frequently, and try to meet in person.* My suggestion is once a quarter is fine, and twice a year is acceptable. If members are too far distant, either pay their transportation fees or use technology to allow them to interact from a distance.

- *The maximum meeting time should be a day, with a planned agenda.* A half day with a working breakfast or lunch also is fine, and less onerous.

- *You should not pay a fee to your advisory members.* If you wish to make a donation to their favorite charities, that's fine. Do buy the meals and refreshments, including a dinner the evening before if that makes sense logistically.

- *Never put clients or prospects on your advisory board*—it's a clear conflict of interest.

- *Meet in a formal conference room*, not a restaurant and not your home. Create a business atmosphere. Dress appropriately for your business, your members, and your circumstances. For example, if you expect someone might show up in a suit, don't dress in jeans.

- *Either record the meeting (with everyone's permission) or hire someone to take notes (minutes).* Don't try to do this yourself, you'll miss too much. Hire from a temp agency, someone who knows how to take and transcribe notes. Circulate these notes to the members when they are completed and make them a part of your company proceedings. They could be important legally in some instances.

- *Don't allow the board members to have veto power.* They are advisory. They can't demand that you do or refuse to do something, so long as it is ethical and legal. Don't take votes.

- *An ideal range is probably five to seven members.* That way you can still have a good meeting if one or even two can't be present. Schedule your meeting well in advance to get on everyone's calendars.

- *Between meetings, keep the members apprised* of new business, financial or legal actions, new offerings, and so forth. Make them feel a part of your business and not merely members of an occasional meeting.

> *Expertise: If you can secure a "name" on your advisory board, all the better, and describe the board on your site and in other collateral.*

- *Create "term limits."* I'd suggest two years, which may be renewed if you and the other person wish, but which also gives you an opportunity to remove someone who isn't working out. (See the next list to make sure you choose the right people to begin with.)
- *Describe the board's presence and composition to the public:* to prospects, in collateral, on your site, and so on. Encourage members to provide a "guest column" for your blog or newsletter.
- *Invite the members to activities between meetings.* For example, a marketing event, reception, workshop, or party would be excellent vehicles to mix your board members with clients and prospects. Put them in positions where they can informally "evangelize."
- *Call on them for help.* Make sure you have permission to judiciously ask them individually for help and counsel between meetings, especially on subjects relevant to their expertise.
- *Refer people to them.* Whenever possible, reciprocate by sending prospects to your board members, making it clear that you are the source.

People

- *Past clients* are fine for your board provided that you are not going to be actively pursuing them for future work. Retired buyers are especially good candidates when possible.
- *Do not assume your attorney and CPA are good candidates.* They are often wonderful at their specialties but horrible business people. (Almost all charge by the hour and work far too hard as a result.) You can always call them for legal and financial advice, and you're better off paying their hourly fee rather than wasting space with them on your board.

- *Do not include family members, period.* Do not allow your spouse or partner to sit in on the meetings.
- *If you can, secure a "name"* (not necessarily a household name, but someone well known in your field). Many successful people are surprisingly generous and just have to be asked.
- *Create a valuable dynamic.* In other words, attractive people attract others like them. If you can obtain one or two key people, others will be more prone to accept. And if they benefit from meeting others they otherwise wouldn't meet, all the better, you are responsible.
- The ideal "type" of board member has these characteristics:

  Runs or has run his or her own business

  Has connections that can help you, leveraging the person's value to you

  Has expertise you do *not* have such as marketing, technology, finance, media, promotion, and so forth

  Will commit at the outset to your meeting schedule

  Possesses interpersonal adeptness—doesn't dominate a meeting, can deal with differing opinions, has a sense of humor, abides by the rules

  Someone you like to be around and respect—a person who can give you candid feedback, positive or negative, in a professional manner

- *Choose people you would "trust with your wallet,"* because that's what you'll be doing. They will know the intimate aspects of your business. If you hold anything back from the board—through embarrassment, mistrust, or paranoia—you're defeating the purpose and might as well disband it.

You don't *need* an advisory board, and you might have one at some points in your growth and not others. The bottom line is that it should be a net contributor to your well-being, not another "meeting to take" or job to do! It should serve you actively (meetings, advice, participation) and passively (making people aware that it exists). It can give you a sense of more "heft" in the practice, but you can also outgrow it.

If your personal predisposition is not consistent with this kind of group, don't do it. If it is, a board can be helpful and dynamic and intrinsic in growing the business and giving you strength.

On the other hand, I've never had one.

LEGACIES AND EVENTUALITIES

I've discussed previously the two types of business models (solo practitioner and boutique firm owner) and the pros and cons of each. Let's examine now the various forks in the road, unexpected detours, and express lanes that you may encounter.

Lawsuits

You may be sued. Take a breath. It happens.

This is why you need a very good litigator among your legal team members. And it's why you *must* carry errors and omissions (malpractice) insurance and liability insurance.

You may be sued by a client who believes your advice caused grievous harm. You may be sued by a client employee who believes that his or her termination or demotion was based on your inappropriate advice. You may be sued by anyone who trips over a power cord from a projector that you are using to show slides, irrespective of whether you own the projector. And you may be sued by other experts who feel you have appropriated their work without permission.

Aside from the insurance, which is a contingent action, the preventive actions are these:

- Document your discussions with your buyers and key others, even if for your personal records and not theirs. Make notes of meetings immediately after the session or phone call. When appropriate, send your buyer the meeting summaries and ask him or her to indicate that they are accurate.
- Always give attribution to others if your idea or model was learned elsewhere. I frequently say, "I'm not sure who came up with this originally, but here's where I read it . . . ." Or I'll say, "I'm using this with the permission of Joan Jones, who originated this." I once received a large financial settlement from

someone who incorporated my entire proposal template into his own book, without referencing me at all or acknowledging my copyrights. His editors missed it or didn't ask.

- Ensure that your advice is being carried out accurately and not distorted, and that you're not being claimed as the source for actions that you never endorsed. Stay in close contact with both your buyer and the implementation people.

- Do not accept jobs as "temporary" CFO and sales vice president. You will have responsibility but not authority, and these are ethical minefields. Turn them into normal consulting assignments, but don't allow yourself to become a de facto employee.

When in doubt, check with your attorneys first, not after the fact.

Financial Options

Make sure you have a healthy line of credit. Your bank should be prepared to advance you $100,000 or more. Demand overdraft protection on your accounts. Place all of your business—mortgage, investments, savings, checking—with one institution if it will increase your leverage.

Expertise: If a bank lends you $10,000, you're a customer. If a bank has millions at stake with you, you're a partner.

Maximize your tax-exempt retirement funding every year. I've met too many people in their fifties with $300,000 in the bank and that's it.[1] Create a slush fund for unexpected events. Make sure your corporate bylaws are maximally attractive for paying expenses out of pretax dollars. Consider these cash needs:

- Retirement savings
- College/wedding/special event expenses
- Slush fund for uninsured losses, impulse vacations, and so on

---

[1]$100,000 isn't what it used to be. About 25 years ago there were a handful of cars costing $100,000, and they were exotics. Today, there are dozens, some quite pedestrian.

- Paying off all debt outside of mortgages and car loans
- Increasing lifestyle choices (house, car, travel, clothes)
- Philanthropy

There is nothing wrong with debt for short-term needs if you have a plan to repay it in the short term. In fact, it will usually improve your credit score. If you have debt now, divide it all by 12, pay it off that way over a year, and incur no new debt, use cash.

You should be able to use your bankers to help you find the best way to fund your needs, not debate with them.

Ownership and Annuities

You may well develop passive income that would continue after you leave the business—be it retirement, sales, or death. You should work with your attorney to determine how such annuity income would be handled in your estate and among your beneficiaries. This isn't morbid, it's prudent. You've established valuable intellectual property, sales, trademarks, and relationships, and these assets should be protected.

It is much likelier that you will become disabled during your prime working years than die. That's why I've advised disability insurance that will pay you *until you can return to your normal work*, not just any work.

It is also likelier that you will become bored with your business rather than run out of business.

In Figure 15-1 you can see the "ambiguous zone," which I define as a period in time, now or in the future, when you aren't sure of the route even though you are clear on the destination. (This applies to your clients as well as to you.) You have to be comfortable with the ambiguous zone, trusting that you will find the way, that you have enough light, that you can correct an errant path.

This enables you to constantly "reinvent." Consultants and practices often fail because they become stale. The original enthusiasm and passion are gone, replaced by a workaday mentality of the "same old, same old." Organizations as large as Sears, Radio Shack, and Netflix have had these troubles. Netflix was able to reinvent itself as a movie production source and popularized "binge watching" after losing over

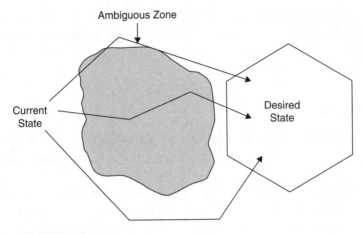

Figure 15-1 The ambiguous zone

600,000 subscribers on its traditional CD rental business. Not everyone has that eventual resilience.

At one point, 3M had a corporate strategy that included 25 percent of its billions in revenue originating from products not in existence five years ago. Traditionally, 75 percent of my income emanates from services that didn't exist three years ago.

You have to be clear on your future state—which is often a moving target—*and* be comfortable enough in the ambiguous zone on the way to get you there. This isn't a profession for the risk averse or overly conservative. One eventuality is that you lose enthusiasm, your work suffers, and your prospects decline, forcing you to seek clients you don't really find appropriate. Avoid this eventuality by becoming comfortable in the ambiguity of the journey to new conditions.

THREATS AND RESPONSES

The first time I was told that I had a greater chance of becoming disabled than of dying, I said, "Hey, great. Wait. What?"

Over the years, exactly three clients have asked me what would happen if I died, and two of those were when I was in my forties! (Today I say, "Well, I'm Catholic and like to think I'd go to heaven.")

As a conscientious professional, you should look at threats in light of preventing them and ameliorating the effects if prevention fails or is impossible. So, in no special order, let me try to both help you protect yourself and put your mind to rest.

1. Disability

You can be disabled by anything from a car accident to a deer tick. In any case, you won't be able to market or deliver. Here are some stratagems.

- *Obtain disability insurance as soon as you can.* The younger you are, the cheaper it is (and it can get very expensive). It's very difficult to obtain inclusion in a group policy, so purchase an individual one through an agent with a strong company. You want a *long* waiting period (e.g., 90 days before benefits begin, which lowers your premium), *and the provision that you must be able to return to your prior work before benefits cease.* You don't want to be able to return to *any* work, but *to your prior work.* These policies will pay up to 80 percent of prior annual income, so document income carefully. If you "hide" income to lower your taxes, you'll also be undermining your disability benefits should you need them. These polices are generally renewable automatically to age 65.

- *Establish ties with other consultants* who may be able to deliver existing contracts for you with some kind of split of the revenues (and you would of course reciprocate for them). This can be an important source of continuing income for the near future.

- *Create important passive income.* If you make money from licensing, royalties, commissions, sales of intellectual property, downloads, subscriptions, product purchases, and so forth, these sources can continue while you are infirm. But they have to have been created well before disaster strikes.

- *Maximize retainer work.* If you are serving as a sounding board and offering access to your "smarts," you may be able to continue doing that even if you are physically incapacitated. Again, this must be germinated long before you experience disability.

- *Maximize your ability to work at home.* Many of us have home offices, but some prefer shared suites or even owned private quarters. At least have a backup office in your home and be prepared to operate at least part-time on that basis with a real or virtual assistant.

- *Utilize technology.* Use Skype and similar options instead of physically visiting. Use dictation software instead of a keyboard.

- *Create backlogs.* If your business utilizes newsletters, blog posts, hard-copy mailings, electronic notifications, and so on, create a two-month or more supply "in the bank" at any given time. These can be used to maintain continuity while you recover.

2. Theft and Infringement

Yesterday I saw a LinkedIn post from someone I've coached for a long time using my IP without any attribution. This isn't uncommon. Some good people use my materials so diligently that they take them for granted. Others, like a guy in Australia, simply steal my stuff and require a legal torpedo in the bow.

There are rip-off sites all over the web (I won't give them publicity here). Surprisingly, an attorney can stop most of it, though it will cost you. So the question is, when do you grin and bear it, and when do you unfetter the main batteries?

My advice is to build your brand so strongly that your clients and prospects recognize your "stuff." Create brand imagery: Marshall Goldsmith's "What got you here won't get you there"; Seth Godin's "purple cow"; David Maister's "We know what to do but still don't do it."

I mentioned earlier that among your legal team should be a first-class litigator. Ask him or her for direction on these issues. Don't explode because someone has appropriated your material. First, find out if it was accidental or deliberate. Second, if deliberate, ask to what extent it's actually hurting you. The chances are, not much.

Don't create partnerships or alliances that can allow your intellectual property and trademarked material to be readily used by others without tight legal restraints. (Never assume a "friend" wouldn't ever steal from you. That's why people have ex-friends.)

3. Overwhelm

Your business can take over your life in one of two ways.

First, as you seek to build it or take it to the next level, you'll face challenges and obstacles that are often significant. You'll think "working harder" is the answer.

Second, as you grow you'll enjoy the feeling of independence and creating wealth so much that you'll become addicted, never turning down business and chasing money—*all* money.

I've talked throughout this book about support from those close to you, advisory boards, and investment in self-development. Keep your priorities straight:

- You are in business to build a great life, not applying life to build a huge business.

- You can always make another dollar, but you will never be able to make another minute.

- TIAABB: There is always a bigger boat—don't waste your time trying to have the biggest.

Million dollar consulting is about having the right *mindset*. If you can't achieve that yourself, acquire help from colleagues, coaches, or counselors.

> *Expertise: You may endure pain, but you do not have to suffer. Pain is usually external, suffering is always internal. Direct your energies toward resolutions, not retribution.*

4. Boredom

The reason I talked about reinvention earlier is that it's easy to get bored without realizing it if no one is pursuing us to change, create, abandon, and innovate. Once you get bored you get stale. You don't take chances, you rely on the same old interventions and speeches, and before you know it, you're in the "success trap." As explained in Chapter 14 (Figure 14-1), the point is to "leap" to the next period of growth while the acceleration of current growth is still strong and sustainable.

About 75 percent of my multimillion-dollar business is derived from offerings *that did not exist three years ago*, and that's a rolling figure. If you're not growing, you're stagnant. Or as humorist Will Rogers pointed out, "Even if you're on the right track, if you're just standing there you'll get run over."

Notice that I haven't mentioned as threats "no business," "unhappy clients," or "too much competition." That's because if you do well and you follow my advice, these aren't threats at all.

Remember: no guilt, no fear, no peer.

Welcome to my world.

APPENDIX

TIPS FROM THE MILLION DOLLAR CONSULTING COMMUNITY

Instead of questions and answers, I thought I'd include tips garnered from the Million Dollar Consulting Colleges, the Grad Schools, the Million Dollar Club, Thought Leadership, the Million Dollar Consulting Convention, the Mentor Summits, and the members of the Mentor Hall of Fame (many of whom you've seen contribute throughout the book).

About Us as Consultants and Self-Esteem

- A large proportion of attendees (about 75 percent) felt "alone" when they were very young, either because they perceived themselves to be different from others or because they were somehow not in a "traditional" loving family. And where are we now? In a profession that requires a certain strength to be alone!

- "Lone wolves" don't have much opportunity for exploring emotional issues with trusted peers. Life and work revolve solely around work to too great a degree, and most conversation is centered on work challenges, not personal issues.

- What doesn't kill you makes you stronger. Most successful people have learned from setbacks and turned them into sources of strength and self-worth.

- Forgiveness is critical. If you don't forgive those whom you perceive as having hurt you, you become permanently enslaved to them (even though they might not realize it). If you allow real and perceived slights to fester, your self-worth will suffer.

- Efficacy and self-worth are separate. You can be excellent at a given pursuit but not feel good about yourself, and vice versa.

- Personal relationships are key to the foundation of self-worth. If you can positively and constructively engage in your personal relationships, your self-worth improves. Hence, poor relationships have to be improved or abandoned, not merely maintained as poor relationships.

- You can look at self-esteem as a *verb*—an action, leading to a condition—or as a *noun*—self-confidence.

- People carry far too much old "baggage" around, and it's insufficient merely to drop it. You must throw it "off the train" so that it isn't merely at your feet traveling in the same direction and at the same speed that you are. However, don't jettison everything. Some of the positive baggage makes sense for the trip.

- Positive self-talk is one of the most powerful tools to build self-worth. Stop apologizing and be honest about your own talent and abilities. Don't generalize from a specific: just because you didn't understand a play doesn't mean you're ignorant about art.

- It's not about what life deals you; it's about how you deal with life.

About the Business of Growing in Consulting

- If you don't understand something, do two things. First, question it immediately, because otherwise the ensuing structure will have a weak foundation. Second, try to apply it in your circumstances to integrate the learning.

- People learn in different ways, so notes, recordings, mind maps, and holographic telepathy are all fine with me. But if you don't have three things (or fewer) to move forward on at the end of the day, you may have quantity but not quality.

- "My trademarked approach the 1% Solution: Tools for Change" says that if you improve by 1 percent a day, in 70 days, you'll be twice as good. But if you don't learn carefully and instead become confused, the opposite can actually occur. People can get dumber.

- When creating pragmatic representations of conceptual images, whether brands or graphics or process visuals, it is *always* better to work with a small team that you trust for quicker and higher-quality results.

- Failing, and learning as a result, among peers is better than mind-lessly succeeding among inferiors.

- Emotion is as important as intellect in integrating learning.

- Groups don't bond through dumb icebreaking exercises. They bond through sharing challenge, contributions, disagreements, and socializing.

- All groups claim that they want to stay in touch and reconnect. The ones that do so most successfully always have an organizer or organizers who take on that responsibility.

- If the facilitator isn't learning constantly, she should go into another line of work. Simply doing something well and receiving plaudits for it is like watching people applaud a movie you made years ago.

About the Most Frequent Organizational Issues

- Leadership is inept in that key people are not serving as avatars of the behavior they are seeking in others.

- Team building is sought when, in actuality, the organization has committees and needs committees, not teams.

- There are silos headed by powerful people who are defending their turf.

- Problem solving is prized over innovation, and "black belt nine delta" nonsense takes over people's minds like a bad science fiction movie from the 1950s.

- There is excessive staff interference instead of support, typically from HR, finance, IT, and/or legal.

- There are too many meetings that take too long and are overwhelmingly focused on sharing information—the worst possible reason to have a meeting. The organization's talent and energy are being squandered internally instead of being applied externally.

- The customer's perceptions of the organization's products, services, and relationships are different from the organization's perceptions.

- The reward and feedback systems are not aligned with strategy and are not encouraging the appropriate behaviors and not discouraging the inappropriate.

- Strategy and planning are mistaken for each other.

- Career development and succession planning are not wedded.

- The organization is bureaucratic, in that it focuses on means and not ends.

INTERVIEWS WITH CONSULTANTS

The following interviews contain commentary from varied professionals in my community about their experiences and expectations.

Andy Bass

Name: Andy Bass

Company Name: BassClusker Consulting Ltd

When Founded: 2004

Expertise and Major Markets: I help leaders and their organizations to get better and faster results with resources they already have. I work internationally with clients across a wide range of sectors including manufacturing, media, and financial and professional services.

Employees: None

Website: www.bassclusker.com
Book Published: *The Performance Papers: Incisive Briefings for Busy Leaders* (Bookshaker, 2011)
Country of Residence: UK
Age: 50

1. *Why and how did you enter the consulting profession?*

   I was an academic for a few years after completing my doctorate. I had very eclectic interests, and the university became worried that they couldn't see the pattern in my publishing. When they said, "We can't see what furrow you are ploughing," I knew it was time to leave, since I didn't want a career as a plough-horse. I decided to take my eclecticism into the marketplace. One of the many things it had taught me was that the go-to guy in independent consulting was Alan Weiss. I Googled him, found my way to the mentor program, and signed up.

2. *What was your greatest mistake and at what point in your career?*

   Before I left my university post I nearly got a lucrative job as an in-house coach at an oil major. I had a couple of great early meetings with the director of the function and some members of his team, and he verbally offered me the job, but in an offhand way said, "I just want you to meet this project manager—it's a formality." I totally failed to generate any rapport with her, and the offer evaporated. I learned a hard and expensive lesson about the importance of being able to build relationships with as wide a range of people as possible. That lesson has stood me in good stead in both my marketing and implementation, but it hurt at the time!

3. *What most accelerated your career?*

   Getting Alan's help in implementing the fundamental principles of Million Dollar Consulting. I take those to include, at the *strategic* level, charging for value, building marketing gravity, and establishing peer-to-peer relationships with executive buyers. The most vital *tactical* accelerator was, and remains,

"Never conclude any communication with a prospective buyer without an agreed next step at an agreed time."

4. *How has your practice most changed since inception?*

Well, firstly, the average project fee has increased by an order of magnitude—that's a function of the accelerators I talked about. In terms of what I do when I'm with clients, the emphasis has shifted away from training events toward deeper, longer-term consulting engagements. And I'm working all over the world now.

5. *What has been your major accomplishment in this profession?*

I'd say it's been taking those eclectic interests—the connections among which so baffled my former employer—and parlaying them into direct benefits for my clients, and a fascinating and rewarding career for me.

6. *What is the most important advice you have for colleagues?*

Remember what Mum said: "Eat everything on your plate." I know people who have put bits and pieces of Alan's approach into practice, and I know people who have built their businesses round it. The second group is doing far, far better.

Get a mentor who has "been there and done that." It's unlikely you'll figure out all the ins and outs of how this business works by trial and error alone.

And: never conclude any communication with a prospective buyer without an agreed next step at an agreed time!

7. *What do you believe is the future of consulting?*

I think firms such as McKinsey, BCG, and Bain will continue to thrive—they are magnificent marketers for one thing—and working for them will remain a great start for someone wanting a senior executive career. My view is that things could be more turbulent for the big implementation-oriented shops (and by extension for their individual consultants), because they are more likely to be disrupted by technology and economic cycles. As for solo practitioners and small boutiques, there will be an increasing number, many of whom will just scrape by. For those who can build the right relationships with the right buyers, who can stay close enough to them to understand and meet their real needs, and who are prepared to think and work globally—virtually as well as in person—there is huge opportunity.

Chad Barr

Name: Chad Barr

Company Name: The Chad Barr Group

When Founded: 2001

Expertise: Internet marketing strategy, web application development

Major Markets: Global service providers, successful entrepreneurs, consultants, coaches, speakers, authors, organizations looking to leverage the web for success, thought leaders

Employees: 9

Website: www.TheChadBarrGroup.com

Book Published: *Million Dollar Web Presence* (Entrepreneur Press, 2012)

Country of Residence: United States

1. *Why and how did you enter the consulting profession?*

   In a way, consulting was a profession I stumbled upon. When I was developing software solutions, my clients began to ask me for advice. They would ask for my opinion on how to best leverage software, how to improve their operations and generate dramatic and successful results. I started to realize that I was actually consulting—I realized there was an opportunity for me to provide my clients with powerful value and the outcome was increased consulting projects and revenues.

2. *What was your greatest mistake and at what point in your career?*

   A third of the way into my career, I made the mistake of spreading myself too thin. I was developing software for retail businesses, wholesale distribution companies, and nursing homes. Any opportunity that looked like software development, I would grab it. I was even on the verge of getting into manufacturing businesses. It was way too labor intensive and too much to handle. I realized that I needed to focus on doing what I did best. I began to ask myself, What are my true talents? Who are the clients I am passionate about? How can I provide amazing value to the right target audiences?

3. *What most accelerated your career?*

Realizing my passion for Internet strategy greatly accelerated my career. Fifteen years ago, I began to understand that I had discovered an amazing opportunity to do something that only a few were able to figure out: how to leverage the awesome power of the Internet to increase and accelerate business success. It was a challenge, but I completely fell in love with every aspect of the Internet. The second thing that accelerated my career was when I embraced Alan Weiss's value-based fees and stopped billing by the hour.

4. *How has your practice most changed since inception?*

We've completely changed. We used to be a software development company and have transformed into an Internet marketing strategy company and developer of creative web solutions. The focus of what we're doing has completely changed from software to the Internet. My role has also changed dramatically. I now take much more of an advisory role with my clients rather than being the technical guy. Today, I lead my team and my clients while focusing on the future and how to create value, enthusiasm, and great success.

5. *What has been your major accomplishment in this profession?*

Being inducted as one of the five charter members into Alan Weiss's Million Dollar Consultant™ Hall of Fame was a very proud moment for me. Another major accomplishment was becoming a sought-after global speaker. I dreaded speaking 15 years ago, and I love speaking now.

Arriving to the United States 37 years ago and building my own empire is my biggest accomplishment. Back in 2001, I developed the vision of becoming a global Internet strategy company. It was a dream. Fast-forward nearly 15 years later, and with clients all over the world, the dream has become a reality. We constantly raise the bar to lead our clients with state-of-the-art web development, amazing content creation, and creativity while generating powerful results.

6. *What is the most important advice you have for colleagues?*

You've got to become great at marketing yourself and your company. You should also publish prolifically: books, e-books, articles, podcasts, and videos—a variety of content. You should speak a lot and focus on delivering amazing value to your clients.

7. *What do you believe is the future of consulting?*

More than ever, people need advice on how to overcome challenges and how to become better at what they do. Whether it's a personal or business matter, the best surround themselves with great consultants. They need consultants to help them achieve their dreams. I'm convinced that people will always need great consultants to help them reach their full potential and raise the bar.

Suzanne Bates

Name: Suzanne Bates

Company Name: Bates Communications

When Founded: 2000

Expertise and Major Markets: Executive presence and communicative leadership

Employees: 18 full-time, about 12 associates

Website: www.bates-communications.com

Books Published: *Speak Like a CEO* (2005), *Motivate Like a CEO* (2009), *Discover Your CEO Brand* (2012), and *All the Leader You Can Be* (2016) with McGraw-Hill and *Thoughts for Tuesday* (self-published, 2012); contributing author to *CEO Branding, Theory and Practice* (Routledge, 2015)

Country of Residence: United States

Current Annual Revenue: $6.5 million

Age: 59

1. *Why and how did you enter the consulting profession?*

   After a 22-year career as a television reporter and anchor, I wanted to leverage my experience and establish a course to financial independence. I launched a solo practice, however, there was sufficient demand and soon I had reason to develop a team and establish a niche in communicative leadership. We designed our own approaches to helping leaders influence and make an impact. We invested significantly in training a team to deliver services. Our people and unique IP have attracted top companies, global companies, and executives as clients.

2. *What was your greatest mistake and at what point in your career?*

   Though I've been lucky in hiring and successful in attracting and keeping great talent, I've occasionally hung on too long when people were not performing. This has a significant impact on energy, morale, and resources.

3. *What most accelerated your career?*

   Commercial publishing was the rocket fuel that enabled us to generate media and land speaking opportunities on big stages. This positioned our firm's thought leadership. Our niche in executive presence and communicative leadership differentiated us from hundreds of other coaching and consulting firms. We established brand value that created marketing gravity, diversified our client base, and attracted more profitable business.

4. *How has your practice most changed since inception?*

In 2013 we embarked on an exploratory research project to answer a question no one could answer—what is executive presence? Our goal was to bring science to address one of the hottest topics in leadership development today. As a result we developed the first science-based model of executive presence and operationalized it into an assessment—the first significant new instrument of its kind in more than two decades. It was quickly recognized as a breakthrough. Through innovation we established a new line of business attracting new clients and giving established clients additional reason to engage. We became a first-mover and positioned our company for growth.

5. *What has been your major accomplishment in this profession?*

I've built a successful business by helping other people—leaders—become highly effective in their work. We have transformed careers. This has helped organizations grow and thrive.

6. *What is the most important advice you have for colleagues?*

If an idea has merit, just do it. It will work or it won't. Learn and grow. Keep moving. Keep trying.

7. *What do you believe is the future of consulting?*

The paradox of consulting today is that our approach must be more global and at once more personal. Adopting a global mindset is no longer a choice—whether you are a consultancy of 1 or 1,000—your clients are competing in a global world, and you will only be relevant if you understand what being global means to their business.

At the same time, the speed of business and availability of digital communication today has lulled us all into overreliance on technology. Our clients are utterly fatigued by the impersonal nature of their daily interactions. This lack of intimacy hinders the building of trust among peers, customers, and employees.

As consultants we need to be careful not to succumb to the same bad habits—overusing technology. Our success fundamentally requires us to establish a basis for trust and win the confidence of clients. This only happens when we create the appropriate space for meaningful dialogue.

Steven Bleistein

Name: Steven Bleistein

Company Name: Relansa, Inc.

When Founded: 2012

Expertise and Major Markets: Maximizing growth and change capabilities of organizations to achieve rapid business outcomes. Expert in Japanese organizations in particular.

Employees: None

Website: www.relansa.co.jp

Book Published: *Rapid Organizational Change* (John Wiley & Sons, forthcoming end of 2016)

Country of Residence: Japan

Current Annual Revenue: $750,000 to $1.1 million

Age: 47

1. *Why and how did you enter the consulting profession?*

   I had just left a job as researcher and was seeking new employment. Booz & Co. had begun a hiring process with me but stopped after the Lehman shock. I liked the idea of consulting and was not finding a job, so I decided to strike out on my own instead.

2. *What was your greatest mistake and at what point in your career?*

   Letting fear drive my career choices. One bad business failure as an entrepreneur when I was in my early thirties made me fearful of starting another business. I was miserable as a salaried employee. It took me 10 years before I mastered my fear and started my consulting practice.

3. *What most accelerated your career?*

   Alan Weiss's books. I read a dozen or so of them during my first year of consulting. I went from $70,000 in revenues my first year to over $700,000 in my second by putting Alan's methods into practice immediately as I learned them.

4. *How has your practice most changed since inception?*

Most of my initial business was based on selling training courses and consulting on Balanced Scorecard methodology. I had negotiated a license to represent the Balanced Scorecard Institute in Japan at the time. I now represent no one but myself. I am the brand, and my consulting is my own thinking and intellectual property.

5. *What has been your major accomplishment in this profession?*

Becoming a million dollar solo consultant and being invited into Alan's Million Dollar Club. There are a lot of solo consultants in Alan's community doing seven figures, and every year the number of us increases. However, outside of the community, I know no solo consultants personally doing that kind of revenue.

6. *What is the most important advice you have for colleagues?*

Never hold back saying exactly what you think for fear of how people will react. Boldness gets clients. Congeniality fetches only polite smiles.

7. *What do you believe is the future of consulting?*

People who base a solo business on providing their own expertise to others will increase. The consulting model as defined by the large firms is not the only option, nor an optimal one in most cases, and clients realize this. Clients value rapid results, flexibility, options, and direct immediate access to the expert. These are the hallmarks of the solo consultant.

Ali Brown

Name: Ali Brown

Company Name: Ali International LLC

When Founded: 2005 (started previous business that led to this in 1998)

Expertise and Major Markets: Coaching and consulting for women entrepreneurs and organizational leaders; leadership and profit growth. I have a very international private client group with women from the United States, Australia, the United Kingdom, and Europe.

Employees: 1 part-time employee, 5 part-time subcontractors
Website: www.alibrown.com
Country of Residence: United States
Current Annual Revenue: $2 million
Age: 44

1. *Why and how did you enter the consulting profession?*

   After college I went through six jobs in six years, totally unsatisfied with any of them. At first I thought there was something wrong with me, but then I realized I'd just be happier working for myself. So I took my best skill set at the time—writing—and started a business offering that service in New York City. I literally knocked on doors of ad agencies, made cold calls, wrote letters, and asked everyone I knew for referrals. It got me off the ground. I knew I had to learn more about marketing to stay afloat, so I studied it like crazy—both for my own business but also knowing it would benefit my clients. I didn't foresee how valuable that would become.

   As my venture grew, other business owners asked me for advice on how to better market themselves. It made me a more valuable resource. When I had success with newsletters and online marketing, they asked me about that, so I created e-books and courses for them to purchase online. From there, I developed a large following that led me to create even more coaching programs and workshops. I realized most of my followers were women entrepreneurs, and that's who I specialize in working with today. I've never been happier, because I have a flexible business that allows me to generate a sizable income and work from around the world with my family. (My husband is from Australia so we travel often with the kids, and I can work from anywhere I have Internet.) It also has propelled me as a thought leader while helping others grow their companies, themselves, and their missions.

2. *What was your greatest mistake and at what point in your career?*

Honestly, I grew too big too quickly, just because I could. Our sales were incredible and I was on a roll. At its peak, it all looked great on paper—$6 million in sales, an Inc. 500 ranking, hundreds of people in my coaching programs, over 15 employees, a jam-packed schedule, and tons of media exposure. I was "living the life." But one morning I woke up and didn't want to get out of bed. I'd lost my way because I'd neglected my number one value: *freedom*. (Yes, there's some freedom you earn by growing a large team to support you. But I'd reached a point I wanted to pull back, and I couldn't because I was supporting *them*! I felt like a big mama sow with a litter of 15 sucklings.)

Finally I had to give myself permission to change things. Bit by bit I adjusted the business model to get back to what made me happiest: working with my high-end clients, doing intimate workshops, and being involved with missions and causes I care about. It took me several years to get here, but it was the best thing I ever did. And ironically I'm now netting more personal income than ever before while working less, and seen even more as a thought leader in my industry.

3. *What most accelerated your career?*

Learning about the power of positioning. You can affect how others perceive you more than you may realize. Not in a manipulative way, but to make sure your best stuff gets out there. You don't want your work to be a secret, and you don't want others having to ascertain your worth based on hearsay or scraps of information they find online. You need to control as much as you can. Also, more of my success as of late is letting go of what *does not* fit me anymore. It's the clients and projects I *don't* take on that speaks just as loudly for me as the high end clients I *do* take on. And, energetically, that attracts better. (If you settle for less, that's what you get.)

4. *How has your practice most changed since inception?*

(See question 2 as well.) In the beginning it was about modeling others. I wanted to grow a large company and have a big team and maybe eventually sell the company. But in 2013, when I realized I was pregnant with twins(!), I suddenly had to (and wanted to) work much less, so my model had to change. In fact, I had to throw the model out the window and create my own. I went from running larger group training programs and overseeing a large team to a lean and mean structure. However, it's worth nothing that having the larger company gave me advantageous experience and makes me a better coach today, because I've "been there, done that." It established me as a leader in my field and was a fantastic platform from which to launch future ventures.

5. *What has been your major accomplishment in this profession?*

My coaching has helped create more women entrepreneur millionaires than anyone else in my industry. And many have become prominent thought leaders and change makers. It's a beautiful ripple effect that is changing lives around the world.

6. *What is the most important advice you have for colleagues?*

You're going to get all kinds of advice. Most people out there won't have the guts to do what you are doing, so they are going to question everything. Do what feels right, but also try new things and push yourself. Ninety-nine percent of all this is how you feel about yourself and your abilities. Your brain will always default to the negative, thinking, "Am I good enough? Can I take on this level client? Am I really an expert?" Build upon each success one at time, build up that bio, go help people, share your wins, and suddenly—you're a million dollar consultant.

7. *What do you believe is the future of consulting?*

There will be more demand for worldly wisdom combined with simple common sense.

Steven Gaffney

Name: Steven Gaffney

Company Name: Steven Gaffney Company

When Founded: 1994

Expertise and Major Markets: The only expert in open and honest communication that focuses around getting the unsaid said to help build strong relationships and transform teams and organizations to increase effectiveness, revenues, and profits.

Employees: 4

Website: www.stevengaffney.com

Books Published: *Just Be Honest* (self-published, 2002), *Honesty Works* (self-published, 2006), *Honesty Sells* (John Wiley & Sons, 2009), *The Fish Isn't Sick, The Water Is Dirty* (self-published, 2009), *Be a Change Champion* (2014), *21 Rules for Delivering Difficult Messages* (self-published, 2014), *Guide to Increasing Communication Flow Up Down and Across* (self-published, 2014)

Country of Residence: United States

Current Annual Revenue: $1 million plus

1. *Why and how did you enter the consulting profession?*

   I was running another business and started to give advice on communication and motivation and I saw the impact my advice had on others, and so I gave up my other business and started to focus on the business I currently have right now. What is interesting about this is that when I began this business, I did not even know you could make a living out of doing this. So in the beginning, I didn't.

2. *What was your greatest mistake and at what point in your career?*

   My greatest mistake was not asking for help soon enough. It took running into debt and running out of money to realize that asking for help and recognizing the success of others who would help me. And that made a huge difference!

3. *What most accelerated your career?*

There were three key items.

- It was when I stopped trying to push my content and strategy on potential clients. Instead, I focused on the true needs of the potential clients and connected those needs back to my products and services and how I could help them.
- Allowing myself to be vulnerable and asking for help from others who were more successful and experienced than I.
- Focusing on what I love to do (i.e., helping others to honestly communicate) rather than worrying about what everyone else was doing and trying to mimic them.

4. *How has your practice most changed since inception?*

From delivering one-off seminars into major consulting and coaching projects that help accomplish the organization's objectives and making lasting difference.

5. *What has been your major accomplishment in this profession?*

Crossing well over a million dollars consistently. In order to do that, I had to make substantial difference in organizations' and people's lives.

6. *What is the most important advice you have for colleagues?*

Be vulnerable, ask for help from people who are more successful than you and follow their guidance. People like Alan shorten the learning curve and help you get to where you ultimately want to go professionally and personally in a faster way than you could ever do alone.

7. *What do you believe is the future of consulting?*

I believe the future of consulting is going to be bigger than we can even imagine now. The reason for this is because speed is critical to organizational success. One of the critical ways that companies can increase speed is their willingness to examine the blind spots that are preventing their organizations from moving forward. That is why hiring outside consultants and experts and getting objective help from them can dramatically shorten the learning curve and help the organizations achieve lasting results.

Linda Henman

Name: Linda Henman

Company Name: Henman Performance Group

When Founded: 2004

Expertise and Major Markets: Strategy, succession planning, mergers and acquisitions

Employees: None

Website: www.henmanperformancegroup.com

Books Published: *Small Group Communication: Theory and Practice*, 7th ed. (Times Mirror Company, 1996), *Small Group Communication: Theory and Practice*, 8th ed. (Roxbury Publishing Company, 2003), *The Magnetic Boss* (self-published, 2006), *Landing in the Executive Chair: How to Excel in the Hot Seat* (Career Press, 2011), *Alan Weiss on Consulting* (Alan Weiss, 2013), *Challenge the Ordinary: Why Revolutionary Companies Abandon Conventional Mindsets, Question Long-Held Assumptions, and Kill Their Sacred Cows* (Career Press, 2014)

Country of Residence: United States

1. *Why and how did you enter the consulting profession?*

I began consulting more than 35 years ago, with the Air Force as my first client. In 1978, when women started assuming roles they had not previously held in the Air Force, a friend asked me to help her develop programs to be used throughout the Tactical Air Command—protocols designed to make the changes easier for both leaders and the women themselves.

On the day of my first meeting, eight men sat in a line, senior enlisted men, roughly the age of my father. They had so many stripes on their sleeves, I started to suffer from vertigo. I could see all these stripes because all eight men had their arms folded across their chests, the question on their faces unmistakable: "Honey, what have *you* got to teach *us*?"

I had an epiphany that day: by honoring and leveraging the wisdom in the room, I could help these chief master sergeants make the difficult decisions they faced. My youth and inexperience didn't matter; I had everything I needed to help these men, and the exchange energized me.

Since then, I have experimented with several types of consulting, at one time relying almost exclusively on training as my method of delivery, at another depending on pre-employment screening for most of my revenue. Now, I have returned to my beginnings of helping leaders make the tough calls. The rewards of doing good work in this arena are tangible, immediate, and stimulating. That's why I started; that's why I continue.

2. *What was your greatest mistake and at what point in your career?*

Until the pivotal day in 2006 when I attended Alan's proposal writing workshop, I had led with methodology and priced my services as commodities. When I switched to value-based fees, I started to think of myself differently, to attract better clients, and to position myself as an expert in my field. And I abandoned forever the burden of keeping track of hourly billing!

3. *What most accelerated your career?*

In general, committing to my own professional development has allowed me to accelerate at speeds I previously could not have comprehended. I currently invest about $30,000 and four weeks annually to achieve this objective.

Specifically, learning the skills to reach conceptual agreement with clients positioned me to write better, higher-priced proposals. Most of my current revenue comes from a handful of clients that I started working with *after* I learned this skill. Today, more than half of my income comes from work I didn't do three years ago. I wouldn't be able to say this if I hadn't committed to improving both my content and my processes. Changing my mindset and skills dramatically changed my intellectual property, income, and job satisfaction.

4. *How has your practice most changed since inception?*

Today I do almost no training and very few pre-employment assessments, the two staples of my professional diet until nine years ago. I have also switched from working on projects or initiatives to assuming the role of expert advisor on strategy, succession planning, and mergers and acquisitions. The role of advisor is more interesting and much less labor-intensive.

5. *What has been your major accomplishment in this profession?*

I have influenced decision makers to think strategically, grow dramatically, and promote intelligently, which has resulted in millions of dollars of profit for their companies. To achieve this, I have committed to ongoing skill development, continued learning, and general professional development.

6. *What is the most important advice you have for colleagues?*

Ask clients, "Why?" *Why* do they want to change and grow? If you start at the core of the issue, you'll provide more value, receive fair compensation for your work, and stay squarely focused on outcomes and results—not deliverables.

The inconsequential, emotional, and unimportant frequently distract clients. Therefore, our job is to help them zero in on the critical few objectives and put aside the trivial many.

7. *What do you believe is the future of consulting?*

As the baby boomers retire, much of the expertise will go with them, and fewer people will be able to replace them because the recent recession caused many companies to stop developing their talent. Consequently, companies will rely more heavily on external consultants both to do the work and to teach the next generations. Companies will continue to need process consultants (strategy, change, coaching), but many will also need content experts (sales, operations, finance, IT, succession planning). Consultants who can offer both forms of consulting will be in demand and positioned for success.

Lisa T. Miller

Name: Lisa T. Miller

Company Name: VIE Healthcare, Inc.

When Founded: 1999

Expertise and Major Markets: Hospitals, healthcare organizations, physician practices

Employees: 16

Website: www.viehealthcare.com

Book Published: *The Entrepreneurial Hospital* (to be published in Spring 2016, Taylor & Francis)

Country of Residence: United States

1. *Why and how did you enter the consulting profession?*

   I was a successful hospital sales representative selling surgical products utilized in cases in the operating room, and I consistently saw firsthand the waste, inefficiencies, and disparity in pricing for supplies and services from hospitals within the same geographical range. Why did one hospital pay $75 for an item and another hospital that was five miles away pay $35 for that exact same item? And while I absolutely believe that companies should make a profit, I ultimately believe that money saved goes back to providing patient care and is used to serve the health needs of the community. I wanted to be an advocate for hospitals and provide them with benchmarking data, insights, market trends, innovations, and process improvement support and assist them with negotiation strategies so that they could achieve the best pricing and contract terms available in the marketplace.

2. *What was your greatest mistake and at what point in your career?*

   My greatest mistake was wrongly thinking that I had to "grow" my business and expand with more people, instead of optimizing my business so I could achieve better results with fewer people.

I promoted individuals within my consulting firm, and provided them with larger salaries and gave them "big titles" but didn't equally provide them with the specific responsibilities, measurements, and accountability that come along with these new roles. I made this mistake after owning my company for 11 years. I wanted to grow and take the next step, and thought the reason why these promotions and our expansion wasn't working was due to "growing pains." However, the reason why was because I didn't ensure that I had promoted the right people to these new positions and I didn't set the right expectations in these new roles with a culture of measurement and accountability.

3. *What most accelerated your career?*

Finding exceptional mentors who I could work with on a consistent basis. Mentors were critical to accelerating my career (and still are), and specifically two of them—Alan Weiss and Keith Cunningham. When I realized that I needed a "master" to learn from and who had the real life experiences in business and consulting and not a theoretical view, I was tremendously fortunate to learn from two world-class and successful entrepreneurs and advisors. Mentors (1) gave me the insights to see the things I missed (both good and bad), (2) made me accountable to the goals and standards we set, (3) challenged my thinking and made me uncomfortable so I could really "think," and (4) provided their life experiences and specific examples they encountered as a teaching tool. I was able to see what they experienced and how they handled certain situations and to learn by their example.

4. *How has your practice most changed since inception?*

My practice started off as a solo practice and then very quickly I had two employees and for about half of our first 16 years, VIE Healthcare was a very small firm with seven people and our focus was hospital cost reduction and revenue improvement services. Today, we have sixteen seasoned healthcare experts and our focus is complete performance improvement services for hospital and healthcare organizations which include the financial, operational and clinical areas of an organization. VIE had to change as did all of healthcare these past few years so that we could adapt to the new reform and The Affordable Care Act in order to provide our healthcare clients with the support and innovations they need in order for them to manage to these new regulations.

5. *What has been your major accomplishment in this profession?*

Since 96 percent of all businesses fail prior to their tenth anniversary, my major accomplishment is celebrating VIE Healthcare's 16 years in business. We have been successfully serving and partnering with our healthcare clients in delivering our mission, which is supporting healthcare organizations so they can provide exceptional patient care. It is being competitive with the large consulting firms who each have revenues in the hundreds of millions of dollars and earning the business from small to large hospitals and healthcare systems each year. We have been able to provide our unique thought leadership and we are easily flexible enough to support our clients' goals and mission.

6. *What is the most important advice you have for colleagues?*

Spend time "thinking" and creating your thought leadership. Innovation is foundational for consultants to set themselves apart from others. Our clients want new thinking and innovative ways to solve their problems and to support and optimize their businesses.

7. *What do you believe is the future of consulting?*

Web-based micro-consulting platforms and on-demand expertise advice. You are seeing a huge growth in these platforms, and many solo practices are also engaged in utilizing them as it does provide a network of experts for companies and an additional marketing vehicle for consultants to obtain new business. Sometimes, businesses want a quick burst of expertise, a small-scale consulting project and not 100 consultants from McKinsey deploying on their organization. Or a business might want to perform a "test-drive" before signing up for a large engagement with a consultant—is this the right fit? These online micro-consulting platforms are becoming very successful and resonating with businesses who want their experts vetted, projects started quickly and with performance guarantees in place. These online expert networks are competing with the big management consulting firms as they provide short bursts of professional knowledge and insights and tend to led into extended consulting and larger engagements.

Rick Pay

Name: Rick Pay

Company Name: The R Pay Company, LLC

When Founded: 1999

Expertise and Major Markets: I help my clients accelerate profit and growth by developing and implementing operations and supply chain strategy, introducing disruptive (new) ideas and personalizing these processes for employees so it can be sustained.

Employees: None

Website: www.rpaycompany.com

E-books: *Creating An Action Imperative®—A Game Plan for CEOs Who Want to Emerge Stronger, Smarter and Ready to Thrive in a New Economy*; *Leadership Excellence—Creating Vision, Innovation and Dramatic Results*

Country of Residence: United States

Current Annual Revenue: $300,000 to $400,000

Age: 64

1. *Why and how did you enter the consulting profession?*

   I have always had a keen interest in how business works and the systems and processes that drive success. I joined Price Waterhouse in the 1980s helping companies develop IT resources to support their processes and MIS strategies that provided internal support of the value chain. I enjoy helping companies be dramatically more successful quickly and accelerating profit and growth.

2. *What was your greatest mistake and at what point in your career?*

At Price Waterhouse, I felt that if I did good work, it would be recognized without having to blow my own horn. The problem was that if I didn't blow my horn there was no music. The environment was so competitive that with others blowing their horns, my work was not recognized to the degree it should have been.

3. *What most accelerated your career?*

I became a member of the Alan Weiss community in 2008, and that profoundly altered my view of the value I provide my clients and correspondingly how to propose, develop fees for, and execute my projects. As a result, my clients achieved dramatic results and I earned a higher income. It also gave me the opportunity to become a Master Mentor, which allowed me to learn by teaching others and to give back to the Alan Weiss communities. Being part of a world-class community has helped me immeasurably in my growth and progress toward success.

4. *How has your practice most changed since inception?*

My practice has changed in several notable ways. First, I started as a technician, helping my clients implement processes and techniques. I worked in the lower levels of the organization and, while doing good work, did not provide the level of value to the client that I was capable of. Over time I became much more strategic, helping clients develop strategy for operations and supply chain, ensuring they had the right people in the right seats to implement it, and guiding the executives to provide the vision and leadership needed to sustain the changes.

Second, for many years I used the hourly billing rate model common to the big accounting firms, tracking my time to the tenth of an hour. At accounting firms, utilization and realization were the watchwords vital for success in the firm. Professionals who billed many hours were promoted. After meeting Alan, I switched to the value-based approach to fees, which allowed me to focus on client outcomes and to be fairly compensated for my results. My clients were much happier and so was I!

5. *What has been your major accomplishment in this profession?*

One of my major client accomplishments was a situation in which my work saved the company. The client was struggling with growth and profitability, and my work overhauled the company so completely that the client introduced me to his employees at a success retreat as, "The person who saved our company."

An accomplishment in my consultant community was when I was admitted to the Alan Weiss Million Dollar Consulting Hall of Fame. I remember the announcement and the ovation given me by my peers and appreciate my colleagues' recognition.

6. *What is the most important advice you have for colleagues?*

Focus on value for you and the client. Good things will follow. Everything you do should be focused on providing exceptional value to your clients while maintaining a balance in your lifestyle and labor intensity that allows you to enjoy the fruits of your efforts. By focusing on improving the client's condition while accelerating profit and growth you can increase the value of the company.

7. *What do you believe is the future of consulting?*

The future of consulting is a combination of larger technical firms specializing in services such as IT and innovation and sole practitioner/boutique firms providing exceptional value in leadership, change management, strategy, and operations and supply chain. Because companies need knowledge, time, and political savvy that are often not available internally, consultants will always be a valuable resource to companies of all sizes, types, and industries.

Prof. Dr. Guido Quelle

Name: Prof. Dr. Guido Quelle (Guido Quelle, PhD)

Company Name: Mandat Managementberatung GmbH (Mandat Consulting Group)

When Founded: 1989

Expertise and Major Markets: We help companies to grow profitably.

Employees: 9

Website: German: http://www.mandat.de; International: http://www.mandat-group.com

Books Published: Fifteen books in German, two in English— here are the English ones and most recent German ones: *Profitable Growth: Release Internal Growth Brakes and Bring Your Company to the Next Level*, Management for Professionals series (Springer, 2012), *Plan Lead Grow: Systematic Approaches to Success* (Monsenstein & Vannerdat, Octopus Edition, 2009), *Wachstumsintelligenz—So gelingt Wachstum im Mittelstand* (BOD, 2015), *Wachstum beginnt oben—Treibstoff für unternehmerische Wachstumsmotoren* (Springer-Gabler, 2014), *Profitabel wachsen—Wie Sie interne Bremsen lösen und Ihrem Unternehmen neuen Schub geben* (Gabler, 2011)

Country of Residence: Germany, international offices in London and New York

1. *Why and how did you enter the consulting profession?*

   I was always interested in consulting and had a few conversations with some of the big players when, as a student, a small consulting company, called "Mandat," which I had never heard of before, offered me a part-time job in my hometown in fall 1990. I took the job and decided to stay with Mandat after my graduation from university. Since January 1, 1993, I have been a professional consultant, since 1997 I have been managing director, since 1999 I have been a shareholder, and since August 2005 I have been the only shareholder of Mandat, which I joined as a student.

2. *What was your greatest mistake and at what point in your career?*

Maybe one of my biggest mistakes was to confront my employees with various facts when the firm was in a financial crisis in 2005. In reality, my employees could do nothing to improve the situation, but I told my staff we needed to do better in order to get back on track, in order to manage a turnaround. This caused immense stress for all team members, and it had a negative impact on the atmosphere within the firm. My employees got stressed, since they didn't know how to change the situation, because in fact it was I who needed to get better at building relationships and getting better business. I wanted to involve my team, but they weren't in charge of acquisition, and what they were in charge of—the quality of our projects—was greatly appreciated by our clients. So it was I who needed to change, who needed to focus, and it was I who needed to educate the team members better. I recognized this and did all of the above so that we were able to get exciting business, and as a result we tripled our revenues from 2005 to 2006.

3. *What most accelerated your career?*

People. There were four individuals who influenced me:

1. The founder of the firm had a very positive and energetic influence on me—he was a real role model for me at the beginning of my career.
2. A C-level client with whom I personally worked on dozens of projects in various companies in which he was involved. He gave me so many opportunities to grow that a lot of my expertise—being a leading expert in creating profitable growth today—can be traced back to these projects and his trust in my abilities.
3. Alan Weiss whom I got to know virtually by reading *Million Dollar Consulting* in 2005. I attended a seminar a year later and this led to a relationship that has lasted now for almost 10 years.
4. First and foremost: My wife, Susanne. Without her support I would never be where I am, and she is one of the few people I ask for feedback.

4. *How has your practice most changed since inception?*

My practice has completely changed—which is no surprise over 26 years. Today we are at eye-level with our clients, who acknowledge us as experts and request advice on creating profitable growth and in releasing internal growth brakes, whereas in the first years, the firm was perceived as a vendor or supplier. We do remote consulting, mentoring, coaching; we offer teleconferences, video series, and a lot of other things we never would have thought of in the early 1990s. I have become a sought-after speaker and am asked to give (keynote) speeches and breakout sessions at major conferences on a regular basis. Every one of my consultants today is an expert in his or her specific area. A couple of weeks ago I told my wife that I recently recognized that we now work exclusively with clients we like and respect—a situation that is new (and very pleasant) for us, and we aim at maintaining this position.

5. *What has been your major accomplishment in this profession?*

I hesitate to talk about my accomplishments, because it would not be fair to my colleagues who contribute a lot. I think our major accomplishment is that we have helped more than 160 national and international companies in more than 400 projects to grow profitably and to thrive (again). We have worked with thousands of people, and quite a few of them are still talking about our collaboration even though those projects were completed years ago.

6. *What is the most important advice you have for colleagues?*

Take action, don't just "think," build relationship with buyers, don't waste time with nonbuyers who may be "nicer," don't even try to be perfect, because you'll never be.

7. *What do you believe is the future of consulting?*

Mentoring, coaching, and individual personal development will play a more important role. Dealing effectively with increasing complexity will be a very important issue. Given a comparable level of quality, implementation speed will be one of the most important reasons to hire a consultant. And building relationships with buyers will be even more important than it is now, regardless of the increasing role of compliance, the involvement of purchasing departments, or other fallacies.

Andrew Sobel

Name: Andrew Sobel

Company Name: Andrew Sobel Advisors

When Founded: 1995

Expertise and Major Markets: I help companies grow by developing their clients for life. I deliver strategic consulting, coaching, and training programs for leading service firms worldwide.

Employees: None—I use a delivery network of subcontractors and distributors around the world.

Website: www.andrewsobel.com

Books Published: *Clients for Life* (Simon & Schuster, 2000), *Making Rain* (Wiley, 2003), *All for One* (Wiley, 2009), *Power Questions* (Wiley, 2012), *Power Questions to Win the Sale* (Wiley, 2013), *Power Questions to Build Clients for Life* (Wiley, 2013), *Power Relationships* (Wiley, 2014)

Country of Residence: United States

1. *Why and how did you enter the consulting profession?*

    When I was a senior in college, my father had a friend who owned a large insurance broker. Trying to be helpful, he suggested I take their competency assessment for insurance salespeople. A few weeks after I completed the three-hour exam, he called my dad and got right to the point: "Andrew definitely should *not* go into insurance sales," he told him emphatically. I breathed a sign of relief. Presciently, he added, "Your son seems to have broad interests. Consulting might be a good field for him."

Four years later, I was in my second year of business school and looking at my options. The appeal of project variety, early responsibility, and strong starting salaries drew me and many of my classmates into the large consulting firms. I spent nearly 15 years with the MAC Group, which became Gemini Consulting when we sold MAC to a large French IT firm. I spent much of that time in Europe. I helped to start up our London office and then became country CEO for Italy.

Those experiences gave me a taste for entrepreneurship and for running a business. I left Gemini and started my own independent practice in 1995. I've now had my own firm for 20 years and worked in nearly 40 countries. I've never wanted another job (except, perhaps, to be James Taylor or Paul McCartney).

2. *What was your greatest mistake and at what point in your career?*

   There are three things I wish I had done differently. First—and most important—I wish I had taken more time off for reflection, rest, family, and personal interests. Second, I should have started writing even earlier. And third, a few times I have relied too much on one client. You shouldn't get more than 20 percent of your revenue from any single client relationship—it's too risky and it creates dependence. This caused trouble for me, and I learned my lesson.

   Regarding this last point: I once interviewed Harvard Law professor Alan Dershowitz for one of my books, and he told me emphatically, "To have true independence with clients you need multiple sources of income. You need to get yourself in a position where you can say no to a client and not fear the consequences." I took his advice to heart.

3. *What most accelerated your career?*

   I chose an important topic, very little had been written about it at the time, and I worked relentlessly to become a leading authority in it. In my case, this was client loyalty and the ingredients of great professional-client relationships. A second key success factor for me has been building C-suite relationships. You may do much of your work for functional executives, but having senior-level client relationships confers huge, multiple advantages.

4. *How has your practice most changed since inception?*

I've gone through three phases. The first phase was in "big consulting" where we did a lot of highly analytical studies and produced big reports. The second phase was becoming more of an individual advisor who still did some analysis and reports, but who focused more time on advice, coaching, and training. The third, current phase represents a dramatic shift toward licensing my intellectual property, creating highly successful mobile learning programs, and doing more one-on-one advice and coaching with C-suite executives.

5. *What has been your major accomplishment in this profession?*

It's been helping people all over the world get better at something that's incredibly important to professional success and personal satisfaction: developing strong, trusted relationships. Many of those individuals have been in consulting and other professional services, because that is a large market for me. A second, related accomplishment has been creating an extensive, recognized body of work on how to build clients for life. This includes eight books, which have been translated into 17 languages and sold over 250,000 copies worldwide.

6. *What is the most important advice you have for colleagues?*

First, choose an area to specialize in and build a "flywheel" around it—continually deepen and broaden your expertise, and publish incessantly so you build an ever-stronger brand and reputation. Create a "family" of articles, books, and frameworks around your core subject. Be original—come up with your own ideas and synthesize others' ideas into new frameworks. Then clients will come to you.

Second, build knowledge breadth around your core expertise. Develop broad business knowledge and commercial acumen—otherwise you risk being a commodity. You need to be able to show how your expertise enables important business outcomes. Otherwise you become what I call an "expert for hire" rather than a client advisor.

Third, become the kind of person that senior executives want to spend time with. In order to get top executives interested in having a relationship with you, you need to be seen as someone with bold, fresh ideas and the willingness to take a stand on important issues. Especially with top executives, you have to take some risks and play to win—if you play not to lose, you will lose.

7. *What do you believe is the future of consulting?*

Don't believe all the predictions of seismic change in consulting such as a wholesale shift to success fees (the truth is, large corporate clients actually like predictable budgets).

The consulting business is evolving, however. Like many markets, consulting will continue to polarize around large, full-service, global firms and smaller boutiques that are highly specialized in a particular subject or area. Corporations are reducing the number of major suppliers they will deal with, and this trend favors the large firms for big projects and outsourcing. Midsized firms, in fact, are getting bought up or in some cases going out of business. But there will always, however, be a great market for nimble, independent consultants and small firms that offer a singular value proposition and deep, specialized expertise.

Phil Symchych

Name: Phil Symchych

Company Name: Symchych Consulting Inc. operating as Symco & Co. Management Consultants

When Founded: Originally from 1996 to 2002. Restarted as a new corporation in 2004.

Expertise and Major Markets: I am an expert in business growth for privately held small and medium businesses that serve the business-to-business market. Expertise includes growth strategies and financial strategies that accelerate profitable growth and build wealth for business owners.

Employees: None

Website: www.symcoandco.com

Book Published: *The Business Wealth Builders*, with Alan Weiss (Business Expert Press, 2015)

Country of Residence: Canada

Age: 52

1. *Why and how did you enter the consulting profession?*

   When I was a teenager, my parents and aunt and uncle purchased a 22-room seasonal hotel called Clear Lake Lodge. Although none of them had any business experience, they wanted to own and operate this 24/7 business in the summer months to pursue their entrepreneurial dreams. These dreams quickly turned to nightmares when interest rates climbed into the low 20 percent range, and we nearly lost everything. Every year, my parents and aunt and uncle went to the accountant's office in the big city. I'm not sure if they asked for business advice and I'm positive they didn't receive it, because we continued to suffer. One comment that was repeated at home was that the accountant was amazed that everyone wasn't bankrupt. That wasn't very useful advice. It was at the point, during those painful discussions over dinners of macaroni (again), that I decided to become a professional advisor for privately held businesses. I went to business school and initially became a CPA. After a couple of years of looking backward at what happened in their business from a financial perspective, I quit the accounting profession and joined the consulting profession. Now, I was advising clients on how to look ahead and how to create the ideal futures that they wanted for themselves and their families.

2. *What was your greatest mistake and at what point in your career?*

Early in my professional career, my greatest mistake was thinking that my clients—business owners—knew what questions to ask. They didn't. They were focused on their day-to-day operations, on serving customers, on cash flow, on payroll. They didn't think very far ahead very often. But they all wanted to grow their business and increase their wealth. But they didn't know exactly how to ask for advice on how to grow their business since proactive, professional advice had probably never been available to them or offered to them before.

3. *What most accelerated your career?*

Three things shifted my career. First, leaving accounting and focusing on consulting elevated my value to my clients because, instead of reporting on the past, I was now helping them to create their future. I advised them how to grow their business and build their wealth. Next, completing my MBA gave me more professional tools to use in order to provide a wider range of advice in areas of strategy, marketing, organizational development, and leadership. The final thing, which dramatically accelerated my career, was becoming involved with Alan Weiss and being active in his professional community of global consultants. I've learned so much from Alan and from my peers around the world that it has changed my life and also the lives of my clients.

4. *How has your practice most changed since inception?*

My practice has most changed because I've stopped relying on checklists and overengineered methodologies that the large accounting and consulting firms still use to generate billable hours. Instead, I've shifted to applying my expertise to empower my clients so they achieve the best results in the shortest period of time possible. It's all about speed and leverage. Everyone wins.

5. *What has been your major accomplishment in this profession?*

My major accomplishment and contribution to the profession of consulting is writing a commercially published book, *The Business Wealth Builders*, along with Alan Weiss as my coauthor. *The Business Wealth Builders* advises business owners of mid-market and small businesses on how to accelerate their top-line revenues and bottom-line profits, how to build their wealth, and how to leave a legacy. It gives other consultants and business advisors tools to use with their clients and to grow both their own and their clients' businesses. It's exciting to make a positive economic difference in the lives of entrepreneurs around the world. A one percent improvement in entrepreneurial output will impact half the economy in the top 17 countries in the world. That's exciting!

6. *What is the most important advice you have for colleagues?*

The most important advice that I have for my professional colleagues, and for any business owner or manager, is to quantify the value and results that you create for your clients and customers. This is the premise of my book, *The Business Wealth Builders*, as most businesses don't measure the results they create for their customers. That's a huge mistake. You can say, "I can grow your business," or you can say, "I increase revenues 377 percent!" The latter is much more powerful to your prospect, to your client, and to your ability to attract great clients and generate excellent fees . . . because you deliver results!

7. *What do you believe is the future of consulting?*

The future of consulting is the same as for entrepreneurs around the world: speed and leverage will help deliver superior results to your customers and clients. Combined with the strong personal relationships and ability to be highly responsive and innovative, solo consultants and boutique firms will be able to outmaneuver much larger rivals who are busy completing checklists and charging by the hour because they have a warehouse full of bodies that they need to be chargeable. The consulting profession has a great future because expertise is highly fluid and can easily cross time zones, borders, and cultures, and because most of the global economy in the top nations is driven by entrepreneurs who can benefit from their advice. It's a great time to be a consultant!

Kim Wilkerson

Name: Kim Wilkerson
Company Name: Wilkerson Consulting Group
When Founded: 1990
Expertise and Major Markets: Consultant, coach, and speaker: real-time, high-impact, mission-critical consult and coach who creates both dramatic organizational progress and profound individual growth.
Employees: None
Website: www.kimwilkerson.com
Book Published: *The Language of Success*, with Alan Weiss (Business Expert Press, 2016)
Country of Residence: United States

1. *Why and how did you enter the consulting profession?*

I worked in a variety of organizations and industries. In each role, I loved the work but always came to the point where I couldn't deal with "the system." I was at a crossroad in my last corporate position of proactively resigning or the likely outcome of eventually being fired. (How's that for anticipating the future?)

While contemplating the situation, I had the proverbial epiphany that there was only one common element in each of my previous employment scenarios of "not being able to deal with the system." That common element was that *I was not a good match for the system and, most likely, not ever for any system.* It was in that very moment that I realized the time was right for me to be "my own system." And, with that, a solo consultant was born.

Backstory: In my early days of employment while in my twenties, I knew I would "someday" be on my own. At the time, I figured I needed a few decades of corporate experience to be credible. I surprised myself when I took the leap 20 years earlier than even I expected. Ironically, the very characteristics and traits that were my "Achilles heel" while employed became the foundation of my success as a consultant. It's an interesting dichotomy.

2. *What was your greatest mistake and at what point in your career?*

Not thinking *big* enough early in my career. ("Early" being the first 10 years!) Not a fatal mistake, but it certainly made for missed or diminished opportunities. I didn't think big enough in regard to the scope of what I could offer organizations (beyond what I was currently providing), the additional value I could provide, and the associated fees relative to that value.

3. *What most accelerated your career?*

Reading *Million Dollar Consulting* (1992 edition!) and joining Alan's Million Dollar Consulting community in 2001.

I was in business for over 10 years prior to joining Alan's community. There were few, if any, resources available in the nineties for solo consultants. Alan's mentor program, workshops, and variety of unique offerings, along with his one-of-a-kind community for solo consultants and boutique firms, filled that void for me. Fifteen years later, I continue to "accelerate" my career through his advice and the ongoing interaction with the consultants in his community.

4. *How has your practice most changed since inception?*

In the early years, projects were focused on "fixing something that was broken or not good enough." Regardless of whether it was people, processes, or productivity, the focus was on problem solving and remedial work.

While there's still some of that work, in today's world the client focus and need have evolved to being more opportunistic and innovative (instead of merely fixing something). The need is for a trusted advisor and partner, not merely a hired hand or vendor providing a service. The work and the relationships are extremely collaborative.

Today, the best of the best (executives and organizations) seek this expertise and consider this type of advisory partnership an integral element of their success.

5. *What has been your major accomplishment in this profession?*

My business has been based on unsolicited referrals, which speaks to my clients' testimonials of our work together.

However, my major accomplishment is very self-focused. While I am the catalyst for my clients successfully "getting from here to there," my best accomplishment is that this role as a solo consultant positioned me and allowed me to create and live the life I want.

6. *What is the most important advice you have for colleagues?*

Many consultants and coaches can easily demonstrate their value while on the job, but struggle with actually communicating it to prospects and clients. To that point, it's essential to know your expertise, recognize and realize your value, and then "own it." Be able to communicate it, not just demonstrate it. Have the confidence to be fearless in who you are, what you do, and the value you provide.

The opportunities are, and will continue to be, endless. It's a great place for those who want to contribute to the success of individuals and organizations while being in control of one's own destiny. Create the work you want to do, and, most importantly, create the life you want live.

7. *What do you believe is the future of consulting?*

Consulting and coaching in my arena have evolved from being "prescriptive based work" to partnering with clients who want to be breakthrough, opportunistic, innovative, and successful.

Being in an advisory role based on your particular expertise, while at the same time being viewed as a trusted partner, will be in greater demand and of greater value to the client.

> *The Very Final Thought: I've found that about 10 percent of people who voluntarily expose themselves to new thinking—in a book or a workshop—actually take affirmative action quickly. Yet you need only 1 percent improvement a day to continually double your effectiveness. As you reach this final word, you'll understand the driving force required to become a million dollar consultant: you.*

INDEX

Abundance mentality, 107
Accelerant Curve, 19–22, 20*f*
  fees and, 61
  new services and, 136–137, 136*f*
  TL and, 144
Accelerators, 252
  authority and, 258–259
  career, 234, 236
  conceptual agreement and, 246
  focus and, 244
  mentors and, 249
  people as, 255
  positioning and, 241
  tactical, 231–232
Accountabilities:
  joint, 76–77
  systems, 75
  translating into, 12
Accounting, 113, 262
  colleagues, 96
  reducing debt and, 5
  systems, 160
Acquisition costs, 9
  unsolicited referrals and, 135
Action, 88
  contingent, 218–219
  taking, 256
Administrative assistants, 188
The Adventures of Koufax and
  Buddy Beagle, 207
Advertising, 17
  spending, 116
Advice, 232, 237, 239

breakthrough relationships
  and, 33
core subjects and, 259
numbered lists and, 101
on-demand, 250
publishing, 235
questions for clients and, 247
retainers and, 63
success and, 242
trust and, 43
value and, 253
Advisors, trusted, 75
Advisory boards, 75, 97,
  214–215
  people and, 216–218
  protocols, 215–216
Advisory roles, 267
Aerodynamics, 147–148
Affection, 97
Affiliations, 55
Affordable Care Act, 250
Air clubs, 32*f*
Air Force, 245
Airlines, 32
Alan Weiss on Consulting
  (Weiss, Barr, Henman
  & Shahar), 245
Ali International LLC, 239
Alive, 105
All for One (Sobel), 257
All the Leader You Can Be
  (Bates), 236
Allergan, 22

Alliances, 18, 200–202
  ethical issues and, 161
  global, 138
  supplanting, 167–168
Ambiguous zone, 220, 221*f*
American Council of Life
    Insurers, 54
American Express, 207–208
Andrew Sobel Advisors, 257
Anecdotal measures, 51
Annuities, 220–221
Annuity income, 220
Anomie, 96
Anticipated need, 190
"App" principle, 117–118
Apple, 24
  Genius Bar, 32
Archimedes, 199
Armstrong, Lance, 45
Arrive, 105
Artisans, 83
Assertiveness, 197*f*
Attention, 55
Attrition:
  expense, 74
  undesired, 9
Authority, 258–259
Autonomous control, 91
Availability, 62
Avatars, 178
Avocation, 123

Backlogs, 223
Baggage, 228
Bain, 232
Balanced Scorecard Institute, 239
Barr, Chad, 233–235, 245
Barrier to entry, 19
Bartering, 208–209

Bass, Andy, 230–233
BassClusker Consulting Ltd, 230
Bates, Suzanne, 235–237
Bates Communication, 235
BCG, 232
Be a Change Champion
    (Gaffney), 243
Behaviors:
  observing, 45
  sales, 197*f*
Bennis, Warren, 145
Bentley, 32–33
Berkshire Hathaway, 179
Best practices, 74, 131
  subcontracting, 203
Bidding wars, 72
Billing, 77–78
  ethical issues and, 160
  of expenses, 163–164
Bills, 213
Binge watching, 89
"Black belt nine delta," 229
Bleistein, Steven, 238–239
Blogs, 117, 122, 194
  testimonials in, 34
BMW, 90
Boards, 118
Body of work, 180
Boilerplates, for RFPs, 66
Boldness, 239
Book publishing, 148, 174
Bookkeepers, 191, 207
Booz & Co., 238
Boredom, 224–225
Bounce factors, 19, 20*f*
Boutique consulting, 147–148
  branding equity and, 26
  future of, 232–233
  as sweet spot, 12

Branding, 22–25
aggressive, 150
building, 24
creation, 23–24
differentiation, 62
elements of, 25*f*
equity, 24, 26
imagery, 223
monitoring, 25
peer-level relationships and, 98
pyramid, 24*f*
retainers and, 140
sequence, 23*f*
value and, 90
Breakthrough relationships, 33
Briefings, 119–121
British Standards Institute,
172–173
Brown, Ali, 239–242
Buckingham, Marcus, 13,
143–144, 148
Buffett, Warren, 179
Bureaucracy, 230
Business. *See also* Relationship
business
acquiring, 42, 129
communication, 45–46
delivery, 129
globalization of, 174
of growing, 228–229
internal referral, 131
international, 171–175
losing, 150
methodology, 129
outcomes, 49
parachute, 19–20, 20*f*
potential, 132
repeat, 130–132
solicited, 133–134

streamlining of, 8
sustaining, 127–130
theft, 168*n*3
turning down, 168–169
unsolicited, 134–136
Business cards, 214
Business media:
platforms, 116–121
websites, 117–118
The Business Wealth Builders
(Symchych), 261, 263
Buy lists, 129
Buyers. *See also* Clients
clicks to conversions for, 53–55
corporate, 111
dynamics, 32–33
executive, 99
ideal, 10, 11*f*, 13, 31
life cycle, 37–39
maintaining contact with, 130
networking with, 54
new, 130
peer-level relationships with,
98–100
personal objectives of, 154
push back on, 35
rapid transformation of, 34–36
response to proposals of, 80–82
retail, 53*n*2
RFPs and, 65
wrong, 11
Buzz, 150

C. K. Louis, 90
Calendars, 212
Calgon, 141–142
Calmness, 99
Capitalism, 83–84
Career development, 230

Carey Limousine, 193–194, 207
Carville, James, 144*n*1
Case Communications, 172–173
Case studies, 34
CEO Branding, Theory and Practice (Fetscherin), 236
Chad Barr Group, 233
Challenge the Ordinary (Henman), 245
Change, 149
    thrive and, 106
    value philosophy and, 89
Change management, 152
Checklists, 262
Chron folder, 212
Cialdini, Robert, 144*n*1
Citibank, 172–173
Clear Lake Lodge, 261
Clicks to conversions, 53–55
Clients. *See also* Buyers;
        Customers
    advisory boards and, 216
    competitors, 166–167
    condition, 4
    confidence, 95
    confidentiality and, 164
    delegation of work to, 8
    dynamics, 32*f*
    engagement, 132
    focus on, 253
    foreign, 172
    needs, 71
    new, 128
    as prospects, 36–37
    prospects distinguished from, 31
    questions for, 247
    remote access for, 92
    request, 6
    touch points with, 39*f*
    traveling for, 171–175

Clients for Life (Sobel), 257
Clothing, 99
Coaching, 256
    Accelerant Curve and, 21–22
    global, 110
    women, 242
Codependencies, 4
Coke, 24
Cold calls, 129
Collaborators, 4
Colleagues, 96
Collins, Jim, 143
Comments, 117
Commercial publishing, 16
Commissions, 171
Commitment:
    compliance compared to, 145
    fees and, 86–87, 86*f*
Common sense, 242
Communication:
    business, 45–46
    clear, 9
    digital, 237
    time and, 231–232
Community, 138
    new services and, 137*f*
Compatibility, 201
Competency, 8–9, 189–190, 189*f*
Competition:
    avoiding, 151–154
    external, 152–154
    internal, 151–152
Competitive strategies, 12
Competitors, 166–167
Complaints:
    on projects, 33
    reducing, 74
Compliance, commitment compared to, 145

Conceptual agreement, 49–53, 50*f*
  accelerators and, 246
  fees and, 60
  presentation of proposals
    and, 80
Conceptual images, 229
Conference rooms, 215
Confidence:
  client, 95
  efficacy and, 95
  showing, 35
Confidentiality, 160, 164
Consultants:
  community, 227–230
  definition of, 2–5
  interviews with, 230–267
  self-esteem and, 227–228
  ties with other, 222
  traits of, 4
Consulting:
  changes in, 234
  future of, 232–233, 235, 237,
    239, 244, 247, 253, 260,
    263–264, 266–267
  interactions, dynamics in, 3
  remote, 256
  unified theory of, 26–29
Content knowledge, 4
Contingent actions, 218–219
Contracts:
  proposals as, 79
  subcontracting, 204–205
Contrarian, 145–146, 153
Conversations:
  controlling, 48–49
  guiding, 35
  sales, 10
  testimonials in, 34
Conversions, clicks to, 53–55
Conviction, 41

Core subjects, 259
Corporate help, 192
Covey, Steven, 13
Craftsmen, 83
Creating an Action Imperative
  (Pay), 251
Credibility, 41
  statements, 110–111
Credit, 219–220
Crossover, 33–34
Cunningham, Keith, 249
Currency, 172
Customers. *See also* Clients
  complaints, 9
  existing, 128
  new, 128
  products and, 128*f*

Daily planners, 212–213
Daily promotion, 126
Daily routine, 211–214
David (Michelangelo), 9
Debriefing, 76
Debt, 220
  reducing, 5
Decision making, 148
  influencing, 247
Defense contractors, 31
Delegation, of work to client, 8
Deliverables, 51
  distrust and, 44
  outcomes compared to, 73
  RFPs and, 64
Delivery, 139, 197
  business, 129
  fees, 129
  marketing and, 27–28
  mechanisms, 13
Deloitte, 1
Delta Airlines, 90

Demographics, shifting, 190
Deposits, 139
Dershowitz, Alan, 258
Design outsourcing, 206–207
Digression, 147
Disability insurance, 193,
    222–223
Disaffection, 96
Discover Your CEO Brand
    (Bates), 236
Discussions, 46
Disruption, minimal, 91
Distraction, 27
    for solo practitioners, 184
Distrust, 44
Doom loop, 93
Driving strategic force, 12
Drucker, Peter, 143, 147, 181
Drucker Leadership Institute, 147
Dynamics, advisory boards
    and, 217

E-mail, 211–213
    testimonials in, 34
Earnings before interest,
    taxes, depreciation, and
    amortization (EBITDA), 185
Efficacy, 95
    self-esteem and, 95*f*, 228
Einstein, Albert, 26
Electronics, 194
Elevator pitches, 4*n*2
*Eliminating the Refraction
    Layer: Achiever Change
    When Change Is Impossible
    in Japanese Companies*
    (Bleistein), 238
Elites, 138
Emotion, 229
Emotional connections, 43

Employees, 185–187, 211
    evangelism, 74
    mistakes and, 255
Empty suits, 96
Endorsements, 17
Engagements, 2
Enterprise Rent-A-Car, 85
The Entrepreneurial Hospital
    (Miller), 248
Environmental issues, 161
Ernst & Young, 101
Errors and omissions insurance,
    193, 218
Estate planning, 192
Estimates, conservative, 53
Ethical dimensions, 158*f*
Ethical issues, 159–161, 169
Evangelism, 33, 38
    employee, 74
    as marketing, 111–112
    opportunities, 54
Eventualities, 218–221
Evidence, 45
Evolution, 149
Exaggeration, 45
Examples, 153
Excel, 133
Execution, 75
Expenses, 60
    attrition, 74
    billing of, 163–164
    reimbursements,
        77–78
    for solo practitioners, 184
    subcontracting and, 203
Expertise, 2, 142
    diverse, 186
    expanding, 4
    independent, 3
    knowledge base and, 260

Exploration, 71
Exploratory research, 237

Facebook, 112, 121
Failing, 229
Family, 96
  advisory boards and, 217
  ethical issues and, 160
  feedback systems and, 255
  self-esteem and, 227
  traveling and, 165–166
Fanatics, 47
FAR. *See* Federal Acquisition
  Regulation
Fear, 238
Federal Acquisition Regulation
  (FAR), 66
FedEx, 85, 90, 194, 207
Feedback systems, 230
  family and, 255
  periodic, 22
Fees. *See also* Value-based fees
  Accelerant Curve and, 61
  advisory board protocols
    and, 215
  based on value, 4
  basis for, 59, 83
  commitment and, 86*f*
  conceptual agreement and, 60
  declining labor and, 19
  delivery, 129
  equitable, 83
  ethical issues and, 159–160, 162
  hourly, 57, 252–253
  increasing, 7*f*, 85, 232
  labor and, 61*f*
  maximizing, 6
  options and, 68–69
  personal interactions and,
    137–138

sharing, 201–202
subcontracting and, 129*n*1, 203
terms and conditions
  and, 77
thought leaders and, 144
TL and, 149
undercharging, 59
value following, 150*f*
Ferrari, 24
Fetscherin, Marc, 236
Field, Eugene, 121
Field of Dreams, 15
File backups, 214
FileMaker Pro, 133
Filofax, 212–213
Financial help, 191
Financial options, 219–220
Financial planning, 191
Firms, 185–187
Fiscal responsibility, 163–164
*The Fish Isn't Sick, The Water
  Is Dirty* (Gaffney), 243
Fishing expeditions, 152–153
Flexibility, 180–182
  mutual, 33
Florida Power & Light, 34
Flywheels, 259
Focus:
  accelerators and, 244
  on clients, 253
  on Internet, 234
  on ROI, 150
  self, 266
Focus groups, 8, 167
  joint accountabilities and, 76
Follow-up, 80–82
  for unsolicited referrals, 135
Forbes, 117
Foreign concentration, 171–172
Forgiveness, 227

Formulating strategy, 12
Forums, 117–118
Freedom, 241
Frequent flyer status, 32*f*
Friends:
  abundance mentality and, 107
  virtual, 97
Fripp, Patricia, 201

Gaffney, Steven, 243–244
Gardner, John, 145
Gemini Consulting, 258
Genealogy charts, 132
General Electric, 31
Gilded Age, 91
Gladwell, Malcolm, 148
Global alliances, 138
Globalization, 174, 190
Godin, Seth, 13, 138, 143, 145,
  148, 223
Goldsmith, Marshall, 13, 143–144,
  144*n*1, 147, 223
Gooding, Cuba, Jr., 200
Google, 17, 24, 124
Gossip, 45
Grad School, 227
Gratification, 13
Groups, 113
  creating, 116
  growing and, 229
  Q&A discussion, 125
Growing, 228–229
  mistakes, 248–249
  multidimensional, 177
  pains, 249
  too quickly, 241
Guide to Increasing
  Communication Flow Up Do
  and Across (Gaffney), 243

Hang tens, 10
Harvard Business Review, 117
Hawking, Stephen, 26
Hayes, Woody, 67
Healthcare, 249–251
Help:
  asking for, 243
  corporate, 192
  financial, 191
  legal, 192
Hemingway, Ernest, 161
Henman, Linda, 245–247
Henman Performance Group, 245
Hewlett-Packard, 7, 37, 101, 131
Hobbies, 156
Home offices, 223
Home pages, 111
Honesty, 42
Honesty Sells (Gaffney), 243
Honesty Works (Gaffney), 243
Hospitals, 248
House sitters, 194
How to Write a Proposal That's
  Accepted Every Time
  (Weiss), 71
Huffington Post, 117
Human resources, 83
Humor, 43

IBM, 105
Ideas, borrowing, 163
Identifying codes, 167
Illustrative speech, 47–49
Impact, 123–124
Implementation, 58*n*1
Imposters, 29, 95
Income. *See also* Passive income
  annuity, 220
  employees and, 187

maximizing, 58
multiple sources of, 258
new sources of, 136
prospering and, 180
relationship business and, 177
taxes and, 222
Independence, 177–180
financial, 236
multiple sources of income
and, 258
overwhelm and, 224
Independent experts, 3
India, 172n1
Indonesia, 172n1
Infringement, 223
Innovation, 229, 250
The Innovation Formula
(Robert), 41
Insecurity, 185
Instagram, 112, 122
Insurance, 192–193, 218–219,
222–223
Integrated learning, 157f
Intellectual property (IP):
continuous, 150
factors for developing,
154–157
infringement of, 223
irrelevant, 155
posting, 123
producing, 149
provocative, 54
subcontracting and, 203
sweet spot and, 13
weekly, 156–157
Interference, 230
Internal people, 151–152
International conferences,
173–174

Internet, 109–110
focus on, 234
international business
and, 175
marketing, 113–114
needs, 194
outsourcing, 206
research, 194
thought leaders and, 143–144
Interruptions, 48–49
trust and, 43
Interventionists, 4
Interviews:
with consultants, 230–267
joint accountabilities
and, 76
print, 18
radio, 17
television, 17
Investment squabbles, 152
IP. *See* Intellectual property
iPhone, 85
IRS, 189
bartering and, 208–209
subcontracting and, 206

Jerry McGuire, 200
Joint accountabilities,
76–77
Joint ventures, 54
Jujitsu, 101
Just Be Honest (Gaffney), 243

Key influencers, 66
Kinko's, 193, 207
Klout Scores, 55, 115
Knowledge, content, 4
Knowledge base, 260
KPMG, 188

Labor:
 declining, 19
 fees and, 61*f*
 intensity, decreasing, 5, 135, 205
 minimizing, 58
 reducing, 7–8, 7*f*
*Landing in the Executive Chair:
 How to Excel in the Hot Seat*
 (Henman), 245
Language, 45–49, 172
 closing, 197
 directionally oriented, 46–47
 external, 102
 martial arts of, 100–103
 peer level, 46
The Language of Success
 (Wilkerson & Weiss), 264
Las Vegas, 90
Launch, 80–82
Laws, RFPs and, 66
Lawsuits, 218–219
Lawyers, 61
 advisory boards and, 216–217
Leadership. *See also* Thought
 leadership
 inept, 229
 skills, 9, 28, 145
 TL and, 145
 trade association, 17
*Leadership Excellence—Creating
 Vision, Innovation and
 Dramatic Results* (Pay), 251
Learned Optimism (Seligman),
 102*n*4
Learning:
 curve, 244
 failing and, 229
 growing and, 228
 integrated, 157*f*

Legacies, 218–221
Legal help, 192
Lencioni, Patrick, 145
Leverage, 199
 alliances and, 202
 speed and, 262
 subcontracting and, 202
Liability, 193
 insurance, 218
Lifestyle, 78*n*3
Limousines, 207
LinkedIn, 112, 114, 116–117
Litigation, 192
Litotes, 48
"Lone wolves," 227
Long term care (LTC)
 insurance, 193
Longevity, 75
LTC insurance. *See* Long term
 care insurance
Lucas Engineering, 172–173

MAC Group, 258
Magazines, 213
Magic bullets, 28–29
The Magnetic Boss (Henman), 245
Maintenance outsourcing, 208
Maister, David, 223
Making Rain (Sobel), 257
Malpractice insurance, 193
Mandat Consulting Group, 254
Manners, 99
Mapes, Hal, 134–135
Market gravity:
 active, 18
 creating, 15–19, 16*f*
 passive, 18
 TL and, 149–150
Market need, 189–190, 189*f*

Market segments, owning,
  151–154
Marketing:
  delivery and, 27–28
  evangelism as, 111–112
  Internet, 113–114
  mass, 125
  online, 240
  to prospects, 38
  remote, 125
  sales and, 111–112
Markets, new, 92
Maslow, Abraham, 104–105, 181
Mass mailings, 129
MBA students, 1, 262
McKinsey, 1, 105, 232, 250
Measures of success, 51–52.
  See also Metrics
Media campaigns, 75
Meetings, 99
  advisory board protocols
    and, 215
  evaluating, 22
  organizational issues and, 230
  periodic, 22
Memberships, 138
Mentor Hall of Fame, 227
Mentor Summits, 227
Mentors, 232, 256
  accelerators and, 249
  master, 252
Mercedes, 90
Merck, 37, 131, 161, 173
Metaphor, 47–48, 153
Metonymy, 47–48
Metrics, 43, 51–52
  anecdotal, 51
  clicks to conversions, 55
  controversial views on, 149

in proposals, 73
scientific, 51
Michelangelo, 9, 154n3
Michelangelo Factor, 154, 187
Micro-consulting, 250–251
Middle management, 22
Miller, Lisa T., 248–251
Million Dollar Club, 227, 239
Million Dollar Consulting:
  metaphor of, 5–8
  power, 7f
Million Dollar Consulting
  College, 19, 227
Million Dollar Consulting
  Convention, 227
Million Dollar Hall of Fame, 253
Million Dollar power, 7f
Million Dollar Web Presence
  (Barr), 233
Mindset, 224
  changing, 246
  global, 237
Mirrors, 99
Mistakes, 233–234, 236
  employees and, 255
  freedom and, 241
  growing, 248–249
  questions and, 262
  value-based fees and, 246
Mobile access, 113
Modeling, 242
Monday Night Football, 141
Monetization, estimated, 88
Money, withdrawing, 107
Morita, Akio, 85
Mossberg, Walt, 143–144
Motivate Like a CEO (Bates), 236
Motivation issues, 42
Multidimensional growth, 177

National Speakers Association
Hall of Fame, 36
National Trade and Professional
Associations of the United
States, 17
Need, 8–9, 85
Negotiations, 71
of terms and conditions, 78
Netflix, 220–221
Networking, 18
with buyers, 54
Newsletters, 125, 240
brand building and, 24
testimonials in, 34
Nike, 24
Nonbuyers, 11
Nondisclosure agreements, 76
Nonprofitable growth, 146
Nordstrom, 89
Numbered lists, 101

Objections, 102
Objectives, 43, 49–51
converting to value
and, 88
metrics and, 51
personal, 43, 154
of proposals, 72–73
value and, 52–53
Observation, 8
Obsolescence, 109
Occupation, 123
The Odd Couple*, 201
Office needs, 193–194
Office sitters, 194
Offices, 191
Opinions, 101
Opportunity, 34
new, 131

Options, 66–69
binary, 67
offering, 102
in proposals, 74–75
Organizational issues, 229–230
Outcomes, 51
business, 49
deliverables compared to, 73
Outside environment, 181
Outsourcing, 206–208
solo practitioners and, 188
Overdelivering, 59
Overdraft protection, 219
Overpromising, 162
Oversight, 75
Overwhelm, 224
Ownership, 220–221
Oxygen mask rule, 14

Pack members, 96–98
Packing, 99
Pain, 224
Parachute business, 19–20, 20*f*
Partners, 201–202
prescriptive based work and,
266–267
supplanting, 167–168
Passion, 8–9, 189–190, 189*f*
Passive income, 124, 222
delivery and, 139
products and, 18
Passive listings, 17
Patents, 192
Pay, Rick, 251–253
PayPal, 124
Peer-to-peer dynamic, 35
People:
as accelerators, 255
for advisory boards, 216–218

Per diem, 162
Perceptions, 230
The Performance Papers: Incisive Briefings for Busy Leaders (Bass), 231
Personal development, 256
Personal interactions, 137–138
Philanthropy, 220
Philippines, 172*n*1
Phone numbers, 214
Physical addresses, 214
Pink, Dan, 144*n*1, 147–148
Pitching, 4, 46
P&L responsibility. *See* Profit and loss responsibility
Plagiarism, 163, 167, 172*n*1
Plan Lead Grow: Systematic Approaches to Success (Quelle), 254
Planning, strategy and, 230
Plateaus, 199–200
Politics, 152
Popularity, 55
Positioning, 241
Positive psychology, 12*n*5
Power Questions (Sobel), 257
Power Questions to Build Clients for Life (Sobel), 257
Power Questions to Win the Sale (Sobel), 257
Power Relationships (Sobel), 257
PowerPoint, 43
Pre-employment assessments, 247
Predictions, 149
   future of consulting and, 260
Prescriptive based work, 266–267
Presence, 142
Presentations, critiquing, 22

Preventive actions, 218–219
Price Waterhouse, 251–252
Principle, 100
Print newsletters, 17
Printing, 193, 207
   interviews, 18
Priorities:
   calendar and, 212
   maintaining, 212–213
   overwhelm and, 224
   wastes of time and, 121–123
Private life, 115
Private ownership, 84
Pro bono work, 16
Problem solving, 229
Products. *See also* Services
   customers and, 128*f*
   existing, 128
   knowledge, 197
   new, 128
   new clients and, 128
   passive income and, 18
   relationship, 32
Profit, 52, 60
   perceptions of value and, 91
Profit and loss (P&L) responsibility, 10, 31
Profitabel wachsen—Wie Sie itnerne Bremsen lösen und Ihrem Unternehmen neuen Schub geben (Quelle), 254
Profitable Growth: Release Internal Growth Brakes and Bring Your Company to the Next Level (Quelle), 254
Projects:
   chunks, 213
   complaints, 33
   implementation, 6, 152

Projects: (*Cont.*)
  oversight, 6
  size, 28
Prophets, 147
Proposals:
  acceptance of, 79
  as contracts, 79
  definition of, 71
  joint accountabilities and,
    76–77
  methodology, 74–75
  metrics in, 73
  objectives of, 72–73
  options in, 74–75
  presentation of, 79–80
  response of buyers to, 80–82
  steps for, 71–79
  terms and conditions of, 77
  timing in, 76
  trust and, 43
  value in, 73–74
Prospects:
  clients as, 36–37
  clients distinguished from, 31
  marketing to, 38
Prospering, 180
Prudential, 134–135
Public exposure, 148
Public hearings, 65
Public sector, 64
Public square, 150
Publishing, 148, 174, 193
  advice, 235
  commercial, 236
Push back, 35, 42

Q&A discussion groups, 125
Quasi-consultants, 2
Quelle, Guido, 254–257

Questions, 81
  for clients, 247
  for converting to value, 87–88
  mistakes and, 262
  rhetorical, 102

R Pay Company, LLC, 251
Radio, 17
Radio Shack, 220
Rainmakers, 187, 195–198
Rapid responsiveness, 125
Readiness, 157*f*
Reagan, Ronald, 102
Recession, 247
Recognized field, 147–148
Recovery, 80–82
Recruiting:
  system, 75
  time, 74
References, 34
  distrust and, 44
  external competition and, 153
Referrals, 18, 132–133
  advisory board protocols
    and, 216
  asking for, 38
  lowering labor intensity
    and, 135
  solicited, 133–134
  unsolicited, 134–136, 266
Reframing, 100–101
Regulations, 66
Reinvention, 220–221
Relansa, Inc., 238
Relationship business,
    109–112, 177
Relationships:
  authority and, 258–259
  breakthrough, 33

building, 257
creation, 197
ethical dimensions and, 158*f*
language and, 46
peer-level, 98–100
peer-to-peer, 35, 231
product, 32
self-esteem and, 228
Reliability, 41
Remote access, for clients, 92
Remote marketing, 125
Remote phone support, 21
Remote work, 124
Republic of China, 172*n*1
Request for proposal (RFP),
  6, 64–66
Research:
  autonomous control and, 91
  Internet, 194
  subcontracting, 188
Respect, 97
  peer-level relationships and, 100
Responses, to threats, 221–225
Responsiveness, 140
Rest, 99
Retail business, 113
Retainers, 6, 60–64, 139–142
  access to, 62, 140
  acquiring, 141–142
  duration of, 62, 140
  maximizing, 222
  scope of, 62, 140
  value, 140
Retention rate, 73
Retirement plans, 184, 219–220
Return on investment (ROI), 43
  focus on, 150
Reward systems, 230
RFP. *See* Request for proposal

Rhetorical permissions, 49
Risk, 148
Robbins, Tony, 138
Robert, Mike, 41
ROI. *See* Return on investment
Rudeness, 116, 118

S-curve dynamics, 200*f*
Sales, 147–148
  assertiveness and, 197
  behaviors, 197*f*
  closing time, 9
  conversations, 10
  marketing and, 111–112
  skills, 197
Santayana, George, 47
Savings, annualized, 87
Schein, Edgar, 18
Scientific metrics, 51
Scripts, 46
Search engine optimization
  (SEO), 112–114
  ignoring, 194
Sears, 220
Self-actualization, 181
Self-confidence, 228
Self-development, 224
Self-esteem, 29
  as constant, 94*f*
  consultants and, 227–228
  efficacy and, 95*f*
Self-help books, 12
Self-talk, 100–103
  positive, 228
Self-worth, 93–96
Seligman, Martin, 12*n*5, 102*n*4
SEO. *See* Search engine
  optimization
Serial developers, 10

Services. *See also* Products
  creation, 137*f*
  new, 136–139
  new clients and, 128
Shadowing, 22
Shahar, Aviv, 245
Sharp right turn, 153, 154*f*
Shell Singapore, 172–173
Shipping, 194, 207
Simile, 47–48
Singapore, 172–173
Sir Speedy, 193, 207
Situation appraisal, 71–72
Skills:
  alliances and, 201
  autonomous control and, 91
  building, 91
  issues and, 3*f*
  leadership, 9, 28, 145
  sales, 197
  self-worth and, 96
  transfer of, 3–4
Skype, 97, 110, 124, 213
Slush funds, 219–220
*Small Group Communication:
  Theory and Practice*
  (Henman), 245
Smile sheets, 149
Smith, Mark, 19
Sobel, Andrew, 257–260
Social media:
  benefits of, 112–113
  disadvantages of, 113–114
  guidelines, 115–116
  platforms, 112–116
  time and, 214
  wastes of time and, 121–123
Social mores, 190
Society for Advancement of
  Consulting, 110

Software development, 233–234
Solo practitioners, 183–185,
  264–265
  future of, 232–233
Sony, 85
Sophistication, 172
Southwest Air, 85
Speak Like a CEO (Bates), 236
Speaking, 17, 234
  engagements, 36
  events, 54
  testimonials and, 34
Speech, illustrative, 47–49
Speechwriting, 161
Speed:
  future of consulting and, 244
  integrated learning and, 157*f*
  leverage and, 262
  perceptions of value and,
    90–91
  sense of, 35
Spouses, 165–166
Staffing, 190–194
Stair steps, 148, 148*f*
Staples, 193, 207
State Street Bank, 173
Stationery, 214
Steven Gaffney Company, 243
Strategy:
  formulating, 12
  planning and, 230
Streamlining, 8
Strengths:
  building on, 12–14
  self-esteem and, 227
Subcontracting, 6, 8, 127,
  202–206
  fees, 129*n*1, 203
  research, 188
  solo practitioners and, 188–189

Success. *See also* Measures
  of success
  advice and, 242
  exploiting, 180
  learned, 103
  loop, 94, 94*f*
  outside environment and, 181
  perception of, 104
  self-worth and, 93–96
  trap, 199–200, 225
Succession planning, 230
Summation, 71
Summit Consulting Group, 180
Surveys, 8
  anonymous, 167–168
  confidential, 167
Survive, 104–105
Sweet spot, 12–13, 12*f*
  identifying, 154–157
  revisited, 155*f*
Symchych, Phil, 260–264
Symco & Co. Management
  Consultants, 260
Synecdoche, 48

Tactical Air Command, 245
Taleb, Nessim, 148
Talent crisis, 74
Talent stability, 74
Taste, 100
Taxes:
  income and, 222
  professionals, 191
Teaching, 18
Team building, 229
Teamwork, 92, 146
Technology, 83
  as augmentation, 109–110
  overuse of, 237
  utilizing, 223

Teleconferencing, 125
Telemarketers, 9
  trust and, 42
Television, 17
Temporary jobs, 219
Term limits, 216
Terms and conditions, 77
Testimonials, 34
  external competition and, 153
  on home pages, 111
  video, 38
Texting, 125
Theft, 223
Thinking, 250
Third-party endorsements, 17
Thought leaders, 13, 143–146
  creating, 250
Thought leadership (TL), 143, 227
  creating, 147–150
  fees and, 149
  market gravity and, 149–150
  scaffolding of, 145*f*
  stair step example of, 148, 148*f*
  traits, 149
Thoughts for Tuesday (Bates), 236
Threats, 221–225
3M, 221
Thrive, 105–106
Time:
  abundance mentality and, 107
  bartering and, 208
  communication and, 231–232
  shifting, 121
  social media and, 114, 214
  use, 157*f*
  wastes of, 121–123
  wealth and, 142
Timeliness, 45
Timing, in proposals, 76
Titles, 249

TL. *See* Thought leadership
Tolerances, tight, 146
Touch points, 39*f*
Trade association leadership, 17
Trademarks, 192
  infringement of, 223
Training:
  minimal, 247
  for solo practitioners, 184
  solutions, 50
  subcontracting, 8
Transference, 32
Transportation, 193–194
Traveling, 171–175, 207–208, 240
  ethical issues and, 160
  family and, 165–166
  first class, 162–163
  lifestyle and, 78*n*3
Tribes, 138
Trust:
  creation of, 41–45
  indicators of, 43–44
  lost, 45
  pack members and, 97
  peer-level relationships and, 98
  pyramid, 44*f*
Trusted advisor, 75
Truth, 41
Turf issues, 152
Turnover, reducing, 91
*21 Rules for Delivering Difficult
  Messages* (Gaffney), 243
Twitter, 112–114, 121

Uber, 85, 193
Undercharging, 59
Understatement, 48
Unified field theory, 26–29
United Airlines, 90

United Kingdom, 172–173
UPS, 194, 207
US Marines, 90
USA Today, 65
Utilities, 31

Value, 43, 52–53
  advice and, 253
  branding and, 90
  converting to, 87–88
  creating, 83
  declining labor and, 19
  distance, 84*f*
  establishing, 12
  estimating, 58
  following fees, 150*f*
  meaning of, 84–87
  offering, 4, 35
  origins of, 83–84
  perception of, 89–92
  personal interactions and,
    137–138
  philosophy of, 88–89
  promoting, 83
  in proposals, 73–74
  qualitative, 89
  quantifying, 263
  retainer, 140
  statement, 11
  uniform, 22
Value-based fees, 4, 8*n*4, 246, 253
  formula, 58
  fundamentals of, 57–60
  Value-Based Fees (Weiss), 58*n*1
Value propositions, 9–11
  on home pages, 111
  recognition of, 13
Veto power, 215
Vick, Michael, 106

Videos:
  subscription, 110
  testimonials, 38
  watching, 116
VIE Healthcare, Inc., 248–250
Vigilance, 131
Viral buzz, 150
Virtual communities, 54
Visual sharing, 124
Visuals, 193
Voice mail, 213
Volunteering, 97
Vulnerability, 244

Wachstum beginnt oben—Treibstoff
  für unternehmerische
  Wachstumsmotoren
  (Quelle), 254
Wachstumsintelligenz—So gelingt
  Wachstum im Mittelstand
  (Quelle), 254
Walkman, 85
Wall Street Journal, 143–144
Watertight doors, 103–105, 104*f*

Wealth, 5
  overwhelm and, 224
  time and, 142
Web development, 235
Web presence, 17
Web surfing, 214
Webinars, 110, 125
Websites, 109–111
  business media, 117–118
  physical addresses and, 214
  testimonials in, 34
  web presence and, 17
Wilkerson, Kim, 264–267
Wilkerson Consulting Group, 264
Williams, Brian, 45
Wisdom, 146
  pyramid, 146*f*
Women, 242
Word of mouth, 17
Word-of-mouth buzz, 150
Work streamlining, 188
Wright, Steven, 27

YouTube, 110, 112, 116, 122

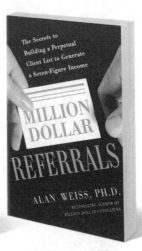